John-Paul Flinton attended a
Comprehensive from 1979 to 1986. He is
now a journalist, living in London.

LADBROKE GROVE

E

LATIMER ROAD

E

A

SHEPHERD'S BUSH

HOLLAND ROAD

D

OLYMPIA

A	POSH PEOPLE'S STREETS
B	INTERNATIONAL EMBASSIES
C	KENSINGTON PALACE
D	CARDINAL VAUGHAN SECONDARY
E	TOUGH ESTATES (FORMERLY SLUMS)
F	CENTRE OF 1958 RACE RIOTS
G	HIPPIES FORCE ME TO SMOKE DOPE
H	CARDINAL VAUGHAN BOYS ATTACK GIL
I	BECKY SNOGS ME IN THE PUB
J	GIL WITNESSES SHOOTING IN POOL HALL
K	MANUEL PUKES TO ESCAPE ARREST

N

HAMMERSMITH ROAD

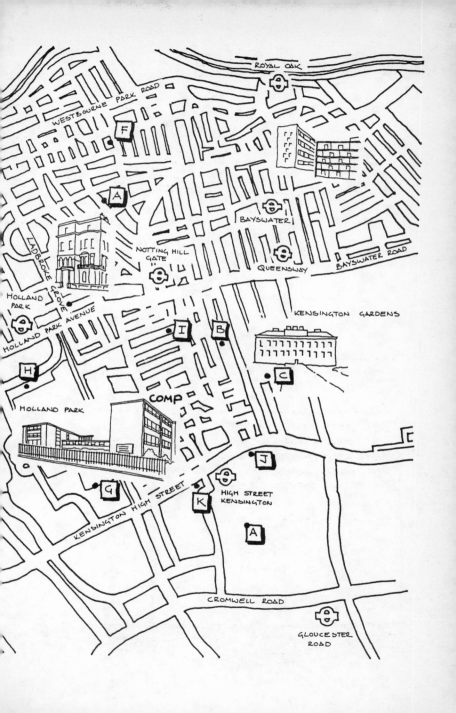

JOHN-PAUL FLINTOFF

Comp

A Survivor's Tale

INDIGO

First published in Great Britain in 1998
by Victor Gollancz

This Indigo edition published in 1999
Indigo is an imprint of The Orion Publishing Group Ltd
Wellington House, 125 Strand, London WC2R 0BB

A CIP catalogue record for this book is
available from the British Library.

ISBN 0 575 40162 1

Printed and bound in Great Britain by
Guernsey Press Co. Ltd, Guernsey, Channel Isles.

Extracts from Gavin Ewart and Tony Benn reproduced by kind
permission of Hutchinson; extracts from Tom Wolfe, Amanda Craig and
Martin Amis reproduced by kind permission of Picador, 4th Estate and
Jonathan Cape respectively.

99   10 9 8 7 6 5 4 3 2 1

For Harriet

Acknowledgements

During my research I spoke to many pupils and
teachers, as well as former pupils and teachers.
Unless indicated otherwise in the text, they
preferred not to be identified; I am grateful to them
all.

The most useful archive turned out to be my
brother. Crispin also deserves credit for keeping me
company at school – rather more so than this book
suggests. My sister Anna gave helpful advice on the
manuscript.

Thanks too to Hugh Barnes; to Simon Trewin and
Emma Gibb at Sheil Land; and to everybody at
Gollancz, particularly Sara Holloway.

Finally, thanks to my parents for having the
imagination to send me to Holland Park. Sorry I
was naughty.

Most of the names have been changed.

Contents

UPPER SCHOOL

PART III

Foreword to Indigo edition

Within days of *Comp* appearing in bookshops, I received a threatening telephone call. Naturally this alarmed me, but in retrospect I can see it was a good sign – because while the book had remained only theoretical, nobody seemed terribly interested.

'I'm writing a book,' I'd tell friends, 'about my time at school.' And their eyes glazed over.

But then the book came out, and the following Saturday – after midnight – I received the call. A voice, unidentified save by a West Indian accent, addressed itself to my answering machine: 'Ras clat, Flintoff. We read what you wrote about us and we comin' after you now.'

That was certainly the book's most succinct review. Another, slightly less direct, came in the form of a handwritten letter from a classmate, identified in the book as Melissa. Contesting certain statements of fact, she demonstrated once again my old friends' preference for omitting the second barrel of my forename: 'You always were a fucking liar, John.'

Then there was the former Holland Parker – a couple of years younger than me – who came to interview me for a newspaper. Startlingly, he described himself at one point as 'the most violent person I know'. But despite quibbling with this and that in the book, he conducted himself professionally and did not feel the need to demonstrate this extreme characteristic.

Some months after publication, then, I seem to have escaped actual physical punishment for writing *Comp*.

'She has a job, she seems very neat in her habits – I mean, these council flats are squalid little places, but hers is very orderly . . .'

'And the boy – he's not going to blow up in our faces, is he? I believe he's some sort of honor student?'

'By the standards of his school. I'm not sure how he would fare at Holland Park Comprehensive.' Fallow smiled. This was a school in London. 'He's never been in trouble with the police. That's so unusual in these council flats, they talk about it as if one's bound to be impressed by this remarkable fact.'

'What do the neighbours say about him?'

'Oh . . . that he's a pleasant . . . well-behaved sort of boy.'

Tom Wolfe, *The Bonfire of the Vanities*

When my daughter Jane went to the Holland Park Comprehensive
she sat with two friends who had been at her Primary School –
because they were bourgeois (one of them even an aristocrat)
they all three spoke the BBC's standard Southern English,
without a trace of the surrounding glottal Cockney.
At once they were mimicked, called toffee-nosed and snobs.
The slurrers and h-droppers christened them Snobs' Corner
(and indeed they weren't Cockneys, Irish or West Indian).
This was all – in a roundabout way – good for them,
to meet unprivileged, poor people on equal terms.
But what I ask is, wouldn't it be better
if instead of the Two Nations, the Posh and Dustbin education,
free or fee-paying, some effort was made to spread it all equally?
To get the rulers and the ruled on the same side of the fence?

Gavin Ewart, *Sonnet: Snobs' Corner*

'It's middle-class socialists like him who destroyed the grammar schools while educating their own children privately,' he said. 'If your father had sent you to your local comprehensive, you bet it would have had to pull its socks up.'

'Oh, but, my dear, Holland Park was much too expensive,' said Amelia. 'The drugs you had to buy to keep up there cost the earth.'

Amanda Craig, *A Vicious Circle*

PART I

Week Zero (1)

Cor. There are millions of children here, nearly as many as in my whole primary school. They're crowded in separate lines right across the giant concrete space. But it's hard to count them because there are tons of parents too, and it's a pretty massive playground.

I catch the eye of a boy with really, *really* blond hair in one of the lines beside mine. I try some funny faces: I go cross-eyed and stick the edge of my nose up so the nostrils look huge, like a pig's. Then I try some better ones, showing my front teeth and raising my eyebrows right up. I suck in my cheeks, and pull my eyelids apart, so he can see all the red wiry bits around my eyeballs.

All he does is, he keeps staring at me, but he doesn't pull any faces. Then he gobs on the floor between us.

I woke up too early this morning, excited about my new class; at about half-past six.

I lay in bed trying to work out what my best friend would be like. In my part of London he could be posh or poor or black or white or even Indian. Or maybe even a girl, I might have a girlfriend: that's what you have at secondary school.

Crispin was asleep, with his mouth slightly open. He wasn't excited because his school doesn't start yet. He's still at primary school. He can't be very excited, because he's got the same people in his class as last year.

I'm a lot older than Crispin.

I kept my legs under the sheets, and just sat up to look at the clothes Mum had laid out for me on the toybox. I told her what I needed, last night.

I jumped off my bunk past Crispin and dropped my pyjama trousers, kicking them across the room. Then I sat on the toybox and pulled up my pyjama top to look at the hairs near my dick, just above it. There are more of them, but not as many as Barney had on school journey. I've got about fifteen hairs now.

Barney is two and a half months older than me, but school journey was three months ago, at the time of the general election.

Barney's going to a private school.

All around me are children and grown-ups from every race on the planet, nearly. At primary school there was practically nobody whose background wasn't English, but here there are black boys and girls, and Chinese (or maybe they're Japanese), and Arabs, and Indians (or Pakistanis), breaking up the majority of white people. I can't see any Red Indians, though, or Eskimos or Aborigines.

Even the whites are mixed up too: beside me there is a podgy, round boy wearing spectacles whose mother is giving him instructions in what sounds to me like Italian or Spanish – or possibly Greek.

Nobody pays me much attention.

The non-white children are no different from us. In fact, if anything they are probably much better, because they've been victimized for years. I know that, but I'm not sure I like the look of everyone. They're a bit too different and scary.

As for some of the white children, well, they aren't much like me either. Lots of the white children in my line have got pasty complexions and grey under-the-eyes. Mum says they probably don't eat healthy food or get enough sleep. I expect they're from the sort of tough background which might make them hate me.

They might be like the boys from the estates who bully you in the park if they're bigger than you; who steal your football and eat your Polos.

Their accents are amazingly Cockney. Cockneys use a glottal stop: my dad told me. It means they drop the T in words like 'kettle' and 'Scotland'. 'Keh-all,' he said, 'Scoh-land.'

He didn't know why they did it: I asked him.

Cockneys also drop the H at the beginning of some words, and some of them say F instead of TH. 'Arf' instead of 'half'. 'Fink' instead of 'think', 'fick' instead of 'thick'. Words sound ruder if they begin with an F.

All around me I can hear people talking like this.

Ms Edwards sounds quite posh, though, but not too posh. She's my new tutor and she sounds about as posh as my parents. She's wearing a flowery dress with the same autumn colours as the trees around the school grounds, and in the park next door: orange and brown and a bit of dark green. Next time the trees have new leaves, it will be the 1980s, which is exciting.

If you look over there, on the far side of the playground, you can see some of my old classmates from primary school: David and some of the others. They're standing in their own lines, and if you think about it, you can tell from the way they stand that they're only *pretending* they aren't scared of their new tutor-sets.

I pulled on my pants and my jeans, which are patched at the knees. I'd torn the denim here and there by diving spectacularly on the concrete playground, playing football and cricket. Mum sewed the leather patches on herself; they're hard to get the needle through.

Before anyone woke up, I even polished my shoes. They're Clarks shoes, and lots of people laugh at them because they're sensible shoes and not trainers. But I've got wide feet, and Clarks shoes let my feet grow. Mum likes Clarks shoes.

I decided to wear the jeans with the patches, and the Clarks

19

shoes, so I can think of Mum when I'm at school. But I didn't tell her that when she got up. She'd only think I'm worried about the new school, and although I am a bit, I'm not.

I sat on the toybox for hours, just thinking. Years ago, Granny came into my bedroom to find out if I was dressed yet, but I was just sitting there thinking, like this morning. Without lifting a finger, she said.

Granny thought I'd be a philosopher when I grew up. There aren't that many philosophers, I don't think, and the ones there are must be pretty famous. Granny died when I was young. Maybe I'll be a philosopher just to please her; in case her ghost is still watching.

At nearly seven o'clock, Crispin still wasn't awake.

I pulled my pyjama top over my head like a T-shirt. I never use the buttons, it's easier without. I leant over and grabbed my green Scout shirt, then slipped it on.

I've already got three badges.

Beautiful dream

February 1964. As they watched a black boy murder a well-spoken white girl, then kill himself, teachers, parents and pupils recalled a beautiful dream. Holland Park Comprehensive had been purpose-built, towards the end of the previous decade, to provide an all-round education for everybody in its richly diverse catchment area, west London. It would serve all social classes, both sexes and any ethnic group.

In principle, accommodating every kind of child under one roof was not, by the date Holland Park opened, in 1958, such a radical idea. As far back as the Second World War, the government had decreed secondary education compulsory, in a generous effort to merge the 'two nations' of educated and uneducated Britons into one fact-crammed, sharp-witted whole. In principle, that meant both sexes, and all classes and races, were entitled to a good education at no direct cost to parents.

But theory isn't the same as practice. In practice, Rab Butler's 1944 Education Act wasn't all it was cracked up to be; it failed to bring the two nations together. Children were sorted into wheat and chaff by exams at the end of primary school, at the age of eleven. In practice, only children from comfortable homes were admitted to grammar schools to learn esoteric subjects such as Latin and Greek, while children whose backgrounds provided fewer advantages were packed off to secondary moderns, where the schooling might help them to pick up blue-collar jobs.

Attlee's post-war Labour government, preoccupied with major reforms in other areas (creating the National Health Service, for example), had left the Butler Act in place; and the Conservative government which took over in the early 1950s didn't accord state education much importance – presumably because, as so often in Tory Cabinets, most of its members shopped in the private sector. But as the years passed, the number of British schoolchildren mounted higher and higher: between 1947 and 1954 it rose by one million. The Prime Minister, Anthony Eden, realizing that one million more pupils could mean as many as two million more anxious parents (that is, *voters*), upgraded the minister in charge of education to full Cabinet status. But he didn't tamper with the system.

The problem of overcrowding in state schools became acute. Early in 1958, at a conference of the National Union of Teachers, a motion demanded that classes should be limited to thirty pupils. That motion, endorsed by the entire union, was proposed by teachers from west London. Not that their own education authority was indifferent. In fact, it was one of the most progressive in the country: along with just a couple of others (including, incidentally, Tory-run Leicester), it had already concluded that secondary moderns were unjust. Indeed, it was closing two of them: teachers and pupils at Kensington West Central, in Olympia, and North Kensington Central, off Ladbroke Grove, prepared to migrate to a pioneering comprehensive on Campden Hill.

With 1750 children studying together in one building, Holland Park Comprehensive would cater for the increased pupil numbers and help to eliminate the old two-nations divide. Different pockets of society would learn all about each other (that white girl, Jenny Abramsky, would meet her slayer, the black boy, Colin Prescod); and given the right attention and effort late developers, far from being written off at eleven, could drag

22

themselves up from the lower streams. That was the beautiful dream.

Children from the condemned schools threw off their old uniforms, then marched their parents to Daniel Neil in Kensington High Street, the new school's official outfitter.

Initially, the navy-and-grey uniform (cap and trousers for boys, beret and skirt for girls) would succeed in concealing the differences between pupils; but as the weeks and months passed, umistakable signs of poverty presented themselves. Some parents' incomes, after all, wouldn't stretch to buying more than one shirt from Daniel Neil, and that shirt, after frequent laundering, inevitably looked greyish, tatty and frayed beside the clothing of classmates who had a separate shirt for each day of the week. Poorer children would also continue to squeeze into uniforms long after they'd outgrown them, while others popped back to High Street Ken to take the next size up.

The children in tatty shirts, stretched tight over rapidly expanding bodies, tended to come from the north, from the blocks of terraced housing between Latimer Road and Bayswater which remained down-at-heel until they were yuppified, street by street, in the late 1980s. Since the war, housing had been a government priority, but even into the 1960s thousands of locals had to put up with slums – in west London as elsewhere. All the same, even then Kensington contained pockets of vast wealth: tucked into the side of Kensington Gardens, just three hundred yards from Daniel Neil, members of the royal family loafed about in Kensington Palace. The contrasting lifestyles within the area were hard for some inhabitants to swallow. One elderly woman, interviewed by the *Kensington Post and West London Star* as the council rehoused her, asked the reporter: 'How can anyone call these filthy, disgusting streets, with their crumbling houses, part of a Royal Borough?'

Slums weren't exclusive to the northern part of Holland Park's catchment area. Stretching west and south into Hammersmith and Fulham, houses, and even entire streets, were gradually pulled down and replaced over the following years by blockish council accommodation. And much of that blockish council housing, in turn, became filthy and crumbling by the time, two decades later, my classmates called it home.

At least housing was tackled: other elements of public infra-structure were sorely neglected under the Tories in the 1950s; not a single hospital or prison was built in the UK during those years, and crumbling schools were patched up slowly.

On the rare occasions when new buildings were planned, they generated huge excitement – they actually hit the headlines. One scheme which fascinated the *Kensington Post and West London Star* was the widening of roads and pavements in Notting Hill Gate itself. The old Midland Bank, among other buildings, was sacrificed to the increased flow of traffic and pedestrians. Architects planned to throw up a 'tower' block – a concept so new that the *Post and Star* handled the word in inverted commas. Other new buildings on that enlarged pavement, on the corner of the Gate and Pembridge Road, included the boxy United House – within which, many years later, the manager of W. H. Smith, wearing tinted spectacles, dug through my brother's damp swimming gear in a successful search for stolen confectionery.

Week Zero (2)

You know what, I saw Ms Edwards once before, at a special parents' evening last term. And some of the other people in the North Playground look familiar too.

One of them's Gilbert Alkan, over there. He's a bit scary, with his slick black hair, fat lips and snaky eyes. Beneath his tight jeans, he's wearing black Dr Marten boots: he isn't a skinhead, but usually only skinheads wear Docs. Gilbert Alkan used to be at St James Norland, one of the toughest schools in the borough. They beat us 5–1 in the league. He scored one, and when David banged his head on the goalpost and the ref stopped play, Gilbert laughed at us.

That match was embarrassing because we had two cheerleaders, Alison and Sasha, and they kept singing songs about us winning – even when we were losing badly.

'Two, four, six, eight, who do we appreciate?' they began. 'Fox!' Fox was my old school's name. 'Two, four, six-and-a-quarter, who are we going to slaughter? St James!'

And that was when we were 4–0 down.

Gilbert Alkan refused to give us three cheers at the end of the match. My primary school only played one other match that year, and lost 6–0 to a team with just black boys in it. We played both matches on Wormwood Scrubs, near where the prison is. But we played too far away for prisoners to watch from their cells.

That's David, on the far side of the North Playground. He's

pointing at Gilbert and trying to say 'Hard luck.' Gilbert's wearing an Arsenal scarf and singing, 'Wemberley, Wemberley,' because Arsenal won the FA Cup.

I wouldn't be very surprised if Gilbert Alkan has even more hairs near his dick than Barney.

For breakfast, Mum gave me special home-made muesli, with grated apple and yoghurt on top: she always provides healthy food. She designed a smiley face on top of the yoghurt, with raisins that she'd soaked overnight to make them more juicy. I didn't like to break up the face, because it seemed unkind to Mum, but it would be all right if I ate one raisin at a time (the mouth first).

Crispin kept looking at me enviously over breakfast. But he'll jolly well have to grow up a bit before joining me at secondary school.

'You must wear a jumper, Bop,' said Mum, combing my hair for me. Mum calls me Bop; I don't even remember why.

'But I want to wear my Scout shirt.'

'Well, you can take off the jumper when you get inside if you like.'

I pulled on my favourite jumper, my cricket jumper, nearly pushing a finger through the elbow. Crispin watched my every move. I pushed up the sleeves to look a bit more sophisticated. It's the first time I've ever gone to a different school from him, but I said goodbye as though it was nothing special: 'See you later.'

In the car, I warned them not to call me Bop, or Jompy, like they do at home. 'And you mustn't kiss me goodbye unless I give you a signal that it's all right,' I added.

In my back pocket I had the letter from my head of year. I'd already read the letter about four million times. It told us to assemble in the North Playground. At primary school there was just one playground, but now maybe there'll be one at every point of the compass.

Before we arrived, I rehearsed things to tell my best friends, to make them admire me. There were lots of things that sounded good: I came top of the class in each of my exams; I've lived abroad, and still speak French with a convincing accent; I can draw funny pictures; and I was in the school team.

But I rehearsed it in my head, quietly.

We parked the car just outside the school gates, near an old-fashioned building with stones stuck on it, called stucco. In the distance, you could see the tarmac bend round a newer building, built of yellowish bricks, and behind that was the North Playground, full of people.

I led my parents past the edge of some gardens, where the mud was baked hard like pottery, and there was a murky pond, with a couple of ducks swimming about. Further on, we walked between two buildings. On the left was the main part of the school; it had to be the kitchens because there were some giant dustbins on wheels covered in bits of old sauce. On the right was the yellow-brick block. Looking through the windows you could see lots of machines, for woodwork, most probably.

Connecting the two buildings was this glass-covered bridge on first-floor level, for people to walk along like in a science-fiction future world, as if they couldn't breathe the normal air. This was a pretty modern school, I'd say.

We were nearly in the North Playground.

A few other boys my age walked in the same direction, with their parents. They looked at me sort of sideways, to see if I might be their friend I suppose. I walked like this, sort of swaggering like a cowboy, to show everyone how confident I was, early on. Then they'd grow to like me a lot and laugh at my jokes in class.

Ghastly gargantuan gasometer

Builders, delayed by bad weather during the summer of '58, camped out in huts on the South Playground. They didn't finish the swimming pool till half-way through the first year.

Altogether, Holland Park Comprehensive cost a grand total of £1 million – at a time when the government's entire expenditure on education amounted to just £485 million, or £43 per child. The school's design – incorporating stairwells cased in glass, glass-covered walkways leading to the sports blocks and the technical block, and a view of park or gardens from every classroom – was conceived by the architectural genius behind London's Festival Hall, Leslie Martin, a future Slade Professor at Oxford University and Knight of the Realm.

Not everybody welcomed the glittering construction. Prosperous residents of Campden Hill, on the strip of expensive land that divides the leafy expanses of Kensington Gardens and Holland Park itself, lobbied hard to prevent the state school being built. They sent stern letters to the local papers decrying the comp. One such epistle described the school as an 'educational abortion, a vast factory, mass-producing units for the prefabrication of the classless dictatorship of the proletariat'. Another described it as a 'ghastly, gargantuan gasometer' – and that was before the building had even been designed.

In the best traditions of middle-class protest, the school's opponents founded a pressure group, the Campden Hill Preservation Society. Members included the South African High

Commissioner, the widow of a former governor of the Bank of England and the future Poet Laureate, John Betjeman. All of them opposed the idea of grubby teenaged rowdies, and angular, 'modern' municipal buildings, popping up in their midst – but each of them had other arguments too. The South African Commission, London-based apologist for a regime founded upon racial segregation, can't, presumably, have been chuffed at the thought of 'blecks' mixing with whites. Lady Norman opposed the plan because it involved a compulsory purchase order on her own home, Thorpe Lodge. Here, after a hard day in Threadneedle Street, Her Ladyship's late husband Baron (Montagu) Norman of St Clere had tried to take his mind off the complexity of the gold standard, and the sheer effort involved in keeping sterling a hard currency; he'd sit with Her Ladyship, beside the grand Medici fireplace, cheerily admiring the works of art they had collected, or the rare species of tree and flower they'd assembled in the garden.

And that's where the conservationist poet stepped in: John Betjeman was anxious about the effect of boisterous schoolchildren on certain pleached limes, a wall-trained fig, a wistaria and a tulip tree. He allowed his anxiety to be published, but after a public inquiry the purchase order was pushed through. By way of compensation for losing her home, Lady Norman was dignified with an additional title: chairman of the governors. This was a symbolic role; she had little more to do than launch the occasional fund-raising drive.

Having lost the battle to prevent the school opening, snooty local residents opposed Holland Park ever afterwards, consistently displaying a greater enthusiasm for private schools than parents in any other part of Britain. With a handful of exceptions, local families which can afford to send their children to the private sector have done so. Consequently, rich children at Holland Park have always tended to be conspicuous, like a boy from South Kensington who joined the school's first sixth form:

George Castell drove to lessons in a sports car (at a time when many teachers could scarcely afford a bike), and his tailor-made blazer was a lighter shade of blue than everybody else's. An article in the school magazine indicated that Castell's parents had a villa in France. He was the exception that proves the rule.

So much for Holland Park's project in bringing together all social classes, its project in *comprehensive* education.

Week Zero (3)

The other boy I recognize is Robert Lester. Mum touches my arm and nods at him in the line before me. 'We've seen him before,' she says.

We saw him at the special parents' get-to-know-you last term, where I first saw Ms Edwards. I was wearing my Scout uniform because troop meetings were on Fridays: I wasn't going to be late, because my troop meets in this school's gym, near one of the other playgrounds.

At that special parents' evening I had a seat all of my own, by the wall. Crispin sat on Mum's knee. Some of the other people in my class had to sit on their parents' knees because there weren't enough chairs. The grown-ups looked silly because the chairs were too small, but they were bigger than the chairs at Fox. The woman in front of us had lots of shopping bags from Tesco on the table in front of her; the stuff at Tesco is really cheap. If you have bad trainers, they're called Tesco trainers. We shop at Tesco sometimes because Mum thinks it's stupid and immature to say things like 'Tesco trainers'. But I don't have any Tesco trainers; we only buy food there, sometimes.

After everyone'd settled down, the teacher started her talk. She told us how this school is different from primary school because we get a separate teacher for every subject.

I knew that already.

Ms Edwards is called Ms because I don't think she wants to tell us if she's married or not. She made 'Ms' sound a bit like

31

'miserable', but without the end bit. My old teacher at Fox was married and we called her Mrs Brown; but that was funny too because her hair was grey.

Ms Edwards is going to be our tutor, she told us, which means she'll look after us if there're any problems, and she'll always take the register for our class in the mornings and after lunch. And she might teach us French.

While she was talking, half-way through that parents' evening, there was this bang on the door.

'Come in,' said Ms Edwards.

The door opened slowly, as if the person outside wasn't exactly sure about coming in.

A very small boy peeked round the edge of the door. He had a huge hairstyle, like Arsenal's Alan Sunderland (who I *hate*). The hair looked too big for his body, but it wasn't a perm because the boy was black and black people's hair does that naturally. It was an afro. But this boy wasn't exactly black, he was light brown, like milky tea.

'Is this the right room for Class 1.5?' he demanded.

'Yes,' said Ms Edwards.

'Am I supposed to be in here? My name is Robert Lester.'

She checked the list, then said yes again.

Robert stuck his arm back out of the room and tugged.

'Come on, Mum, it's in here.'

Everyone in the room, children and parents, watched closely as this really dirty white-skinned woman tottered in after him.

She was the most alarming woman I'd ever seen, except on telly. She wore a mouldy fur coat. Her hair, as pink as bubble gum, lay in grubby strands over her face. And she was horribly drunk, smelling from miles away like a bottle of paraffin or something.

I was pretty sure she was a prostitute. She looked like the ones on *The Sweeney*: my sister Anna had showed me them. I'm not 100 per cent sure about prostitutes; I only watched *The*

Sweeney once, but Anna used to baby-sit for a prostitute called Birdie, so she knows.

I hoped Robert Lester and his mum wouldn't sit near us. Luckily, she just grabbed the nearest table, plonking herself next to a horrified Pakistani mother-and-daughter. For the rest of the meeting, she kept interrupting, challenging tons of things Ms Edwards told us, and laughing wildly at information about time-tables and school dinners.

'Shut up Mum!' Robert complained, sticking forward an ear from under his massive round hairdo. 'I'm trying to listen.'

Walking home that night, I asked Mum why Robert Lester's mum was like that. She didn't exactly say, because she probably thinks prostitutes aren't appropriate.

But she did worry about Robert. 'He must be a very unhappy little boy.'

Mum said I should try to be a good friend to him. As I was wearing my Scout uniform, I felt like helping other people; and I said I would.

Not all Scouts are like that though. My patrol leader Tim goes to this school, but he looked really worried when I told him I was coming here. He told me never to speak to him, or even say hello, when he was with his sixth-form friends.

In the playground, my parents keep trying to tell me things, not to worry and all that, but I don't really want to listen because there are too many people to look at.

I'm watching Robert Lester. He's sort of mucking around, trying to entertain the boys on each side of him with a spitting contest. His mum, who looks quite sober now, wearing a rain-coat, isn't even paying any attention.

Spooks

North Kensington wasn't just poor, it was positively macabre: close by Ladbroke Grove tube station – and one of the secondary moderns that faced closure, North Kensington Central – was Rillington Place, where the greatest ghoul of the post-war years, Dr Christie, had strangled several women, and had sex with them afterwards.

Notting Hill in the 1950s was the domain of ruthless, hard-nosed landlords. The most notorious of them, Peter Rachman – who really did send the boys round if you were late with rent, and sometimes even if you weren't – was flushed out in the 1960s, brought to the nation's attention as an indirect result of the Profumo affair. Rachman was one of the first villains to be destroyed by television: most of the country watched with astonishment as the young David Frost quizzed him, on *That Was the Week That Was*, with such vigour that Rachman actually did wriggle in his seat.

You won't find Rillington Place in the *A–Z* because they knocked it down years ago. Christie's house was one of hundreds sacrificed to the Westway, the elevated motorway that snakes from White City to Marylebone. Anna took me for a walk, when I was ten, round the streets near our flat. She showed me where Christie had lived, and told me what he'd done, providing the raw material with which I would later construct, in my sleep, many colourful nightmares.

Week Zero (4)

At half-past nine my parents kiss me goodbye and leave the playground. I don't mind the kiss: when I realize they're actually off, I suddenly get a bit worried and wish they wouldn't go. I nearly beg them to stay, in fact, or to take me away with them. But I can't say it without someone hearing me.

I watch as they walk back to the car: I don't take my eyes off them for a single second, because then everything will be OK. I sometimes think that if you take your eyes off your parents as they are going away, they'll die in a car crash.

They stand and wave before getting in and driving off. I wave back, tears pricking my eyes but just about under control.

Now I just stand here with my hands deep in my pockets, kicking the concrete with the toes of my shoes. The floor has lots of chewing gum stuck to it, and there are faded paint lines going in all directions.

I don't exactly feel like talking to anyone yet.

We wait in line, as Ms Edwards works her way down the register. After that, she promised, we'll be conducted to our classrooms.

Looking behind me, to the back of the queue, I see a bricked wall patterned into pits and bumps. This must be for Sports classes to practise rock-climbing techniques. I sort of think about grappling my way over it now, before it's too late and there's no way out.

'John Flintoff,' calls Ms Edwards, shattering my dreams of escape.

But even though I'm sad, I can't stop sounding like a know-all:

'Um, it's John-*Paul*, actually,' I say, taking my place up the line after a girl called Yemisi Fatodu.

We file out of the playground and into the school's main entrance. Then along a corridor and up the stairs. Each stairway has a different colour, says Ms Edwards, so you can easily tell where you are. Our stairs are covered in blue.

I take care not to run my hand on the banister. Anna doesn't usually talk to me much, because she's older and more sophist-icated; but she did warn me about this: for a joke, older pupils sometimes dig razorblades into the banisters and leave them there, cutting first-years' hands to shreds. She said: 'School's not like *Just William*, you know.'

After a few paces, I hear a voice behind me, calling: 'Actually! Oy, Actually!'

I turn round, and see Gilbert Alkan, crowing the new name he's made for me: 'Oy, Actually!' he laughs, making his snaky eyes small.

'Oh, very funny,' I sneer, sarcastically.

Gilbert Alkan slams me into the wall, grabbing my shirt at the neck. He's so close, I can feel his breath on my face. 'Do you want a fight?' he asks.

I say I don't.

Tons of the new classmates that I wanted to impress slow down to watch, enjoying the show. One has eyes too close together, and smiles with big front teeth, like a rat. A lardy boy stands beside him, zipped up in one of those polyester parka jackets with fur round the hood. He's smiling, too.

Robert Lester pushes through them and scowls at me as though I've done something to upset him: 'Don't let him do that to you, boy,' he says to me. 'Lick im!' Then Robert grabs my

36

arm by the elbow and swings it in Gilbert Alkan's direction, as if I was trying to punch him.

But Gilbert Alkan has more: 'I can beat you up in any way of fighting,' he menaces. 'Boxing, wrestling, kung fu or normal. So don't forget it.' Then he saunters off.

I don't cry, but there's water in my eyes like when it's blowing a really cold wind. But I'm actually pretty hot too, at the same time. I just want to hit him, but I can't because I'm scared. God, I want to hit him, I really do. But if that's how he reacts to grown-up sarcasm, what would he do if I hit him? Just a few minutes at my new school, and I'm scared stiff and humiliated.

In the classroom, I'm paired at a desk with this girl Yemisi Fatodu, a girl from Kenya whose surname is just before mine in the register. She takes the pairing badly: 'Oh miss, why! He is a bwoy!'

I reckon I'll win her round eventually. I could have made a similar complaint, about her being a girl and everything, but it would have been rude. Anyway, there're a couple of girls in the class that I wouldn't mind sitting beside. One of them's Alison, the cheerleader from Fox school. I snogged Alison for days on school journey, under a bush, then dumped her because I wanted to play cricket with my friends. She was always trying to make me perform the songs from *Grease* with her; she thinks she's Olivia Neutron Bomb. Looking to the back of the class at Alison flirting with unfamiliar, tough-looking boys, I wish I hadn't dumped her.

In the next lesson, the tutor-set is all mixed up, and I sit next to Desmond, the tallest boy in the class. Desmond's black, and I've never had a black friend before. Even though school uniform was abolished years ago, Desmond wears this dusty, threadbare blazer with the old school badge, showing a fox running around with a rose or something in its mouth. And he has a really

37

impressive black plastic Adidas sports bag; it's huge. Judging by the rattling noise, though, it's only got about one new pen in it. (It has to be a pen, because pencils are only for kids, at primary school.)

For the first time in our whole lives, we're allowed to leave the school grounds for lunch, so that's what we do, me and Desmond. We decide to go to the park beside the school. To get there, you have to walk under the gym's glass-covered walkway. It's like the other walkway, the science-fiction transporter near the North Playground and the woodwork block.

Outside the school grounds, groups of older people – third-years most probably, or even fourth-years – stand about smoking and spitting. They stand there every breaktime. Wherever you go in this place, there's cigarette ends and big puddles of gob on the floor.

One of the groups is about seven punks wearing zippy trousers: one has yellow hair and another has a ring in her nose. Some of them aren't punks but skinheads; they wear two-tone trousers and bomber jackets. They are all white, while the other group is all black boys. They aren't standing that far apart, but they aren't talking to each other.

One says to me: 'Oy, first-year, have you been mugged yet?'

I reply: 'Not really,' and we keep walking.

Race riots

As Holland Park Comprehensive prepared to usher in a new epoch of mutual respect and understanding, blacks and whites began to clobber each other in the streets. The new school opened in the same district, and the same week, as the Notting Hill race riots, the first of their kind in Britain.

If any part of Britain was ripe for this novel form of violence, it was Notting Hill. Oswald Mosley, the leader of British Fascism – who'd failed in an attempt to march his Blackshirts through Cable Street in London's East End in the 1930s, and endured a spell of wartime incarceration for sympathizing with Germany and Italy – now turned his attention towards west London. This area, and Notting Hill in particular, had attracted a substantial number of immigrants, many of them lured by vigorous British recruitment campaigns in the West Indies. Mosley and his sympathizers didn't like bleedin foreigners and dirty blacks, and no law prevented them from expressing their distaste: West Indians, seeking accommodation on arrival, would first have deduced the hostility by reading signs in boarding-house windows: NO IRISH, NO DOGS, NO BLACKS.

After years of having their bones broken by touring groups of teddy-boys, the immigrants fought back; several young blacks led the campaign from a house on Talbot Road, between Portobello Road and Kensington Park Road. That location helps to explain why the riots won so much newspaper coverage: if you walk south up the hill towards Notting Hill Gate from

Talbot Road, you'll immediately notice the grand communal gardens at the centre of every block. The Notting Hill riots weren't confined to some slum: they took place within a stone's throw of prosperous homes – and lots of people were throwing stones.

This was several years before America's civil rights movement caught the popular imagination. In Britain, several years would go by before mainstream opinion took a stern line on racism (the Race Relations Act wasn't passed until the following decade). But the blacks of Notting Hill felt righteous: they'd shown the Fascists. So they must have puzzled long and hard, months later, about who they should vote for when Oswald Mosley contested the local parliamentary election. Immediately after the riots, the sitting MP – a representative of the Labour Party, at that – had uttered a speech that could have been written by Mosley. George Rogers told the press: 'Immigrants must be limited.'

Not all foreigners at Holland Park were immigrant West Indians. When the flagship comp opened, its pupils represented thirty-five nations: many were the offspring of diplomats, living comfortably on the school's doorstep in Campden Hill or nearby. As it was then, so would it continue: statistics have consistently demonstrated Holland Park's astonishing racial diversity. Between them, Holland Parkers speak more recognized languages and dialects at home than the pupils of any other school in Britain.

Colin Prescod, the black boy who murdered Jenny Abramsky, had arrived in North Kensington from the West Indies only weeks before the Notting Hill riots. A fantastic athlete, he could cover a hundred yards faster than any woman alive (he'd beaten every women's record); at Holland Park, he established himself as all-London champion. With several years of rigorous colonial education behind him, he impressed teachers too, notching up terrific exam results. In the sixth form, Prescod was appointed deputy head boy. Among staff and pupils alike, Prescod proved so much more popular than the actual head boy, Roy Jose, that almost at once everybody spoke of the pair as 'joint head boys'.

All the same, Prescod resented Jose's eminence. Could this explain his mad attack on Jenny Abramsky? Or was the school's experiment in unisex, cross-class, multi-racial education doomed from the start? And what happened afterwards – did they close the school, revert to the old system of grammar school and secondary modern, send the black children to a school of their own? Back to the West Indies?

Not at all: in fact, the murder of Abramsky was applauded wildly by the pupils, staff and parents who witnessed it. Prescod (whose son Adam joined Holland Park a year after me, enabling Colin to become the first former pupil among the parent governors), looks back on that evening's work with pride. National newspapers splashed the story the next day: this was a triumph for Holland Park, the first school ever to cast a black boy in the role of Othello against a white girl's Desdemona.

Week Zero (5)

The park is really amazing, because there are so many different bits. At one end, to the north, it's quite wild, with weeds and probably even blackberries and stuff. But if you go the other way, which me and Desmond do, you come to these sweeping lawns and row upon row of flowerbeds. There are ornate benches by the flowerbeds, and peacocks and exotic kinds of ducks just wander around the place.

There is also a shop. 'Shall we get an ice lolly?' asks Desmond.

'Actually, I've got some sandwiches, and I don't have any money,' I say.

Desmond buys an ice lolly, then we sit on a bench – looking out for pigeon crap first.

I eat the sandwich Mum made me, cheese and tomato on wholemeal bread, and a Granny Smith. I tell Desmond lots of things about me, like about how ancient my sister Anna is, and how Crispin's too young for secondary school. Desmond tells me his blazer used to belong to his older sister.

We're both Man U supporters, which is pretty amazing; but neither of us has actually been to a match yet.

Desmond is still hungry. He buys a hot-dog, so I ask him: 'Do you want to hear a joke?'

'Yeah.'

'Well it's about three men who went to a hotel, one English, one Scottish and one Irish. The Englishman, right, was on the top floor and he needed a shave, but there wasn't anywhere, so the hotel woman told him shave out of the window. The Scottish man, on the floor below, wanted to go to the loo, but there wasn't a loo so the hotel woman told him to just do it out of the window. And on the ground floor the Irishman wanted to eat a plate of beans but there wasn't a table so he sat at the window to enjoy the view.'

'Yeah.'

'But the Englishman dropped his razor. It fell on the Scottish man that was having a piss's dick, and cut it right off!'

Desmond laughs.

'The dick, and lots of blood, fell right into the Irishman's plate. He said: "Yum! What lovely sausages in these beans! And what lovely tomato sauce."'

It's quite a good joke, but it didn't put him off his hot-dog.

I'm practising my accent, to sound less posh in case people pick on me. First of all I've changed the way I say Gary; I call him Gow. If there was someone called Barry, I'd call him Bow.

I made an appointment to meet Gow at breaktime. He said: 'Meet me at the loins near the South Playground.'

I knew what he meant: it was Cockney for 'lines'. I went to the South Playground but there were lines *all over the ground*, yellow ones for basketball, white ones for soccer, and other ones in red and blue that I didn't recognize. They stretched all over the place and I couldn't see Gow.

After waiting nearly all of the break, I started to walk back to the West Block for my next lesson.

'Oy, I'm up ere, where were ya?'

I looked up a line of steps and Gow was sitting on top of a little statue of a roaring lion. That was what he meant; but he pronounced it 'loins', so I didn't find him.

Everyone is well behaved in class. If you think about it, lessons can be good fun. In Music, we play a song by the Police called

'Message in a Bottle' on xylophones. I kept the sheet with the music on it so I can try at home with my old recorder. The Music teacher has a silly moustache, and enormous glasses big enough for a welder. He looks grumpy when we get the notes wrong, and in fact he is Scottish, which somehow makes him seem even more grumpy. But the lesson made most of us laugh.

Maths isn't exactly fun, but I normally like it. I write notes *amazingly* neatly in my blue exercise book, taking down stuff about long division which I already know. The teacher looks even worse than in Music. This one has sloping shoulders, damp brown eyes and a nearly bald head. The hair at the sides hangs down like a spaniel's ears, almost to his neck. In fact, he looks exactly like a really sad dog.

Our English teacher hobbled into the lesson with a bad limp. She's my friend David from primary school's mum and I like her and everything. Nobody makes fun of her walk, because she came out and told us straight away that she got polio when she was young. Her mother dreamt she'd get it, the night before.

Whatever lesson we're in, nearly everybody puts their hands up, even for boring questions. You have to shout, 'Please, miss . . .' or 'I know this one, sir . . .' I think the teachers have got the message about how keen I am on their subjects. My work is going to be about the best in the class I think.

Very Important Person

Holland Park had scarcely got going when a Very Important Person enrolled his child there. When Prince Philip visited the school in 1964, as patron of the Duke of Edinburgh Awards Scheme, his own children's schooling seemed fixed. Prince Charles, the future head of state, had been sent to a tough private school of the duke's choice, Gordonstoun in Scotland. And Princess Anne was at Benenden, an expensive private school in Kent.

But how long would they stay there? Other children from eminent families had switched from private schools to Holland Park – and flourished. Polly Toynbee, daughter of the author Philip Toynbee, had scored badly in exams at Badminton, picking up just four O levels. Her English teacher at Holland Park, Mr Stedman-Jones, assured her she was bright enough to get into Oxford. One of many excellent teachers attracted to the new school by a strong belief in equal opportunities and the comprehensive system, Stedman-Jones coached Toynbee at lunchtime, helping her to crack Oxford entrance – with a scholarship to St Anne's thrown in.

Many middle-class parents hadn't liked the look of the lower school, but A levels were different. Sixth-formers alone had the run of Thorpe Lodge, with its kitchen at the back, separate common rooms for the upper and lower sixth, and plenty of wood-panelled rooms for extra-curricular activities. These sophisticated outsiders astonished home-grown sixth-formers. Some, like George Castell, impressed with material wealth; others just seemed terribly intelligent (one, a school legend, introduced herself to classmates with 'Oh my goodness, don't you know Debussy's work?'). With people like that around, the sixth-formers acquired a distinct sense of superiority. One home-grown talent, Leonard Hobbs, adapted for A levels by poshing up his accent and general demeanour; another boy suggested that sixth-formers should sport a special tie, to distinguish them from the grotty children in the lower school. But Robin Black-burn, the son of an MP, rubbished the tie proposal as absurd élitism. Easy for him to say: Blackburn was one of many sixth-formers who had no personal experience of the lower school.

As well as dying in *Othello*, Jenny Abramsky did one other thing to get the papers writing about Holland Park. She told the Very Important Person all about the school, persuading him to send his children there.

Compared with today, Holland Park in the 1960s sounds like some old-fashioned grammar school. The headmaster, Mr Allen Clarke, having little clue how to direct this novel educational drama, had fallen back on old-fashioned props: not just the uniform for pupils but also gowns for those teachers who were graduates; a Latin motto, *'Floreat semper scola'* ('Let the school always flourish'); a school badge; a system of eight 'houses' for pastoral care; corporal punishment; and streaming.

On the badge, the badge I first spotted on Desmond's hand-me-down blazer, Allen Clarke gestured at a little local history: Holland Park had once been the private gardens of Lord Hol-land, an eighteenth-century politician who'd started his career as plain Henry Fox. King George III had conferred membership of the aristocracy on Fox, for statesmanship, but Fox had additional claims to fame. One related to his gardens. According to history books, Lord Holland did the same for dahlias as an earlier globe-trotting nobleman, Sir Walter Raleigh, had done for potatoes: he imported them to Britain. Hence the school's symbol: a fox *rampant*, bearing a dahlia in its mouth.

Pupils advertised the house they belonged to by means of a coloured ribbon stitched into the blazer pocket; all eight houses were named after dead white men, including the eighteenth-century politician Fox (his house colour green) and the twentieth-century bank governor Norman (light blue). Streaming, from A to E, was rigid, with little movement between the top and the bottom.

Corporal punishment was perfectly acceptable; some teachers stalked about with canes inside their gowns, while the head of PE, a retired member of the Parachute Regiment, preferred to wield the slipper. Discipline was good. Pupils stood up when someone came into the class; and left their belongings in open desks, or in lockers which were never actually locked. If something was reported missing, a polite announcement went out on the tannoy: 'Somebody has mistakenly picked up a black umbrella belonging to a first-year. Would they please hand it in at the office.'

The range of subjects was broad: not just English, Maths, languages, Geography and History, but Woodwork and Metalwork for boys and Domestic Science for girls, Music for everybody, and PE too. Less everyday subjects included Economics. And, in his study, the headmaster taught Chaucer to sixthformers. Holland Park, as a comp, really did offer an amalgam of the two kinds of schooling previously served up separately by grammar schools and secondary moderns, a mixture of academic and vocational.

The Inner London Education Authority had declared Notting Hill an educational priority area, but Holland Parkers proved good at exams. Of two hundred or so first-years who joined in 1962, only twelve had passed their Eleven Plus, and yet eighteen departed with three or more A levels. Altogether sixty-six pupils in that year achieved 129 A-level passes. Studies by the National Educational Association compared this with Hendon County Grammar School, where just seventy-nine pupils out of ninety who had passed their Eleven Plus managed to gain an A level. And the NEA, far from seeking this outcome, was a pro-grammar-school, anti-comprehensive pressure group.

If it hadn't been for Holland Park, these local Eleven Plus failures would never have had the chance to study in a sixth form; but at Holland Park the sixth form numbered two hundred pupils within four years. Leonard Hobbs, who'd joined Kensington West Central after failing his Eleven Plus, was admired at Holland Park for his eloquence in Senior Society debates. He went on to study at Cambridge. Another like him was Julian Aston (the society's secretary, prime mover behind an impressive list of guest speakers, including Trevor Huddleston, Johnny Dankworth, Mary Goldring and Penelope Mortimer). Aston pipped Hobbs to the prize for best essay on Kensington, funded out of campaign leftovers by Lady Norman's Campden Hill Preservation Society. And more revered even than these two was the first head boy, Luath Grant Ferguson, who carried that title with him from the lower sixth to the upper. He performed the lead role in *Becket*, to the satisfaction of (among others) my father, an actor, who found himself in Grant Ferguson's audience though I was not yet a member of the school; in fact I wasn't born until some years later, and even my older sister was just a toddler.

Outside school hours, besides performing plays, and music, Holland Parkers took part in many activities. Not just the Duke of Edinburgh Award scheme: Holland Park was new, pupils felt they'd been given a fresh chance; they were excited, *involved*. One group was photographed by *The Times*, on a march to Aldermaston with the Campaign for Nuclear Disarmament. For their earnest hobbyism and puritan work ethic, A-stream and B-stream pupils such as Hobbs, Aston, Grant Ferguson and the

CND supporters were characterized by less committed children as eager beavers and eggheads.

Impressed? So was the Very Important Person.

The VIP, of course, was not the Duke of Edinburgh. His children, including Prince Charles, the future head of state, were not entrusted to state schooling. But a senior Labour Party figure, living on the school's doorstep, did back the new school. Tony Benn was soon to be Postmaster General, then Minister of Technology. He had a house between Notting Hill Gate and Shepherd's Bush, on broad, leafy Holland Park Avenue; to which he invited Abramsky, as head girl, to discuss with him and his wife – over tea – the new school's advantages.

The Benns put Holland Park firmly at the centre of attention. By 1964, Labour had been out of government for twelve years, but Tony Benn was rather better-known than the average opposition MP. He was a folk hero.

As an MP when his father died, he'd inherited a peerage which forced him to quit the House of Commons. He tried to renounce his title, but wasn't allowed – so he stood as Viscount Stansgate in the by-election and the voters backed him. Turning up at the House of Commons, he was refused entry. But the public backed the reluctant peer, and eventually a joint committee of Lords and Commons recommended the changes Benn wanted. During the decades that followed, Benn remained hugely influential. In the 1970s he helped to introduce yet another constitutional change: the use of a referendum (to determine Britain's entry into the European Common Market). And, at the height of his career, he narrowly missed winning the party leadership.

Benn's endorsement of Holland Park might have carried more weight if he'd been Minister of Education. But his wife Caroline was to make up for that. For more than thirty years, since Jenny Abramsky popped round to extol the merits of Holland Park, Caroline Benn has shown endless commitment to education.

The holder of two postgraduate degrees, she has written several books on the subject; laboured as a university teacher and school governor; and held significant posts within the education section of the UNESCO Commission and the Inner London Education Authority.

The Benns withdrew their oldest son, Stephen, from his private school, Westminster, and packed him off to Holland Park. Tony noted in his diary: 'I hope it does something to get comprehensives moving.' After Stephen, the Benns sent three more children (one of them overlapped with my sister).

Just as the Tory Lords Home and Hailsham swiftly copied Benn in ridding themselves of politically inconvenient titles, so plenty of politicians and media figures followed his endorsement of Holland Park. Roy Jenkins, who dwelt in a grand square off Notting Hill Gate, towards Queensway, and whose career was to include stints as Home Secretary, Chancellor of the Exchequer and Chancellor of Oxford University, sent a son (Charles Jenkins joined the sixth form in the mid-1960s for just one year, studying Maths, Economics and English).

Tony Crosland was another Labour minister who lived around the corner from the Benns. As Minister for Education, Crosland was the originator, in 1965, of the celebrated government circular, 10/65, which urged local authorities to introduce comprehensives instead of grammar schools and secondary moderns; and to many minds he was the only holder of that job ever to have considered seriously the harmful effect of a flourishing private sector on state education. But Crosland never sent a child of his own to Holland Park. It was his *step*daughter, offspring of the journalist Susan Crosland, who was told by an angry Holland Park teacher: 'Just because your father is Minister for Education is no reason to think you can do anything you like.'

Week Zero (6)

From the fourth day, class behaviour gets worse. The teachers don't actually look surprised, but I am. Some of the tough-looking boys are pretty naughty. They leap around from desk to desk in Maths, shouting, putting innocent boys' heads in a neck clamp or kicking the backs of their chairs. 'Those bwoys are so stupid,' mutters Yemisi, angry about boys still. I feel less welcome than ever beside her.

Desmond stops wearing his sister's blazer and just wears a normal jumper instead, with an old Fred Perry underneath.

One morning Alison comes over to my desk in registration and makes Yemisi laugh by being rude about my clothes. 'You are so unfashionable,' she says. 'Those trousers are flares.'

She also sneers at the leather patches Mum sewed on my jeans, and says my shoes are 'crusty'. For Christ's sake, I think: it was *me* who dumped *you*, not the other way round.

Alison is nice-looking and everything, but she's also got this mole on the back of her right hand, as large and dark as a melted chocolate chip. I hate it, it put me right off her, on school journey. When I dumped her, I told her it was only because I wanted to play cricket with my friends instead of snog her all the time, but the truth is I blame her mole for putting me off. But I can't turn the attack back on her, because Alison's already going home with a big boy called Sean, holding hands and snogging him on the bus. So I *still* don't mention her mole.

I try to argue using the facts, instead. 'They aren't flares. If I took them off and you measured them all the way down, they don't get any wider at the ankles,' I explain. 'And I have to have patches because I always make holes in my jeans playing football.'

She doesn't make fun of Robert Lester though. He came into school this morning without his beach-ball-sized afro. Instead, the hair stood in short, thick plaits; it made his head look like an exotic, prickly fruit. Or a small planet, like in *Le Petit Prince*. Nobody laughs at Robert because he's tough, but you can tell he's pretty embarrassed. He swears quite a lot about his aunt for doing his hair like that.

After break, Robert comes out of the second-floor toilets (I don't call them 'loos' any more, except at home) with the plaits untwisted, and the afro restored. But he hasn't got it quite right, it's wonky: the smooth, round edges dented here and there, like a ball that hasn't been fully pumped up.

Yesterday afternoon in Maths, my new friend Desmond sat next to Gilbert and Robert. After a few minutes he laughed, then stood up and pointed at me and shouted: 'Oy, Actually!'

I have to be friends with Alexander and Daniel now. They are scruffy boys that I never paid much attention to at primary school, because they are also useless at football. Alexander and Daniel have picked up a new friend here, the round boy with glasses who stood beside me in the playground on the first morning. His name's Diego, and he doesn't speak a word of English.

After all, I have to be friends with somebody, and they're probably flattered that I thought of them. But Alexander and Daniel and Diego can be dangerous friends because most people like to pick on them.

At the end of the first week, I walk home with Alexander and Daniel and Diego. Leaving the school building, we cross the North Playground. At the beginning of the week it was really full but now it's nearly deserted.

In one corner there's a group of punks smoking and spitting together. In the other corner there's a couple of first-year boys. One of them's the really, really blond boy I pulled faces at. I know his name because he's in a couple of my lessons where the tutor-sets are split up; it's Andrew. I don't think I like him. The other boy is Andrew's best friend, Hanif, who's even taller than me. They call themselves the Two-Tone Posse, but two-tone's meant to be white and *black*, not white and Asian.

When we are nearly past them, Andrew stops Alexander, who sort of shuffles when he walks and looks good to pick on.

Andrew's pretty Cockney, and he says: 'Whatchoo looking at?'

Alexander says he isn't looking at anything.

'Yes you were, you were looking at me,' says Andrew. 'Wanker. D'you wanna fight?'

That question again!

'No,' says Alexander, looking down at Andrew's feet all the time to show he doesn't mean trouble. But Andrew moves closer, virtually touching noses, and spits right in Alexander's face. If you look you can see the frothy bit just under Alexander's eye. But Alexander just stands still until Andrew turns away, chuckling with Hanif.

Andrew must be pretty brave, because there were four of us, and just two of them. But that sort of thing, with the spitting, is really nasty.

I'd expected to be pushed about by older children, but not by my own age-group; it's really a horrible surprise. I can't understand it.

From their accents, I guess Andrew and Robert Lester are working-class, but they aren't exactly the noble underdogs I expected from what I hear at dinner, at home.

What am I supposed to think?

Centre of crime and violence

Lower-stream pupils – deadbeats, drips and dilutees, to use the 1960s terminology – began to feel excluded. All too often, they missed out on the dedicated, experienced staff, only to be fobbed off instead with temporaries and student teachers.

Looking back on the 1960s, it's easy to conjure up a process of decline. In politics, everybody's darling, JFK, was replaced by bullying Lyndon Johnson, then the degenerate Richard Nixon. In pop music, the Beatles abandoned their sharp suits in favour of kaftans and shaggy beards. Whether such trends had any effect on Holland Park is open to question, but it's certainly true that the school's bright, earnest, world-challenging ethos changed into something less heroic.

The following details serve to suggest the school's emerging counter-culture: pupils started to smoke in the toilets (and not just cigarettes), regularly setting off the fire alarm; a gate leading directly into the park was bricked up after outsiders broke in, closing up the school like a prison; slogans such as 'Johnny loves Sandra' were carved into the trees which John Betjeman and the Campden Hill Preservation Society had fretted about. And some time in the mid-1960s a young teacher said the word 'fuck'. A teacher of languages (appropriately enough), Mr Coggle had always tended to be outspoken. Favoured pupils actually knew his first name, Paul, even if they didn't use it in school. One morning he walked past a desk on which a pupil had scrawled the forbidden word. 'What is this?' he asked. 'What do you mean, sir?' asked the pupil, pushing it further. 'Why is this word "fuck" on the table?' replied Coggle (who much later, incidentally, wrote a book entitled *Do You Talk Estuary?*).

The headmaster, Allen Clarke, became increasingly remote. Sixth-formers studying Chaucer were one thing; but pupils making a noise outside his office were another. The head established a system whereby pupils walked the long way round his study, or shuffled up one set of stairs and down the next one. Like the Wizard of Oz, Allen Clarke communicated as a disembodied voice through the school's whiz-bang, up-to-the-minute tannoy technology, broadcasting his thoughts to everybody at once.

As the 1960s came to an end, he became unwell; he took to the bottle. His deputy, Dorothy Coleman, took over as acting head. Caroline Benn by now was chairman of the school governors, a body of men and women who took a rather more active part in the school than they had under Lady Norman.

Towards the end of 1970, pupils overcome with radical chic put together a deputation demanding a voice in how school was run. At that point, the media turned against Holland Park; the protest was covered in the national papers; stories suggested that a thousand pupils had gone on the rampage. Tony Benn noted in his diary:

The press arrived in force at the school. Some photographers gave five or ten bob to some of the kids to break windows and others had given them tomatoes to throw ... Nobody has taken any notice of Holland Park for years because it is a very ordinary comprehensive. But when we send our children there it is immediately described as the fashionable Eton of comprehensives, though it never was. You get a bit of trouble like yesterday, the whole thing is built up as being the centre of crime and violence.

Of course, that's not quite true: Holland Park had always attracted a certain amount of criticism. A typical article in the *Daily Telegraph*, in 1963, focused on three pupils who'd experienced a miserable time at school; in response to that, a group of former pupils, studying at the London School of Economics, complained to the *Telegraph*'s editor. He invited them to meet him, and to write a piece in response – but didn't publish it. What changed with the arrival of the Benns was the ferocity of the press attacks, and their frequency. Within weeks of the 'riot' story there was a fresh twist: an article in the *Spectator* suggesting that somebody at Holland Park was operating a call-girl ring.

A permanent replacement for Allen Clarke was urgently required. The departing head told the *Times Educational Supplement* that his successor would need one thing in bucketloads: energy. But the *TES* was more interested in the bucketloads of cash to be earned by running this large and unusually challenging school: it wrote up the vacancy as 'this plummiest of plum jobs: school roll 1,966, maximum salary £4,561 per annum'. Today, the financial rewards continue to attract attention in a sector which isn't renowned for large salaries. The school's current head, Mary Marsh, hit the headlines when she joined because her pay package was reckoned to match that of the Education Minister.

One teacher who sent in his application for Allen Clarke's job was Mr Frost, efficient but uninspiring head of Maths since the school opened. The only serious challenge to Frost was from Dr Rushworth, the school's first head of Languages, who'd left Holland Park six years earlier to become headmaster at Shoreditch Comprehensive in east London.

Rushworth was regarded by colleagues and by pupils as a paradox, a fascinating combination. Vigorously progressive (why else teach at Holland Park and Shoreditch?), he was also a bit of a snob about education, rarely seen without his scholar's gown. The combination owes a lot to Rushworth's own background: he'd 'made it' from humble origins, a grammar school in Huddersfield, all the way to Oxford University. Even in its headmaster, Holland Park matched the spirit of the times: Huddersfield grammar and Oxford was precisely the combination that had taken a near-contemporary of Rushworth, Harold Wilson, to his position as leader of the Labour Party, and then Prime Minister.

After the usual round of interviews and assessments, Rushworth got the job. His entry into public life is recorded in Tony Benn's diary for Thursday 13 May 1971: on that day, Caroline Benn ate lunch with the Secretary of State for Education, Margaret Thatcher; and then, in the afternoon, the Benns were joined at home (for tea) by the new headmaster at their children's school, Dr Rushworth.

Returning to Holland Park after six years in east London, Rushworth found a dramatic difference. Lockers had been vandalized, with doors pulled off the hinges and locks damaged beyond repair. The building was in poor shape; there was hostility between the streams; staff morale was low. *Semper*? Erm, no: *scola* had ceased for the moment to flourish. 'The place was unrecognizable,' says Rushworth now, looking back. Having lost its novelty, Holland Park had also lost its original impetus. It needed shaking up. The radical new headmaster looked at the old grammar-school trappings: the house system, the streaming, the uniform and corporal punishment. He didn't like what he saw. Dr Rushworth wanted something more 'comprehensive'.

PART II

Lower School

Ling

We're waiting for our teacher, and the classroom door opens: it's Captain Caveman! It's this woman with frizzy hair and a stubby nose that points upwards; she often covers lessons when our proper teacher's sick. She's not a genuine cover teacher, she normally teaches Art. She's short, she wears a necklace with giant red balls on it. It's like primitive jewellery, the stuff in history books about man before *Homo sapiens*. That's why we call her Captain Caveman, like the cartoon character.

She looks really depressed when she recognizes our class; her shoulders drop and her eyes roll towards the ceiling; but as for us, we're delighted. Everyone stands up and roars, 'CAPTAIN CAAAAAVE-MAAAN!'

She's good at staying calm, cause we behave really badly when she takes our lessons. Apart from shouting Captain Caveman all the time, we make special noises. One is the call of a peacock. There are peacocks in the park beside school, and this is a special noise, just for our class. Once somebody starts the peacock noise, everybody has to join in. It goes, 'Aaaargh-ah.' Like this:

'Aaaargh-ah.'

'Be quiet,' says Captain Caveman, but it's too late.

'Aaargh-ah, aaargh-ah.' Then everyone's off.

'Aaargh-ah, aaargh-ah.'

And so on.

The other noise to irritate teachers is when you hum with

your mouth open, and teachers can't tell who's doing it except when they lean over and listen really closely – so if they do that, you stop. Sometimes nearly everyone in the class – well, the boys, at any rate, and maybe a couple of girls – gets humming all at once.

We made one woman go round the bend doing that. She shouted her head off at us: 'Get back to the gutter from whence you came!' Another class rule is, if you see that teacher in the corridor, you have to shout her slogan back at her.

Donna Cable invented a game called Ling, with the wooden blackboard rubber. Donna is this black girl who's the biggest person in the class. She snatches the blackboard rubber when the teacher isn't looking, and throws it as hard as she can across the room at someone who isn't looking. The only warning you get is that she shouts as she lets go of it: 'Ling!'

I always sit with my back to the wall; that way I can see anything that's going on. Like spitting. Peter Davies spends hours spitting silently on people's backs. Peter has this amazing technique, he scoops gob out of his mouth with his tongue, sending it flying out in a little loop. Robert Lester too has mastered that technique. Normally they spit on Alexander's back, or Daniel Murphy's, because those two never fight back.

But Peter wears glasses. You wouldn't think he was a big fighter. He looks funny when he takes his glasses off. His eyes don't focus on you properly, as though he can't see *at all*.

The other things I always look out for are drawing pins on my chair, or chewing gum which messes up your jeans. I never sit down without checking chairs carefully – someone might have taken all the screws out, for example, so the chair will collapse. Once, Robert Lester left Superglue on a teacher's chair but it dried before she sat down, because she carried on for hours writing on the blackboard.

After a whole lesson of Ling and making a racket, Captain Caveman looks furious. She shouts at anyone. Robert Lester

64

picked on Kampol Mai Ngram, making him say his name out loud. Robert sat close beside him, with the knuckles of his fist touching Kampol's leg, and said:

'What's your full name?'

'Kampol Mai Ngram.'

But Kampol spoke really quietly, so Robert hit him and hissed: 'Louder.'

Kampol said it a bit louder.

Then Robert hit him again. '*Louder.*'

So Kampol said it fairly loud – but Robert wanted him to shout it out, so he hit him again.

Anyway, it ended up with Kampol shouting out his own name so the whole class could hear it. From Captain Caveman's point of view, Kampol was causing a disturbance. She couldn't really understand it, cause even *she* knew that he's usually shy. So she told him to be quiet.

Immediately after that, Kampol shouted out: 'KAMPOL! – MAI! – NGRAM!'

She gave him detention.

In Needlework classes, you don't need to work hard. You can muck around because the teachers are soft, and never give detention.

Me and Samuel Thomas made headbands out of scrap material, running them up on the sewing machines so the loose threads wouldn't come out. Mine was red and white, Samuel's had blue stripes. The teacher helped us to run up the headbands. Then we chased each other round class with a special rule: you're not allowed to touch the floor. We jumped on the chairs and tables and vaulted over girls' sewing machines.

'Oy, fuck off, you made my fucking sewing slip, you fucking wanker,' said Ellen, slapping Samuel's legs. I twisted and slipped out of Ellen's range. Miss told us to get down – but we don't listen because she never means it.

'Get down,' she said, sighing again. 'I mean it.'

It was early afternoon, and the midday sun was coming straight through the window, from high above the trees in the park. The heat seemed to make everyone cross. Pulling the headbands down over our foreheads, me and Samuel impersonated John McEnroe, that time at Wimbledon: 'You can*not* be serious, miss.'

Most of the teachers who do Needlework are young women. The one who teaches me always wears tight jeans and low-cut sweaters made of that big, hairy kind of wool, angora. When she leans over someone's machine on the other side of the room, you can see her boobs in her bra as clear as anything. She's quite a good teacher.

The best thing I made in Needlework is an excellent green-and-red sponge-bag for putting soap and stuff in when you go away. It's about one foot deep and nine inches across, so I can fit loads of things in; it's going to be really useful on my next Scout camp. It's got a lining as well, made of cloth like net curtains.

Also, each of us made a cushion in the shape of a person. I sewed a red rosette on it, in honour of the general election, and called it Tony Benn because he lives round here and my dad likes him. We stuffed our cushions with snipped-up pieces of foam that were brilliant for throwing at each other and putting down people's backs. Miss kept sighing and telling me and Samuel to pick it up, and then coming over all reasonable and asking if we'd behave like that at home.

Samuel said: 'Yes, miss. I do it all the time.'

In different classes, you have different people to be your best mate. Samuel's my best mate in Needlework. He's not usually in my class, so I normally pair up with someone else. Last term, in Home Economics, I paired up with a thin boy, Ernie Dallas, but Ernie left school last term.

Everyone must do Home Economics, Needlework, and Design

and Technology. You can't avoid it, you have one each term, for two lessons a week. Actually, they're fun. But you should never mess around with Design and Technology teachers – who've mostly got tattoos and look as if they should be in prison. If you mucked around in *their* classes, they'd probably give you a good kicking. Still, they never set any homework. I had Design and Technology for my first term. We spent weeks making metal ashtrays, then melting enamel powder on them so it ran and made patterns, like for hippies. Stupid, because we aren't even allowed to smoke. I gave mine to Anna.

Teachers in Home Economics are completely ancient. My teacher doesn't have any dark hair at all, she's gone completely white. And she's lost her marbles too. When she told us to cook macaroni cheese – she demonstrated it, at the beginning of the class – the food looked so disgusting that I secretly made jammy biscuits again, like the week before. Who wants macaroni cheese, anyway? It's disgusting. If you're late for school dinners cause you've been held in detention, or if you were playing football, the last things left are always those Spam fritters, and macaroni cheese. Nobody likes it. It's a fact.

The best things we made in Home Economics are: apple jam, jam biscuits and a thing called *jalousie* tart, which is French for 'jealousy', because it's got slits in the pastry for peeping through when you're jealous of someone. Well, that's what *she* told us.

The worst thing about Home Economics is: washing up. If you're badly behaved in class, miss gives you other people's washing up to do as well as your own. Normally me and Ernie would try to get rid of our washing up, dumping a wooden spoon in someone else's sink, or a chopping board. But you can't do that with pans: they're too big. Luckily, the teacher never notices whether you've washed something badly, so nobody needs to try too hard. But the bad thing about that is that people in the lesson *before* you also leave pans covered in disgusting stuff, like old flour and eggs. The only exceptions are older people, doing O-level Home Economics. *They* take it seriously, and wash up brilliantly. Once a week we have a class after them, which means the pans are shiny as space ships. I've even seen the older pupils staying in class *throughout break* to wash up, finishing off while my lesson starts.

Most people who do O-level Home Economics are Asian girls, and a lot of them wear headscarves. They wash up properly of their own free will.

You know what? My Home Economics teacher always drinks tea. She never stops. At the beginning of the lesson, while she's demonstrating how to mix something, or how to cook, she always picks on one of the boys to make her a cup. Once she made Gilbert Alkan fix her tea. When he'd nearly finished, he said, 'Miss, do you take sugar, miss?'

'Yes, thank you, dear.'

While she wasn't looking, Gilbert Alkan put in salt, instead. Behind her back, while she was demonstrating, he lifted up the salt cellar as though he was Pat Rice holding up the FA Cup. That way, everyone could see that it was salt. He poured a heaped tablespoon, then another one too, stirred it, and handed it to her really nicely, as if she was his own granny.

'Here you are, miss.'

'Thank you dear, that's very kind.'

And you know what? She drank the lot!

In lessons like Home Economics and Needlework and Design and Technology, we have tons of unusual things to muck around with. In more ordinary lessons such as Maths, there's only a pen and a book. But sometimes in Maths there may be a compass to draw circles with, and there are fun things you can do with a compass. Usually, we play the dare game, putting a hand on the table with the fingers spread out, then moving fast with the compass, stabbing the table in between the fingers. The winner is the person who stabs fastest, with no injury. Alternatively, you can scratch your girlfriend's name on your arm, if you have one, making a thin scar – but that can be painful.

In Needlework, pupils have access to electricity, which is needed for sewing machines. One day, me and Samuel told this stupid, buck-toothed fat boy, Stephen Harris, to stick his scissors in the plug. But he wasn't *that* stupid.

If there's nothing special to muck around with in your classroom, you can make your own fun. One thing to do is play Asteroids – like the arcade game, but on paper.

Take a large sheet of paper, and draw massive obstacles – asteroids, and mines – all over the middle of it, leaving the tiniest passage for you to get through, from the bottom to the top. At the top of the page, draw five or six different bays for the rockets to dock in. And at the bottom, draw an up-and-down zigzag, making plenty of peaks for the rockets to launch from.

Take it in turns to steer a biro with just one finger, touching it on the top. If you use more fingers than that, your rocket will blow up and you lose a life. Steer round the obstacles. If your pen drops before you get to one of the bays at the top of the page, make a tiny cross where the ink stopped, and start again at that cross when it's your next go.

If you become good at this, you can steer a pen round *all sorts* of corners. The secret is to be calm, to take it nice and slow. I'm so good at it now, I can do the whole course in one go. That Thai boy, Kampol Mai Ngram, is best in our class. But he's shy as anything.

To make lessons more interesting, I had to improve Asteroids. Together with Kampol, I designed it so that different bays were worth different points – anything from five thousand points to a hundred thousand. Now it's a race to score more of them.

Asteroids is a good thing to do in lessons because you don't get detention, or go on report, if they catch you. To be frank, they never catch you anyway. Even though they're better than

Asteroids, you can't really play Space Invaders or Pac Man on paper; nobody has invented it.

Stephen Harris can't even concentrate on a game of Asteroids. You go to all the trouble of preparing the game for him, and then he draws dicks all over it. Stephen goes on about dicks all the time. He always draws circumcised dicks, because he says that's cleaner. Every so often, he nudges you and says: 'Look at this willy.' You look at it and say, 'Har har,' then try to get on with whatever you're doing.

I prefer to draw pictures of people. I draw them all over my exercise books – and sometimes on textbooks too. On the front of each exercise book, I draw the teacher who's teaching me. Inside, I illustrate whatever we've been studying in that lesson.

The other week, Alexander got me in a load of trouble in French. He kept pestering me to ask Dr Bowes what a French letter was.

The thing is, I knew Alexander was trying to get me in trouble, because he had a certain smile on his face, and he spoke quietly so nobody would hear him. Anyway, if he really wanted to know, he'd have asked himself. But I didn't mind annoying Dr Bowes because three weeks earlier, after I'd drawn a brilliant cartoon of him staring out of the window and shown it to everyone (they thought it was brilliant), he'd put me on detention.

I didn't know what a French letter was, but as soon as I asked, I could tell Dr Bowes was annoyed. Dr Bowes frowned in my direction briskly, before turning to somebody else, as if he'd spotted a little fly in his soup but didn't like to complain. So I pressed on, asking him again and again.

'Sir, sir . . .'

'Stop that,' he warned. 'Don't be silly.'

I wanted to see what he'd do next. So I shouted out the question again: 'But sir, I only want to know what a French letter is . . .'

And then, as quick as you like, Dr Bowes put me on detention again. I couldn't believe it! I had to collect Crispin from Fox straight after school. I told Dr Bowes it was rather inconvenient.

'You should have thought of that before you started asking silly questions,' said Dr Bowes.

I sat sulking for the rest of the lesson and refused to answer any questions, even though I'm the best in the class at French by a mile (*par plus d'un kilomètre*). I stared at the wall. Someone had written on it: 'I French-kissed Ms Edwards 'ere.'

I didn't know what that meant either.

In History, we study weird tribes in the Amazon, and their rituals. For example, we watch films about natives of the rainforest, jumping out of trees with vines tied round their legs. Then everybody must write it up in their exercise books, explaining that the man who jumps from the highest branch is the bravest in the tribe. I drew some pictures of them jumping, with speech bubbles saying 'Aaaaaaargh!!!'.

The closest we ever get to real history is the ancient Egyptians. At least they had *some* kings and queens. To tell you the truth, I'm fed up that we never study English kings and queens, because I can already tell you what order they go in. Even back to front. I learnt when I was about nine and a half. We got a poster from the National Portrait Gallery; it left out Lady Jane Grey. I can tell you who was related to who, and why they changed from Plantagenet to Lancaster, to York, to Tudor, to Stuart, to House of Hanover, to House of Saxe-Coburg, to Windsor. Half of them I even know the dates for. My poster's got prime ministers on it too, all the way from Walpole; but they're in black and white and it's not up to date because Maggie Thatcher is missing.

Ms Dawson always tells me to shush when I ask why we can't do English history instead of crap about Amazon tribes. 'Don't be so insolent, you ought to know better.' She always says that. Instead of telling me off, she tries to make me guilty.

I never say 'crap' or any other swearwords at home. Last year I said 'crap' in front of my grandfather and he was furious; but 'crap' is nothing at school. At school, it's sometimes a good idea to bung in 'fucking' every so often; you can put it anywhere.

Apology

I never *meant* to act badly at school, it just happened. I misbehave because, if I didn't, everyone would kill me. If you don't join in, and have a laugh, everyone will think you're a wanker. Tons of people have asked me if I want a fight. That includes: Gilbert Alkan, Robert Lester, Peter Davies, Darius Nyland, Desmond Mears, Hanif Ali, Derek Hadeed, Eammon Robinson who does boxing at a boys' club, Andrew Smith, Mark Rooney, this mod called Mark Pye who wears a parka with a bull's eye on the back, Martin Palmer, a boy called Clifford, and about ten others whose names I don't even know. I'm getting used to them asking for a fight, and I know the best approach is to bluff – to act hard so that the other boy chickens out first – but I'm not much good at that, I always back down.

When there's a fight, everybody nearby shouts out, 'Fight! Fight! Fight!' to attract people who are further away; then they make a crowd around you. They laugh if you can't fight well, but if one of the fighters is really violent – if there's blood, for example – the whole crowd holds its breath in awe. And because there's a crowd, teachers can't get in and break it up. I'm scared of the pain, and the humiliation.

In Maths once, even Ernie Dallas told me he was going to beat me up when the bell went, so I pretended to cry and told Ernie my grandfather had died the previous night.

Your dad! Your mum!

One day a cover teacher took our class because Ms Dawson was sick. It wasn't Captain Caveman, it was a man with a blazer who wasn't taking any lip. 'You're going to watch a film,' he said. 'So follow me.'

He led us downstairs to a room in the South Corridor that had a telly and a video machine in it. Alexander said it was the same as his video; they got it for Christmas. There were already a couple of other first-year classes in the room, sitting towards the back. The only chairs available were at the front. I grabbed one near the far wall, so I could watch out if anyone threw anything, or started spitting.

The teachers took nearly fifteen minutes to work out how the machine started. But when it got going, I recognized the film at once. It was early James Bond, and my dad was in it. He'd learnt Russian in the National Service, so in the film he acted as an enemy rocket scientist. He only appeared for a couple of moments, but I thought my friends would be impressed.

I nudged Ian beside me, and Alexander: 'My dad's in this.'

Word got round the whole room, eventually reaching Mark Rooney.

'Who says his dad's in this?' boomed Rooney, staring straight at me.

I told him it was true.

'Is he an actor?'

'Yes.'

'Well, what's your surname – Connery, or Moore?'

I told him my surname, which Mark Rooney pretended not to hear.

'Fartoff? Fuck off.' All round the room people were laughing at me.

Whenever anybody in the film fell over, or got killed, people in Mark's class shouted out: 'It's your dad!' Even boys in *my* class joined in. And when Bond jumped into bed with a gorgeous woman, they yelled: 'It's your mum!'

Samuel Thomas's mum had three children – and each of them had a different dad. Samuel was the middle one. He hardly ever sees his dad, cause I don't think his mum even knew the man very well when she got pregnant. Samuel hates Christmas, cause his half-brother and half-sister's dads always pretend to be his dad too.

He said: 'John, what are you doing on Christmas Day?'

I said: 'Well I'll probably open my presents pretty early and then we'll have a big turkey and stuff, and then watch a good blockbuster like Indiana Jones or whatever. Then just play with my presents.'

'Bor*ing*!' he said.

'Why, what are you going to do?'

'I'm going to have a laugh. Do you want to come? I'm going to Heathrow to muck about on all the trolleys, and the travelators, and nick stuff from the shops, and stuff. Come on, John, don't be boring.'

'I can't, I think all my family will be there, and they'll *kill* me if I go out.'

You know what he did? He telephoned me at nine a.m. on Christmas Day and asked me again if I was going to Heathrow with him. I said I wasn't allowed out, but the truth is I never even asked because I *wanted* to stay in.

*   *   *

Samuel can cycle down the hill in Kensington Park Road without holding the handlebars. Once he even managed it standing on the saddle. He taught us how to steal from W. H. Smith.

Every day, after collecting Crispin from primary school, we nicked tons of chocolates and sweets. We scoffed it before we got home, to destroy the evidence.

We walked out of the shop with the biggest bars that Cadbury makes. You know how we did it? What you never do is try to put stolen goods in your bag or a pocket, cause someone might watch you doing that. Instead, you hold them in your hands and walk round and round the shop. Eventually, when nobody can remember whether you bought the chocolates or not, you wander calmly outside and walk off – never run.

But one day a man pounced on Crispin as he walked out laughing. Samuel was already round the corner, but I couldn't leave Crispin behind. I went back inside.

The man wore blue-tinted glasses, even though he was indoors. He had a white shirt with a name badge, and his skin was shiny. He was dragging Crispin upstairs when I caught up with him. I said:

'Oy, what are you doing with my brother?'

'Your brother is a thieving little toerag,' said the man. 'You can get in here and all.'

I stepped into his private office.

'You've been spotted nicking stuff,' the man said to Crispin, 'and you might as well admit it, if you don't want us calling the police.'

I told Crispin to admit it, and I handed over a couple of Cadbury's Dairy Milks, to show good will.

'What else have you stolen?' the manager asked.

'Nothing,' I promised, offering my pockets.

'Nothing,' said Crispin.

'You'd better be right.' The manager reached for Crispin's

carrier bag, which was full of wet swimming things. Inside, he found a chocolate bar. And another. And then more.

'You idiot,' I hissed, hoping that if I took the manager's side and pretended to be cross with Crispin we might escape. 'How could you be so stupid?'

'Where do you live? What's your telephone number?'

'No – please – our parents will kill us.'

I knew they wouldn't, but they'd be 'terribly disappointed'. I felt sick with guilt.

'You should have thought of that before.'

'It wasn't us. It was another boy who made us do it; he said he'd beat us up if we didn't. His name's Alexander Ford.' He wrote down Alexander's address. But he insisted on our telephone number too. He called Mum at work; and the worst thing is, she's a lawyer, so she doesn't like us breaking the law.

An hour later, Mum arrived. First thing she did was apologize for our appalling behaviour. She said she would pay for whatever we had taken, but he said there wasn't any proof we'd actually got away with anything. But he said he'd seen us in there nearly every day for weeks. He asked her if she'd heard of a boy called Alexander Ford, and Mum said yes. She apologized again, then walked us home. Normally, she'd chat, or play games, but this time she didn't say a word, all the way home. Even when we got there, she didn't speak to us. We sat on the couch without turning on the telly or talking, feeling ashamed.

After a while, I went into the kitchen, where Mum was cutting up vegetables, and said, 'I'm sorry.'

She didn't look at me but said: 'You've probably been doing this for weeks. How much have you taken? I'll have to pay them back for all of it, and we can't afford to throw money away like that.'

'No, it was the first time,' I lied. I could see Crispin in the living room, watching me without saying anything. I was older, I had to sort it out. 'We've never done it before – ever.' I was so glad, I added, that we'd been caught the first time: it taught us a valuable lesson.

When my dad got home, Mum said she had something to tell him, and they talked about it in the kitchen with the door shut. When he came out, he didn't say anything, but at bedtime he came to tuck us in, and said quietly to me:

'Don't ever do that again. You should know better.'

I promised I wouldn't.

That night, lying in bed, I made Crispin join me in an oath not to be good friends with Samuel any more. 'He's a bad influence.'

Ebony and ivory

Ms Dawson keeps being sick, so we've had loads of cover teachers taking us for History. One of them started to tell us about the Holocaust, and how Hitler gassed six million Jews.

Desmond Mears stood up and said: 'Sir, I don't want to learn about the fucking Holocaust. Everyone's always going on about the fucking Jews and the fucking Holocaust, why can't we study something like slavery or the Notting Hill Carnival?'

The teacher went crazy, shouting his head off at Desmond's impudence, and telling him to stand outside the class.

'And don't you move,' he said, as he pushed Desmond out, 'or you'll be in detention for a month.'

As the door was shutting, Desmond shouted: 'It's always the history of the fucking Jews, instead of the fucking history of black people.' And then he grinned at everyone through the glass. The glass was reinforced with wire mesh, like our front door at home. Considered in a certain way, it looked as though Desmond was behind bars; as though he was performing the life of a slave for our History class.

The teacher carried on telling us about how Hitler had gassed six million Jews. Towards the end of the lesson, Robert Lester stuck his hand up really politely till the cover teacher noticed. Then Robert started grinning. He asked:

'Sir, are you Jewish, sir? Sir, are you a Jew?'

Peter Davies was sitting next to him, with his face buried in his book, but the teacher could see he was laughing, so he chucked them both out of the class too.

There are lots of black boys in my class, and black girls too. The fact is, they're the best fighters. I'm not saying they always are, because that would be prejudiced, but in this case it's true. The best fighters in my class, in order, are: Desmond Mears (black), Darius Nyland (black), Sean (black), Peter Davies (black), Gilbert Alkan (white), Derek Hadeed (white). Donna (black) might be able to beat any of them up, but she's never tried. If you did a list for the best at football, it would be nearly the same, but Darius and Gilbert would swap places, and Donna wouldn't be anywhere at all. But the funny thing is, there are only about five professional footballers in the whole League who are black: two at Watford and a couple at West Brom and Viv Anderson at Notts Forest.

Cause they're the hardest, the black boys can afford to be the rudest. No one dares to fight them. Like, lots of people laugh at my trainers cause they're cheap, and they call them bogus. But nobody laughs at Desmond Mears's bogus trainers, which aren't even a well-known brand. With his last pair, he even came to school with the soles attached by Sellotape. He'd wound Sellotape all round them, you couldn't see any leather at all; you'd have thought they were actually *made* of Sellotape.

One day when Desmond was bunking off, we had Sport. We were all sitting on a bench waiting to pick up teams. While the teacher was fetching team-colours, Darius stood up and walked down the line checking out everyone's trainers. He said: 'Let me see . . . Adidas, you're OK . . . Bogus, you get a slap . . .' He slapped Alexander for having no-brand trainers. '. . . Puma, OK . . . Nike, excellent . . . Bogus, slap . . .' Ian was at the end of the line, wearing bogus Green Flash. He placed a sports bag in front of his feet and hoped Darius wouldn't get that far. But he did. 'Move your bag, Ian. Oh God! *Most* bogus plimsolls. Extra slaps for hiding them.' Darius slapped Ian in the face, and on his bare thighs.

If black people are annoyed, they suck their teeth. It sounds like this: tssssk. If they get angry, they call you blud clat, which means blood cloth (like Tampaxes that girls stick up their fannies); or they say boomba clat, which means bum cloth (loo paper). Or they call you batty man, which means botty man (homo). When they're arguing among themselves, they sometimes call each other 'African', as an insult, cause they think black people are only cool if they're West Indian.

Darius is half African, half West Indian, but he's the lightest-skinned of them all, except for Robert Lester (whose mum's white). He's got a pointy afro, like the shape of a candle-flame, which he spends hours combing into shape with a special afro comb, upwards.

Once Ernie Dallas called Alexander a boomba clat, but Desmond and Donna and Peter Davies heard him say it. They came over and started slapping Ernie. 'What you saying "boomba clat" for?' asked Donna. 'You ain't black. I come give you licks.'

Another time, in the playground, Peter Davies tackled Ian Natty and ran off with the ball, improvising a commentary as he did it: 'And he's taken the ball off the Paki . . . !' But Ian Natty isn't a Paki; he told me. His dad's from a South American country called Honduras, and his mum is English (white).

After Peter tackled him that time, Ian said quietly to me, 'I hate that black bastard.'

In registration, Peter called Ian a Paki again, and Ms Evans heard him. She told him not to be racist. He said it was impossible for black people to be racist, cause they're the underdogs. Ms Evans said that wasn't true. Desmond asked her if black people were allowed to call Jews 'yids' and Chinese 'coolies', and she said they certainly weren't allowed to. Desmond said: 'You better not say that when my dad comes for parents' evening, miss – or he'll box you!'

Sometimes Mark Rooney calls Ian Natty a Paki too. Mark's really big, though, so Ian pretends to be reasonable about it. He stands there, shouting after fat Rooney: 'But I'm *not* a Paki, Mark – it's just my dad's from South America!'

On Wednesdays, Mr Raymond, the head of year, and his deputy Ms Hayes take first-year assembly, on one half of the hall. Tutor-set 1.0 sits on the left, with 1.1 beside them, stretching right across to 1.9 at the far end. Mr Raymond usually drones on about punctuality, or why we shouldn't run in corridors, and why we should keep to the left. Ms Hayes doesn't say much, but she always sits on the table beside him, nodding a lot.

On Tuesdays, the entire school crams into hall for assembly together. If you look round the room, you can see every single teacher in the school, all mixed up. One Science teacher over here, in his white coat; and another one over there. One Art teacher in stripy dungarees, with smiley-face badges, covered in paint, behind you; and another in front. I always look to see which of my teachers is with which tutor-set. Our tutor, Ms Edwards, stands beside us, chatting to a hairy Design and Technology teacher who's in charge of 1.6. The Needlework teacher who wears low-cut angora sweaters is in charge of a fourth-year tutor-set; Ms Dawson sits with a class in the fifth year; and Captain Caveman's in charge of a class of third-years.

The headmaster, Dr Rushworth, stands on the main stage on his own. He's short, with white hair, and a squeaky voice. He's been here for years, at least since Anna was in the first year. My parents reckon he's very good, very progressive.

At assembly he wears a gown like Robert Donat in *Goodbye Mr Chips*. Nobody else does. He makes speeches that last about twenty minutes, but they aren't about punctuality or walking on the left. He always discusses important issues. Once he told us the man who drew the Tintin books, Hergé, had died that week, and told us how Hergé came to do the Tintin books.

Another of his speeches was about how all human races have different qualities, but he said they make a great mix if you put them together. To explain, he said if you took the white notes on a piano you could play one kind of tune well, and if you took the black notes you could play some other kind of tune well, but if you wanted to make really *great* music you had to use both kinds of notes. Everyone expected him to start singing like Stevie Wonder and Paul McCartney, cause 'Ebony and Ivory' had been in the charts for ages. But he never mentioned it.

Yemisi Fatodu, the girl who sits next to me because our surnames are next to each other on the register, is African. Her hair's like a squared-off afro, shorter at the sides. During lessons, she spreads her stuff out on the desk. She takes off her watch and rings and lays them out. Then she takes out a pot of cream, scoops a little out, rubs it between her hands, and wipes it all over her face. Once Dr Bowes caught her:

'Yemisi, please put your make-up away.'

She said it wasn't make-up.

'Well, what is it then?'

'It's a special cream, sir, to make my skin paler.'

Darius started jeering. He stood up and pointed at her and said: 'Sir, Yemisi's too black, sir, Yemisi is *African*.' And all the other black boys laughed.

Dr Bowes told him to sit down and stop being silly.

'Please put it away for later, if you really must use it, Yemisi.'

Peter Davies, the blackest boy in my class, has got pink skin on the palms of his hands and under his feet. He had a fight in the north playground with Andrew Smith, and got a big graze on the side of his head. When he picked off the scab, the skin underneath was pink too. It took a few days to turn the same colour as the rest of him.

Telling tales

We were studying nuclear destruction with David Arrowseed's mum. She passed round a pamphlet about nuclear war. It was designed by the Tory government to help people plan ahead. It said you needed lots of tinned food (which Mum hates anyway), and showed how you could construct a shelter with loads of doors and pillows, and a dustbin to poo in.

The information made me depressed. I'm scared about nuclear war. I know how much damage a small bomb did to Hiroshima (we saw a film about it), and these days the bombs are thousands of times stronger.

This government pamphlet had illustrations showing how to build a shelter. You take one of your doors – the bedroom door, say – and lean it against a wall, then put a load of sandbags over it, and you hide underneath with all your baked beans and pineapple. It might take months for the world to be safe again, so you have to be sure you have enough tinned food.

Mrs Arrowseed handed out a textbook with a play in it about what happens if there's a nuclear war. I had one of the best parts in the play, called WILLIAM. Anyway, in the play it says you have to poison your oldest relatives and young babies when the war happens, or else you wouldn't have enough food to go round. So they gave a little green pill to the grannies and grandads. And they left a six-month-old baby in the house (which got blown up).

The main girl's part was given to Alison. She was supposed

to be my girlfriend SANDRA. It was like the old days when we snogged on school journey at Fox, although of course we didn't actually snog this time. We weren't really acting, just reading it out. At the moment in the play when it says *They kiss*, Mrs Arrowseed read out that bit and the rest of the class whistled so that I went red; then we carried on.

Some people aren't very good at reading, so it can be slow work doing a play. People start to lose interest. But we got to this interesting bit where the two main boys in the play had a fight over SANDRA, so everyone in the class was interested. At that moment, two men came into the class. They were young black men and they apologized for interrupting. Mrs Arrowseed didn't get up but beckoned them over to her desk: 'Carry on, John,' she said. (Even David calls me John these days, so his mum doesn't know any better.) The men went and crouched down, whispering to Mrs Arrowseed, one of them on each side of her desk.

I carried on reading:

WILLIAM: But I've been going out with Sandra since before the bomb fell. My life with her extends back to walks in the trees, and by the river. Sandra met my parents before they perished – how can she be interested in *you*?
RUSSELL [played by Gilbert]: That was then, this is now. Sandra's the best-looking girl here, and for the sake of the human race she should mate with a natural leader. I'm in charge of this dug-out; what you say counts for nothing . . .

The two men left the room and Yemisi interrupted the drama to ask what they'd wanted.

'Nothing much, Yemisi, they were looking for somebody and they didn't know what part of the school they were in.'

'But why were they in the school, miss?' demanded Yemisi. 'I didn't like the look of those men, they seemed like ruffians.'

'Shall we carry on, class? Alison?'

SANDRA told RUSSELL that she wanted to stay with WILLIAM, and have his children. I was proud she'd made that decision, even though it was just a play.

At the end of the class, Mrs Arrowseed said: 'Has anybody seen my handbag?'

Nobody'd seen it anywhere. Mrs Arrowseed was about the only teacher everybody liked, nobody would've moved her bag. We searched under our desks, and around the room. Peter said: 'Miss, do you think those men teeffed it when they came in?'

'Well, I do hope not, but it did cross my mind. I don't suppose they'll have hung around if they did.'

Mrs Arrowseed couldn't walk fast so she asked the boys to go looking round the school for the men. 'If you see them, don't approach them, but tell a member of staff.'

We all headed in different directions. I didn't see the men, but I saw David Arrowseed. I thought I'd better tell him. 'Your mum's been robbed.'

'What do you mean?'

'She had her handbag stolen – while we were all sitting in class. These two men came in and nicked it in front of everybody. You'd better go and find her, and see if she's all right.'

Like I said, if you're a boy, you behave badly or you get killed. Look at Alexander and Daniel, who are always gobbed on. But if you're a girl, nobody does that to you. Two girls from my primary school still talk posh, even though the rest of us have changed our accents. And they never swear either. Melissa and Rosalind are best friends, and they hardly even talk to anyone else. Their catchphrase is: 'Boys are *so* immature.' They say it to me all the time, which is *so rude*, cause sometimes I'm only messing around to impress them.

Rosalind is strange; she wears velvet shirts, with big dungarees and coloured Kickers which make her look like one of the presenters on *Rainbow*. She spooked Gow by asking to look at his nails. He showed her, and she keeps asking, every day. He told me he scrubs his nails before he comes to school, so it won't be embarrassing. Rosalind told him: 'Grow them long, nice and long, so they curl.'

The other thing she does is sit in strange postures. I once heard her say to Melissa: 'I want to sit in an interesting pose, how does this look?'

Anyway, one afternoon Gilbert Alkan was sitting on the same table as me and Stephen Harris and Gow and Ian Natty. Gilbert was being funny for a change, without threatening to beat us up, so I said to him: 'Gilbert, do you want to know a secret?'

'What?'

'Melissa and Rosalind are lesbians. They were even lesbians at Fox.' To convince him, I added: 'It's true.'

Stephen Harris was amazed. His buck teeth stuck out in a smile. He said: '*Really*?'

I don't know if Gilbert believed me, but he liked the idea. He called out to them:

'Oy, lesbos! Oy!'

They looked a little confused. They knew he was talking to them, but they chose not to answer.

He put his hand up and asked the teacher if Melissa and Rosalind were allowed to sit next to each other if they were lesbians. 'It's like me having sex with a woman in class, sir.' The teacher told him to stop being silly.

Gilbert carried on calling them lesbians for weeks. One day they both ran out of the class crying, Melissa first, and Rosalind soon after. Melissa stubbed her toes on a desk as she was running out, but didn't stop.

They never even knew I started it.

At the bottom of the stairs, where it's cool and dark cause there are no windows down there, I saw two fourth-year boys hiding.

One of them spotted me. He has a brother in my year, called Damien. In the winter, Damien's brother used to stand at the top of the stairs, with the window open, and drop these giant snowballs, the size of a basketball, with sharp pieces of ice sticking out of them, on people who weren't looking. One snowball landed on this first-year girl, who was taken to hospital with cuts and concussion.

When he spotted me, Damien's brother said:

'Oy, first-year, do you want to see something?'

I said I didn't mind, but not if he didn't want me to see it.

Damien's brother beckoned me into the stairwell and told me to stand by the wall. I thought he was going to run at me and hit me in the stomach, and take my money.

The boy stood there and took a brown bottle out of his pocket. His friend started grinning. I thought they were going to make me drink their piss.

Damien's brother took a swig from the bottle himself, then waved at his friend to hand him something. The friend passed him a cigarette lighter, and Damien's brother sparked it up in front of his own face – then spat out the liquid everywhere, making a giant fireball. For a moment, the whole stairwell was brightly lit. I thought the flames would hit me, but they didn't reach. I stayed where I was, while the other boy did exactly the same. This time, when he got ready to spit, I tucked my bag behind my back in case the books caught fire, and squinted to protect my eyes.

'Do you want a turn?' asked Damien's brother.

'No, thanks,' I said. 'Can I go now?'

The other boy sneered at me and made the wanker handsignal, and called me a little chickenshit. 'Fuck off, first-year,' he added.

Damien's lucky. Even though he's smaller than me, nobody picks on him. If you're a bully, I expect you need to check first whether your victim has older relations, and if they're at all hard.

I bumped into Ms Dawson in the playground outside, and told her what'd happened.

'And are you *really* all right?' she asked, putting a hand on my shoulder because I was shaking. I would have been OK if she hadn't asked, but when she did ask, it made tears go in my eye.

She took me into an empty classroom to get over it before break ended. She just stood looking out of the window, towards Holland Park. She was being kind. I sat at a desk feeling guilty for being rude about the history of Amazon tribes, and for running round making peacock noises in her class.

Please use the lavatory

Diego is the chubby Spanish boy with glasses who can't speak a word of English. Even after nearly a year, he's crap at it. Nobody else wants to be his friend, so me and Alexander and Daniel took pity on him. We let him play games with us, such as catch. Needless to say, he's useless at football.

Diego has a weird problem with his eyes, they shake from side to side all the time. You can watch them, behind his metal-framed glasses.

Even though he's Spanish, he's just as pale as me. His black hair is curly, but he combs it so it makes neat, frizzy ripples across his head. He wears a grey nylon jacket which is always done up to the top. What's more, he wears smart black shoes that his mum bought him. Nobody must have told him you wear trainers in England.

Sitting beside him in class, I asked Diego what his name meant. Sometimes names don't mean anything, but sometimes they do. David's surname, Arrowseed, might mean someone in his family a long way back planted arrows, you never know. It turns out that Diego just means Diego, as simple as that – but his main surname, Domingo, means 'Sunday', and his extra surname, which goes on the end, Rey, means 'king'. I told him his name was Diego Sunday King and he seemed pleased.

'Why did you leave Spain?'

'Because I killed General Franco,' he laughed. I didn't actually know if Franco was alive or dead, but Mum had told me he was a bad lot, so I laughed along with Diego.

If someone in the class makes fun of Diego – for his clothes, or his wobbly eyes – he says: 'Tomato!'

It's brilliant, but we don't know why he says it. We tried him on other fruit and veg, but he said tomato again and again.

If Diego spoke English, he'd probably be a great friend, even though he's a bit chubby and unfashionable. He never argues, or gets shirty. He has a laugh, but he works a bit too. Everyone likes Diego, shouting, 'Tomato!' at him all the time. People pass Diego in the corridor and say: 'All right, Tomato?'

The other Spanish boy in our class, Jorge, is called Bug Eye because he's got huge eyes that look like they might fall out of their sockets if you patted him too hard on the back. He talks English with a Cockney accent, cause he left Spain when he was young (something to do with Franco again).

The only person I know who actually hates Diego is Alexander's mum. She thinks he's dirty. Alexander invited us to his big house after school, to show off his new toy, which had Space Invaders and a few other arcade games on it. It's only round the corner, in Holland Park Avenue, so a few of us went round, including Diego. I've been there before. The house is twice as big as ours, with about five floors, and a garden at the front as well as the usual one at the back. Most of the furniture is old, so the house looks like *Upstairs, Downstairs*, on telly.

Alexander's Space Invaders is slower than the real thing, and there aren't so many aliens to kill. But it's fantastic to have that in your own home and not need to spend so much pocket money on it.

Diego asked where the toilet was, and Alexander pointed to a door on the far side of the hall. But Alexander's mum heard Diego asking, and whizzed off to the kitchen. When Diego finished in the loo, he came out and found Alexander's mum standing right outside with a cloth and a couple of cleaning sprays. He'd hardly got out of there, and she was already inside. She left the door open, so we could see her wiping down the loo seat, and the floor around it. Most of us laughed, but Diego didn't. He looked over at her a couple of times, sort of embarrassed, and didn't join in the computer games. She came out red-faced from bending down, and we quickly looked away, as though we hadn't been watching. She went back in the kitchen to put away the cleaning things. After a minute, Diego said he had to go. Alexander was in the thick of a game, so he didn't show him out; and his mum didn't say goodbye either.

It's not as if Diego's any dirtier than the rest of us, just a tiny bit fatter. I felt sorry for him walking home on his own after that. Maybe he'll think he hasn't got any friends; it's harder for him anyway, cause he can't speak English properly. I said I had to go too, and caught up with him. At the corner shop I bought him a Black Jack and told him not to worry; but he pretended he was only sad because of Spain. He said some soldier had hijacked Parliament and fired loads of bullets. I think he was making it up.

When we went on school journey, to France, it was four to a room. We had to share double beds. I paired up with David Arrowseed, and Daniel Murphy in my class shared the other bed with Samuel Thomas. The beds had dirty orange covers.

My dad loves France. He thinks the French are marvellous, because they elected a socialist, while we got the Tories.

Before she let us into the hotel, the owner had a quiet word in French with Ms Edwards. Then Ms Edwards announced that she had something very important to tell us. We stood listening, blocking up the pavement, so real French people had to walk in the road to get past us.

'In your rooms, you will see a thing that looks like a lavatory, as well as a basin for washing your faces and brushing your teeth. Please remember this is *not* a lavatory. It is called a bidet, so do NOT use it as a lavatory. There is a lavatory at the end of the corridor on each floor, so please use that.'

'Miss, what is a bidet?' asked a girl called Pauline from David's class, who was standing in the road.

'It's a bit like a footbath. For washing your feet,' she explained, before letting us in.

The girls had the top two floors, we had the ground floor and the first floor. Me and David and Samuel ran to pick the best room for ourselves. None of the best fighters came on school journey (apart from Gilbert). Alexander said they probably couldn't afford it. Stephen Harris and Gow couldn't afford it, and nor could Diego Tomato, but they aren't good fighters.

Every night the boys raided the girls' floor. We made them scream by running up and down the corridor and banging on the doors. One night after we did that, we spied into Ms Edwards' bedroom. The main curtains were open, and she'd switched the light on, so we could see through the net curtains. She was standing up, and talking to David and Samuel's tutor, Mr Robins, who was sitting on her bed. He has long black hair and wears a black leather waistcoat, like a Motorhead fan.

Suddenly Mr Robins walked over and gave Ms Edwards a cuddle. We hissed for more boys to come and watch. (Me and David saw it first, then Daniel and Samuel, then Gilbert Alkan and Jorge Bug Eye.)

After about ten minutes standing with their arms round each other, both teachers fell on the bed, and Mr Robins started kissing Ms Edwards on the arm. Then she started waving at the window, looking worried, so he got up and closed the curtains.

We laughed for about twenty-five seconds. Then Gilbert said: 'Do you think he's going to fuck her?' We all said yes.

Two nights after that, I was in bed with David, and Samuel was in bed too. Daniel was standing at the sink in his pants and vest, and big hair. Dan's got more hair than anyone I know, great sandy-coloured curls which make his head look huge; the

93

closest to an afro hairstyle a white boy could get. He's known as Dan Dan the Big Hair Man; and Dan Hair. He finished brushing his teeth, and said: 'Do any of you know how to wank?'

We said we knew how, but never did it. I didn't really know how.

'Give us a demonstration, Dan,' said Samuel. We sat up in bed, pushing up the pillows behind our backs.

So Daniel took off all his clothes and skipped across the room to the bidet. His hair bounced when he moved. He said the bidet wasn't for washing your feet at all (we'd already guessed that), but for wanking on. He sat down on it facing us, as if he was going to do a poo, then said:

'You have to hold your willy in your normal hand, like the hand you use for writing.'

He took his willy and held it the way you hold a pen. He tugged it upwards, as if he was trying to ping a rubber band. 'Then you just rub it up and down.'

We were all laughing our heads off.

Then, before he got any further with the demonstration, the door beside him opened, revealing Ms Edwards.

She looked amazed, but quickly recovered, and said: 'I realize you must be very embarrassed, Daniel. But it's time for bed.' And she walked past him to fetch a towel, so he could cover up again. The three of us hid our heads under the bedcovers and laughed and laughed.

Even though he's got a lot of hair on his head, Daniel's still hardly got any round his dick. Samuel has the most, and me and David are about equal.

Detention, detention, detention

If Stephen Harris sits on your table, you never do any work. He always talks about the fucking Army Cadets. He says he goes out on manoeuvres with them, and tells you about the guns and anti-tank missiles they practise with. He told me he always gets to fire the anti-tank missiles, cause the people in charge think he is such a good Army Cadet.

He says Army Cadets stick fireworks up cats' bums and laugh when they explode. When he's talking to white boys like me, Stephen always goes on about how brilliant Great Britain is, and makes racist jokes; he probably picked that up from his Army Cadet friends. He whispers that Army Cadets hate black bastards and always beat them up if they try to join.

Nobody believes him. Stephen's so stupid. For a start, he can't read or write. He literally never has a pen. Every lesson, teachers ask him why he's forgotten his book.

'I don't know, sir, I just forgot.'

'Well try to remember it next time,' they say, and they've already moved on to someone else.

If you ask Stephen how to spell something he gets shirty. But he's not much of a fighter. He spends his whole life talking about fighting, and the Army – he told me the only thing in the world he is scared of is a heat-seeking missile – but he's never had a fight in the whole time he's been here.

Stephen's part of the group that plays Catch, at lunch, in buildings with lifts. The other people are Alexander and Daniel, and maybe Gow and Ian Natty and Kampol Mai Ngram. It's best at the Kensington Library building cause that's next to the Town Hall, and there are three lifts, and a car park with two floors. You can easily hide.

It's harder to get into other buildings cause they're private.

Stephen and me got into this posh house at the top of the hill – four houses away from the school, in Airlie Gardens – by ringing the bells and pretending to be visiting relations at one of the other flats. Alexander had done it the day before and said the view was superb.

We caught the lift to the roof, and went for a look. It was true about the view. It was a windy day in summer so there were no clouds and you could see for miles. The house is on top of the hill, so you can see all the way round. You could pick out the city's famous buildings – the Post Office Tower, the Houses of Parliament, the Empress State Building in Earls Court and the Exhibition Centre – but you couldn't see my house cause the council tower blocks were in the way.

Stephen said that roof would be a good position for Army Cadets on manoeuvres. Then he picked up a brick which some builders had left over. He leant over the rail at the front of the house, and saw the line of cars.

'How much do you want to bet I can hit that blue Mini?'

'You wouldn't fucking dare.'

'Of course I would, I'm in the fucking Army Cadets.'

'Go on then.'

'How much?'

'Nothing.'

He lobbed the half-brick, shouting: 'ROCKET – TO – THE – MOOOOOON!'

Long before it landed, I ran from the roof's edge to hide. After a long pause, I heard a *crump*, and Stephen started cheering.

'Oy, shut up or they'll see us,' I hissed.

'*Yes!*' he cheered. 'ARMY CADETS! FUCKING AR-MY – FUCKING – CA-DETS.'

'Stephen, is there anyone down there, have they seen you?'

'No.'

I went forward to look, and saw the roof of the Mini severely dented in its centre. The brick had bounced off and landed in the road, breaking in half. I peered left, towards school, and saw everybody heading back for class. Breaktime was over.

'Fuck. Let's get out of here.'

Later that week, the deputy head came to our class with a man dressed in overalls. The man was caretaker at the posh house. He pointed straight at Stephen, and then at me and Alexander.

'Mr Stewart, can I borrow these boys please?' said the deputy head. His name's Mr Lyndon.

We went to Mr Lyndon's office, and the caretaker came too. He said how someone had seen us running out of the building, and he was sure we were responsible for the car's dented roof. Me and Alexander denied having thrown anything, but admitted we'd been in the house. Stephen denied he'd even been in the building.

Mr Lyndon asked Alexander: 'What did you think you were doing in there?'

'We went to admire the view.'

'Don't be funny with me, boy.'

'But it's true, sir,' I said. 'From the top you can see all over London.'

'I'm not having anyone be cheeky. Mr Davies has made a serious complaint, and there's been some very expensive damage to a car.'

But it's *true*, sir,' I insisted. 'I swear I didn't damage the car.'

Stephen kept quiet. Me and Alexander got detention with Mr

Lyndon for the rest of the week, and with Mr Lyndon, you absolutely *have to* turn up.

I'm fed up with xylophones, they sound terrible. You take a good song from the charts, and the teacher hands out the music, and we bang it out: *clunk, clank, clunk*. We did some songs by Madness and yet another one by the Police, and some Beatles songs, but they all sound the same. Without singing, anyway, it's not even a song. That's logic.

Once, Samuel tried singing, but everyone laughed too much. After that, he couldn't do it properly.

Sometimes we have theory lessons about music. We had one all about how pop descended from rhythm and blues, and how that descended from slave songs, and how those came from Africa.

After I'd written up my homework, I drew a picture of Daniel on a bidet, holding his dick. I forgot I'd done it, so I was amazed when miss told me she wanted me to stay behind after the lesson and explain myself.

I asked what she meant, and she showed me. I said sorry.

'Well that's not good enough. Do you know how much the school spends on exercise books?'

'No.' I stared at her big nose; it was brilliant for caricatures.

'Well I can assure you it's a great deal. And the books are not there so that you can draw silly pictures. What do you have to say for yourself?'

'I'm sorry. It's just that I draw when I get bored.'

'You're saying my lessons aren't interesting enough for you?'

'Well, not really, but I suppose so.'

'You've got some cheek. Well, I'm going to confiscate this book, and you can do the work again.'

She tore the book up.

'But that's not fair. Why did you tear it up?'

'Because it's got silly drawings in it, and I don't want you drawing pictures of me on the cover.'

'But it's my book, not yours. And I thought you said the books were too expensive to waste. That book was hardly started. You've wasted the whole thing!'

'Well I'm not prepared to argue about it with *you*. You can do the work again, in detention, or else explain it to the head.'

A man was running after me. Desperate to escape, I charged through the underground car park. The man grabbed my shirt.

'Ow – fuck – get off.'

He cuffed me round the head, yanking me round, then led me towards the kiosk where drivers hand in their tickets when they leave. Gow and Alexander had been caught too. They stared out of the glass, looking frightened.

The man pushed me into the kiosk, locked the door on us and went round to carry on serving people with tickets, lifting the barrier for them.

Alexander sidled up to me, holding a bag of liver-pâté sandwiches. His mum always gave him liver pâté. It looked like dog shit, and he never ate them. If you were about to catch Alexander in the car park, he'd try and slip you up by dropping a liver-pâté sandwich. He whispered to me not to use his name, cause he'd given someone else's.

After a few moments, when I'd caught my breath, I said to the man: 'Excuse me, but why are you holding us here?'

He told us customers' cars had been broken into. 'There have been complaints about kids running about, knocking off wing mirrors. Some very expensive cars in here, BMWs, Mercs and all that. They don't like it. Police are coming.'

'But we haven't broken into any cars. Look in my bag.' I opened it up, and pushed it towards him, but he ignored me.

'Maybe your friends've got something, them that ran off,' he said, handing coins to a driver. 'Thank you, sir.'

'But please, mister,' added Gow. 'We're going to be late for lessons. If we're late, we'll get a detention, and we haven't even done anyfing to the cars.'

Gow has wobbly lips that don't fit around his front teeth. He isn't as buck-toothed as Stephen Harris, but when he talks, he fires bits of spit at people. You could see the spit catching the light in the kiosk, but the man didn't seem to notice the tiny flecks on his jacket.

Two policemen walked into the car park out of the bright street, from High Street Ken. They spoke quietly to the man, then came over to us. One of them asked: 'Which one is Rawson?'

'Me, sir,' said Gow, 'Gary Rawson.'

'And which one is Harris?'

Alexander said it was him, first name Stephen.

'Who are *you* then?'

I told him my real name, with my proper, posh accent.

The other policeman wrote it down with a pencil in a tiny notebook. Why was he doing that? I panicked.

'Are we being arrested then, will you be calling my parents?' I asked.

'No, you ain't been arrested. But you never know what might happen later. Now tell us what you're doin in ere.'

We explained about the game. They asked to see in our bags. Alexander opened his polythene bag of sandwiches and the man in the kiosk, who hadn't been paying much attention, looked up.

'So you're the little bastard that leaves sandwiches all over the place. Do you know someone has to clean them up?'

The policeman with the pencil asked him to let them deal with it.

We told them we were late for our lesson.

'So where's your school?'

'Just up the top of the hill,' said Gow. 'Holland Park.'

'Oh, you go *there*,' said the first policeman, as if that explained it all.

'We'll give you a lift.'

Before leaving, they gave us a long lecture about car theft, and dropping sandwiches, and told us if they ever heard we were back in the car park they'd take the matter further, and our parents would definitely hear about it.

When we got in the car, in Campden Hill Road, loads of people watched. I tried to look as though it was no big deal, and watched out for any of our friends on the way up the hill. We asked them to drop us off right at the front of the school, so everyone would see us get out.

We were three-quarters of an hour late. Ms Dawson was standing beside Melissa's desk, explaining something. She looked up and asked where on earth we thought we had been. Everyone went quiet to hear our excuse. 'Sorry we're late, miss,' I announced. 'But the thing is – we've been under arrest.'

Towards the end of the summer term, Ms Edwards started wearing baggy dresses, so Daniel stuck his hand up to find out why.

'Yes, Daniel?'

'Miss, are you wearing a maternity dress?'

She went white, and snapped at him: 'Don't you dare to be so impertinent. You can come back later for detention, and every day this week.'

Donna, who was sitting on a table behind Daniel, leant over and thumped him in the back – so hard that you could hear the breath pushing out of his lungs. 'Don't be so damn rude, boy,' she said.

But two weeks later, at morning registration, Ms Edwards announced she wasn't going to be our tutor next year. The new one was coming from another school, and he was going to be head of Modern Languages.

Yemisi, who still hates boys, put her hand up and said she didn't want a man for our tutor, and asked why Ms Edwards couldn't carry on in the job.

'Because I'm leaving the school, Yemisi, but I'm grateful for your support.'

'But miss, why are you leaving?' asked Yemisi again.

With a big smile on her face, Ms Edwards said she was going to have a baby. All the girls went aaaah.

Daniel was really pissed off. Afterwards, Dan said 1.6's hairy tutor had made her pregnant on school journey before Easter. I think he was right.

Backing a winner

At the beginning of the second year, the class was chopped and changed, to break up some of the troublemakers. Desmond Mears was transferred to 2.2, and Peter Davies was put in David's new class, 2.6. We still have them in our lessons sometimes, lessons where classes are mixed up, like Sport and Home Economics.

In return for those two, we got a new boy, Justice Gardiner. He was the biggest in our year, and he'd beaten up a sixth-former in his very first term. Cause of the new alphabetical order of the register, Justice sat next to me.

I was well worried. He's already about six feet tall, and in Swimming you can see the muscles on his chest and his tummy, like in the Olympics. I expected Justice would beat me up every lesson, thumping me under the table and giving me a dead arm whenever he felt like it.

In fact he didn't pay attention to me at all. In lessons where we were paired off, he took the table next to me and leant back in his chair, tilting it against the wall. Sometimes he folded his arms on the desk and put his head on them, as if he was going to sleep. Sometimes he *did* go to sleep. Teachers just let him put his head down, cause they were scared of him. Justice always had red eyes, and looked tired.

Then one day, in the morning, he came in and said: 'Look after this for me.'

It was an empty wallet. I said OK, and put it in my bag. I

didn't know what he wanted me to do with it, so I took it to the locker in the East Corridor which I shared with Kampol. Most of the lockers were abandoned, and I'd bought a lock for this one last year, giving one key to Kampol for 25p. The door was badly dented. Neither of us used the locker much: it's easier to take books round with you, from one lesson to the next. If they're too heavy, you just leave them at home, and borrow someone else's.

So I showed Kampol the wallet, and said I was looking after it for Justice, telling him he'd better not let anyone nick it if they sneaked up on him looking in the locker.

The next day, Justice gave me another empty wallet, and told me to look after that one too. Then he yawned, stretching his left arm right across my face, and went to sleep. The teacher saw, and asked:

'Justice, I hate to bore you, but do you have to go to sleep now?'

Justice said he did, cause he was tired.

'Why are you so tired? Why don't you go to bed earlier?'

'I've been having too much sex, sir.' Nobody could believe he was so flash.

After a couple of months, I was getting on well with Justice. I'd been looking after his wallets; and to stop him beating me up, I came up with funny ideas for in class. Once I suggested he should beckon Stephen Harris over to his desk. He did.

Stephen came over, looking scared, but grinning. Justice told him to take his shoes off and put them on his desk. So Stephen got down on his knees and started untying his trainers, while Justice looked away as if he'd forgotten Stephen even existed. That was my idea. Then Stephen placed the shoes on Justice's desk and stood waiting for something to happen.

'All right, fuck off.'

Stephen started walking back to his desk, and Justice took the shoes and threw them at him. The first one hit him on the back of his head, which made him duck, so the next one missed him. Justice shouted at him: 'What you putting your stinking shoes on my desk for, you wanker?'

Justice likes that sort of thing, so I tried to think of more along the same lines. Another trick involved calling people over from the far side of the library. Justice waved frantically at them. Then when they started walking over, he stared at his book as if he was reading it. They got to his desk and stood waiting for him to say something. He let them wait for hours, then looked up, and snapped: *What?!!* Usually, they'd mumble that it was him who called them over, but he interrupted them, telling them to fuck off and stop irritating him, or he'd kill them at break.

As long as I came up with ideas, I'd be fine. But I didn't like it if he played tricks on good fighters, cause they might think I was behind it all, and beat me up. In Chemistry, we were supposed to be testing coloured inks when Justice started staring out of the window and said to me: 'I'm the hardest in our year, ain't I?'

I agreed, but he snarled at me that I was only saying that cause I was scared of him. So I said I didn't think there was anyone who could beat him up but maybe I was mistaken. Maybe some were *nearly* as hard.

'Who? Tell me their names and I'll kill em.'

'No, I don't mean you should fight them just to prove it to *me*. They probably aren't as good at fighting as you . . .'

'Jus tell me their names.'

'Well, maybe *Des*mond would be a good fighter . . .' After all, Desmond was nearly as tall as Justice.

'I'll mash im. Who else?'

'Tony Forrester, maybe, but no one else.' He was big too.

'Come on, there must be more.' He was grinning at me,

making me squirm. I thought of the next tallest person I could think of in our year, who as it happened I really hated.

'Well, maybe someone like Hanif Ali. He thinks he's quite hard.'

'Don't be fucking stupid – that batty man – I could kill im.'

'Well that's what I *said* . . .'

To show the torture was over, Justice gave me a gentle slap in the face and got on with the experiment, squirting ink on to his page.

But that gave me an idea. I proposed a league table of fighting for our class. To make it interesting, the best fighters would start at the bottom of the table, and the worst fighters would be at the top, so the good fighters would have to work their way up.

We didn't know what to do with Donna, so we made it boys only.

Justice and me sat down to draw up the table. Some of the ranking was difficult, especially with people like me who aren't bad at fighting but prefer not to do it. And some people were equally good or bad, so we gave them the same number of points (as if it was half-way through the season). Every so often, Justice called someone over to his desk and said: 'Tell me all the fights you've had.'

They'd list the fights, and tell him which ones they'd won, and which were draws. If a teacher had broken it up quickly, it was a no-score draw, but if they carried on for a while without an obvious winner, but lots of good licks, that was a score draw (but that didn't affect the ranking, it was only for the pools information). In the end, the table looked like this:

Player	Played	Won	Drawn	Lost	Points
Alexander Ford	1	–	–	1	0
Tomato	1	–	1	–	1
Dan Hair	1	–	1	–	1
Stephen Harris	2	–	1	1	1
Ian Natty	2	1	–	1	2
Robin Patel	0	–	–	–	0
John Flintoff	0	–	–	–	0
Kampol Mai Ngram	1	1	–	–	2
Romanian Nabuschko	1	1	–	–	2
Gary Rawson	3	1	1	1	3
Joseph Montero	2	2	–	–	4
Bug Eye	4	2	1	1	5
Peter Davies	5	3	1	1	7
Gilbert	4	4	–	–	8
Robert Lester	5	4	1	–	9
Darius	5	4	1	–	9
Justice	3	3*	–	–	12**

* Includes beating up a sixth-former at start of first year.
** Includes bonus points for beating up a sixth-former in first year.

It was hard to justify putting the worst fighters at the top, when you saw how few points they'd got. So Justice decided not to show anyone the table until there'd been a few new results.

I was standing outside Maths, on the first floor of the West Block, waiting for the teacher to turn up, when somebody whacked me from behind. It stung my ear.

'Oy!'

I still hadn't worked out what was happening when more punches landed in my back, winding me. I swivelled round, and saw Bug Eye giving me licks. He was even aiming at my face – one punch slipped off the side of my jaw, glancing on to my neck.

'Right you cunt, Bug Eye,' I menaced.

I fought back, spinning my fists in front of me like an egg whisk so he couldn't get near me, but it didn't work, cause Bug Eye jabbed through them and hit me on the nose. My eyes filled with water and my nose stung, but I carried on punching. To ease the stinging, I shut my eyes, and kicked too.

Luckily, I could hear the teacher.

'Right, break it up, the pair of you. What's this all about?'

I was glad when the teacher pulled us apart, but I pretended to keep lashing out at Bug Eye – as if I was wild with fury. It might help me pick up extra points.

The teacher pushed us both into the class, and asked for an explanation.

'It's cause Jorge's a total bastard, sir,' I said, standing in front of the teacher's desk.

'I had to fight him, sir, for our league table,' said Bug Eye.

'Don't be facetious, Jorge,' said the teacher.

'Sir, but sir, I'm not being facetious. It's our league table.'

Peter Davies put his hand up and asked what 'facetious' meant, but didn't bother listening to the answer.

'Right, go and sit down, the pair of you.'

I took my seat next to Justice. I didn't want to complain, but I couldn't see why he told Bug Eye to start the fight without even warning me. I was the one who looked after all his wallets.

'So how many points do I get, Justice?'

'Well, I think Bug Eye won that one.'

But I didn't even know it was a fixture! And he attacked me from behind! 'But don't you think it was a draw, cause I came back after he attacked me?' And then I dared to ask: 'Why didn't you tell me I was scheduled to fight Bug Eye? He just attacked me without warning.'

'Cause he had to have home advantage.'

I was bound to get more fights. I asked Justice to be sure they weren't all going to be better fighters than me. He fixed up an easy match against Daniel Murphy. When I told Dan, he said:

'John, don't be such a bastard. We're friends. Why should we have a fight?'

But Justice was sitting beside me, so I sneered: 'What's the matter, are you scared?'

Daniel turned away from me, back to his work. Alexander and Diego and Stephen Harris were sitting on his table, pretending they weren't listening – but they were. They frowned over their books, and Stephen can't even read.

This wasn't one of the lessons where we were paired alphabetically, but there I was, sitting next to Justice all the same. He must actually *like* me. I told him I'd start the fight at break, and I did.

Daniel was walking along the North Corridor with Alexander and Diego and a couple of their softy friends from another class. They knew we were behind them, they kept glancing over their shoulders. Justice pushed me forward, so I ran at Daniel. Before I could reach him, he turned round and said: '*Fuck off*, John.' He began retaliating before I'd really started.

All the same, I was confident I could win this time. Dan's never been strong: sometimes on the tube we hold him down as the train approaches his stop, just me and Crispin, and we don't let him off until he sings 'Bridge Over Troubled Water' at the top of his voice.

Suddenly people appeared from nowhere, shouting, 'Fight! Fight!' We were the centre of attention.

Daniel was surprisingly vicious, fighting harder cause he was so angry with me. Even while he was fighting, I could hear him gasping 'John – you're – *gasp* – supposed – *gasp* – to – be – my – friend!' He tore my shirt, so I pulled on his big hair. I didn't want to aim for his face.

I heard someone heckle: 'Look at the two wankers!'

It was a draw. Later, Justice tried to arrange a fight between

Diego and Daniel, but they wouldn't do it, even when he slapped them a couple of times. So he tried *Diego v. Alexander*, which Gilbert called the 'Clash of the Wankers'. But they wouldn't fight each other either. So Justice slapped them both too.

Cause of his wobbly eyes, Diego always wobbles his head from side to side to compensate. He wobbles it all the time, you don't even notice it after you've known him for five minutes. After Diego refused to fight Alexander, Justice grabbed Diego's jaw and told him to keep his head still. Normally Diego can get out of anything by smiling, and saying tomato, and that's what he tried now. But you could tell he wasn't enjoying this. After all, he'd already been slapped. Justice held Diego's head in both hands, and forced it to keep still. But Diego's eyes still wobbled from one side to the other. Justice slapped him again, knocking his glasses a bit.

Deadly serious, Diego looked at him and said: 'Tomato.' Nobody laughed.

Gow was playing Slaps with me, planting a few good shots on my hands. I never move fast enough, and Gow is pretty good at this. Then Justice came over and offered Gow a match. Nobody could believe it, but Gow said all right, as long as he could go first.

So anyway, they were playing for a few minutes, with everyone watching, and Gow smacked Justice loads of times. He was being so cheeky, you should have been there.

But then his luck ended and Justice moved his hands out of the way.

'My go,' he said, with an evil smile. Gow was bricking it.

So they lined up their fingers and all of a sudden Justice went *clop!* – across Gow's face, hitting him so hard he went flying into the desks.

* * *

In Sport lessons, Justice always wins. The teachers think he's a great bloke, cause they're scared of him too. Even Sports teachers.

If we play five-a-side, the teacher appoints the captains. Gilbert and Justice. Gilbert hates being a captain, cause he'd like to be on Justice's side once in a while. But he's good at football, so the teachers always pick him.

Then they pick teams. Gilbert calls first, and selects a good player. Then Justice calls Diego, or Daniel, or any of the others who hate Sport, like Fat Raphael in 2.3. He ignores all the good players.

But even though Gilbert's got a strong team, he hasn't got a hope. Justice lines up the fatties in his goal so there is no way the ball can get past them. He tells them:

'If you let the ball in, I'll kill you.'

Then he goes out on the field and tries to get the ball off us, on his own. So long as we keep passing it well, like Liverpool, there's no way he can get it, but he isn't a bad footy player, so you don't let him get too close.

If he gets the ball, the teacher shouts out: 'Well done, Justice, good effort.'

Using the arm the teacher can't see, Justice clenches a fist and whispers to anyone who comes near him: 'If you touch it, I'll mash you.' So he dribbles brilliantly past all these defenders who tumble over as they lunge for the ball. Then he gets to the goal, and – using his hidden fist again – menaces his way past the keeper.

1–0 to Justice's team.

'Well done, Justice,' says the Sports teacher. 'What a brilliant run.'

We get so frustrated, the only way we get our own back is to pass really well after the kick-off, and set up a goal-scoring opportunity. Then whoever gets nearest Justice's crowded goal kicks the ball as hard as possible at the fatties, to sting them as hard as you can.

Once, Justice proposed a penalty shoot-out. He came over to our goalies (we were taking each one in turn) and said: 'If you save it, I'll give you two licks later.' As if that wasn't bad enough, he added, 'If you don't even *try* to save it, I'll give you five licks instead.'

I've started supporting Fulham instead of Man U. Fulham's one of the local teams and we prefer it because there is less chance of hooligans than at Chelsea or QPR. Most people from school support QPR (especially the ones from Shepherd's Bush) or Chelsea; hardly anyone likes Fulham. Some people have even started to call me Fulham. When I pass them in the corridor, they say: 'All right, Fulham?'

Or when we play football, if someone's commentating, they say: '...And Fulham's got the ball, Fulham's going to shoot, and – oh! – it's a beautiful goal by Fulham.'

On the estate

There's a couple of new boys in my class. One of them is called John McGuire. He used to be at Isaac Newton School up the road, but they expelled him because he shot a teacher with an air gun. It didn't kill the teacher, but the pellet had to be dug out of his leg.

John's a skinhead and he wears expensive Pringle sweaters. Most days, he wears a yellow one with grey squares on it. Otherwise he wears a pink one with blue squares. He never wears anything else. Also, he's got tassels on his loafers.

Because his name is John, like everyone calls me, I get on well with him. The first time I sat near him, he said: 'Ere, look at this.'

He was putting out his fists towards me, like at the start of a chess game when someone has to choose which colour you're going to be. On the knuckles of John's left hand was the word LOVE (one letter on each finger), and on the right hand it said HATE.

I said: 'How did you do that? Are you ambidextrous?'

'Nah, it's a tattoo.'

I looked closely. 'Oh yeah . . . Brilliant.' I asked how much it cost him.

'It dint cost me nuffin. Me bruvver done it for me with a compass and some blue ink, outer a jar.'

'Didn't it hurt?'

'Course it fucking urt. But it don't matter, I ad to do it.'

'Why?'

113

'One fer me mum, and one fer me dad.'

'What do you mean?'

He lifted up L–O–V–E, and said: 'Me mum,' then lifted up H–A–T–E and said: 'Me ol man.'

'Why do you hate your dad?'

'Cause he's a cunt. He's inside, anyway.'

'What – in prison?'

John nodded.

'What for?'

'Ah, nuffin much, he's just a cunt.'

John asked if I wanted a tattoo as well, but I said I didn't think my parents would like it.

'So what? Fuck em.'

Then he said: 'Ere, John, where do you live then?'

I told him: 'Fulham.'

He said: 'Which estate?'

'Well I don't actually live *on* an estate, but I live quite close to the Clem Attlee.'

'I got a load of mates down there. I'll come down and check you out one day.'

I hope he doesn't.

The other new boy is straight from some country in the Middle East I hadn't heard of before. I forgot the name of the place, but his name's Hanif. He seems all right, but he's definitely the kind of boy you call a plum. After all, he's got wire-framed glasses, and he carries a briefcase. He wears shiny white shirts like a bus driver, and a jacket he probably got at C&A.

This new Hanif can't believe the way black boys behave in class. After he'd been in our class for about a week, he was sitting next to me and Gow, watching Robert Lester mucking about. Hanif leant over and said: 'In my country, blacks have to be polite. They have to say hello to you if you pass them on the street. They must get off the pavement for me.'

*   *   *

I went on a housing estate in North Kensington to follow two boys who'd nicked Crispin's bike and our football while I wasn't there to look after him. I chased after the one on Crispin's bike for a mile, but lost him near an estate. I couldn't cycle too far, cause I had to look after Crispin too.

Then Crispin heard someone on the other side of a wall say, 'Let me see the ball,' and he guessed it must be them. I said it was unlikely, but he insisted. So we went on to the estate where the voices had come from, and walked along a high pathway between the blocks of flats. On one side you had the flats – some of them with broken windows, others smart with flowerboxes – and on the other you had a view over the estate, where people were mucking about below.

Crispin was right. We saw the boy with the bike, and his friend kicking our orange football. We crouched down to stop them spotting us.

We were scared to be on the estate, cause we were posh boys. Not *that* posh, but posh enough to get into trouble. To stop being posh, we agreed to forget John-Paul and Crispin, and stick with John and Chris if anyone asked our names.

We walked past a man smoking a cigarette who hadn't shaved. I held on to my bike really tight, but he didn't say a word. We kept our heads down and followed the boys. The one who'd nicked Crispin's bike looked familiar: he was at school, in the year below me. He had red hair and a pale face, and I'd heard people in his class call him Gypsy.

They went in a block of flats and we ran across the concrete to see where they went next. The concrete was broken up by lots of weeds coming through. They'd gone in a flat on the third floor. I thought we should go home and get Mum, but Crispin expected me to do more than that, so I had to show him how brave I was. We went up and watched them go into a flat, then I ran on tiptoes to the door and checked the number and to see if there was a name.

Then we ran all the way home, in case someone from the estate ran after us. We made Mum go to the flat and tell their mum that they'd nicked Crispin's bike, and the football. We stood beside her at the door, and I saw the gypsy looking out. He looked really scared. His mum said his dad would take his belt to them, and make them bring the bike back straight away.

We were sitting in the front room at home when we saw the gypsy with tears running down his face, wheeling Crispin's bike towards the front door. His friend was red-faced too, and he carried the ball. We didn't dare go to the door, but watched through the window as Mum collected it from them.

She said: 'Thank you so much for bringing it back. I'm dreadfully sorry you've been hurt, but let's hope it's a useful lesson.'

They snivelled, and said sorry.

Lots of the people in my class are from estates. About three-quarters of the boys, anyway. I don't know where most of the girls live. Some of them live on the same estates as each other, like Robert Lester and Bug Eye. I feel sorry for Stephen Harris. He lives on the same estate in Olympia as Mark Rooney, and a couple of hard black boys in other classes. I went round to his flat to see if it was true he had a pool table.

As well as going on about the Army Cadets, Harris has started raving about his pool table. He said he got one for Christmas. I said I bet he didn't have one, and he told me to come round and look at it.

When I got there, his dad was playing on it already. His dad works on a shift in a factory, so he finishes after lunch. As it was quite hot, he was wearing football shorts and no shirt. He had buck teeth like Stephen.

'Hi,' he said, 'who are you?'

I told him I was Stephen's friend, then said my name was John. 'Have you come round to play on the pool table? I expect all Stephen's friends will be round here now!'

I didn't think so – cause, if you think about it, Stephen doesn't have that many friends cause he's so stupid. But I said maybe.

'Do you want a cup of tea, John?' said Stephen's dad.

'Dad, just fuck off and let us get on with a game will you?'

We left the kitchen area. The pool table took up the whole living room. To see the telly, Stephen's dad had to lean over in his chair. But he didn't seem to mind.

We played six matches. Stephen won three, and I won three. His dad watched *Newsround*, then *Blue Peter*.

Death

Justice announced a day of mourning for Bob Marley, but Donna was playing Ling in the History class cause Ms Dawson still hadn't turned up. Gilbert and Robert Lester took Gow's Adidas sports bag and threw it around the room, with Gow trying to get it back.

Someone outside pulled down the doorhandle, so Robert threw the bag directly at the door. A balding man with a beard came in, saw the bag sailing towards him, and ducked out of the way. Gow came to pick up the bag, and the man grabbed him: 'Right – detention.'

'But sir . . .'

'No buts, be quiet and sit down.'

'Sir, where's Ms Dawson?' shouted Donna. 'Is she sick *again*?'

'Everybody sit down and shut up. I've got an important announcement.'

Everybody went quiet, but in front of me Kampol and Stephen Harris carried on playing Asteroids.

'As you all know, Ms Dawson has been very sick for the last couple of years.'

'Sir, is she dead?'

Even Kampol and Stephen started paying attention then.

'Be quiet,' said the bald teacher. 'She has been very sick, and didn't need to come to school, she could have taken sick leave. Some of you will have heard of cancer, and how serious that can be. Well, Ms Dawson had cancer, but she carried on coming to school because she was a highly dedicated teacher, and loved working here.'

'Sir, is she dead?' said Gilbert.

Donna told him to shut up.

'She was very dedicated, and worked right up to the end. Yes, Gilbert – if you could just be a little patient – she died at the weekend.'

Gilbert pulled a face, a bit shocked.

Yemisi asked: 'Sir, did she have any children?'

'No, Yemisi – and before you ask, she was unmarried. She always said the school was her family.'

Too quietly for the teacher to hear, Robert Lester told Gilbert she must have been a lesbian.

'Is she having a big funeral, will we all have to go?' asked Melissa.

'No, it will be a quiet ceremony, just a couple of colleagues and her family. Now, for the rest of the term, I am going to take your lessons, and we'll have to see what happens after that. Who can tell me what you did last week?'

Our new tutor, Mr Bryant, is head of Modern Languages, so he speaks excellent Spanish. When Bug Eye comes in late, he'll say something to him in Spanish and Bug Eye will explain in Spanish why he was late.

Bug Eye doesn't really like speaking Spanish in front of people. After all, he speaks perfect Cockney.

But when Mr Bryant speaks to Diego, Diego says more than we've ever heard from him in our lives.

Peter Davies asked Mr Bryant why Diego always said tomato. Mr Bryant looked puzzled; it didn't mean much to him. Then he spoke to Diego in Spanish and we heard him say 'tomato'. Then Diego spoke back to him, laughing, pushing his glasses back up his nose when they slipped down, and ended his explanation with the word 'tomato'.

Mr Bryant laughed again, then said to Peter:

'He doesn't say "tomato", meaning the fruit. He says "Te mato," which is Spanish for "I'll kill you."'

Euh, aaah, ooh

Ms Smith, our Social Education teacher, had brought in a selection of birth-control devices. The coil, the rubber johnny (Durex), the Pill, the Dutch cap, and other stuff like anti-sperm foam and creams for putting up a girl afterwards (I *think*).

Darius and Robert Lester nicked a couple of Durex each, and everyone told Ellen she should nick the Dutch cap – or else she'd be up the duff in no time. Ms Smith said you shouldn't make fun of people like that.

We'd done sex education before, in Science, but that was the technical stuff, with films showing animal reproduction. Social Education is where they tell you that you shouldn't have sex if you don't feel ready for it, and how you should use birth control. It's much funnier than Science.

Usually Social Education lessons are about subjects like breaking the law, or immigration, or comparing religious beliefs, or debating nuclear weapons. Sex was the funniest lesson in the history of the school.

One girl missed out, a Pakistani girl called Manmeet, who brought in a note saying her parents didn't want her to take part, so Ms Smith sent her along to the library. Some classes have got a lot of Indians and Pakistanis, but not us, we've only got Manmeet and Robin Patel. Manmeet's Pakistani, and has a huge hooked nose, so nobody fancies her. Once Alexander saw her eating her sandwich before lunch, in a class. It was a French-bread sandwich, with cheese. Alexander shouted a rhyme he'd invented: 'Look at the Pak, With the longer-lasting snack.' Darius thought that was really funny, but Manmeet's best friend Sharon, who is black, pointed out that it was racist, so Darius hit Alexander.

Anyway, in this sex lesson I was talking about, Alexander sat on a table with me and Daniel and Gow and Ian. He was holding the Pill, which is actually about *thirty* little pills in a foil packet. He dared Gow to eat one, but Gow told him to fuck off.

'Why don't *you* eat one, Alexander?'

So Alexander said he didn't mind if he did. Gow dared him to eat the whole lot, bet a whole quid he wouldn't do it. Gow's always betting. He's got a bookie system going, with Daniel. He gets people to bet on horse races, but nobody knows anything about racing, so they're mugs. Gow made £15 last week.

So anyway, Alexander took the first one out of the packet, and popped it in his mouth. We all laughed our heads off, so the teacher looked over. 'What's so funny, boys?' she asked.

'Nothing, miss.'

She carried on explaining to Ellen how the Dutch cap worked, so Alexander took another one out of the packet and popped that in his mouth too. Then another. It was difficult for him to swallow, cause he ran out of spit, but after a few minutes he'd eaten the whole lot.

Then he put up his hand.

'Yes, Alexander?'

'Um, I was wondering if you could tell us what is actually *in* the Pill.'

'It's a combination of hormones. Why?'

'Miss, if a man was to eat a lot of them,' Gow asked, 'would he start growing tits?'

'No, Gary. But it probably isn't a good idea.'

'Well, it's too late, miss, cause Alexander's already eaten them all.'

Ms Smith collected up the remaining items of birth control,

and counted the Durex. 'Who's got the other Durex?' she asked, but nobody owned up. 'Well I just hope you know how to use them properly,' she added.

The second sex education lesson, there was another teacher there, a thin bloke called Mr Burkett. He's incredibly weedy, and wears square, metal-framed glasses like Diego's, but he wears his shirts open at the top, so you can see his hairy chest. Every day, guaranteed, he'll be wearing a white shirt open half-way down his chest, as if he was in the Bee Gees. He was there to give a man's perspective on sex education; and he thinks he's a bit cool.

Half-way through the lesson, Gilbert put his hand up.

'Yes?' said Mr Burkett.

'Sir, what is masturbation?'

Everybody laughed, cause everybody knows what it is.

'Do you really need to ask?'

'Yes, sir, I'm not sure if I really understand what it means.'

'Well, Gilbert, masturbation is what you would normally call wanking. Do you know what that is?'

'No, sir.'

Ms Smith joined in. She said: 'Wanking, Gilbert – as you well know – is when people gratify themselves sexually on their own.'

This was too much for Yemisi. 'Oh, miss, that is disgusting, I don't like this lesson. I think I'm going to be sick.'

'Don't be silly, Yemisi,' said Mr Burkett. 'There's nothing wrong with it. In the past, young people were threatened and scared about it. People told them it would make them go blind, but that is absolute rubbish.'

'It's an old wives' tale,' explained Ms Smith. She'd told us about old wives' tales the previous week, giving an example about having sex upside-down to stop you getting pregnant.

'But sir,' asked Gilbert, 'how do people actually masturbate?'

Everyone laughed again.

'Well, for boys, you tend to rub your penis up and down.'

I thought Yemisi was going to faint. She was squealing horribly, going: 'Euh, aaah, ooh – sir, please shut up.' She stuck her fingers in her ears. She was acting as if she was a little girl. But if you look at Yemisi, you can see she's already got quite big tits. I'd noticed, from sitting next to her.

'Sir,' asked Gilbert, 'have you ever masturbated?'

'Well I think you can probably all be more grown-up about this,' said Mr Burkett, still smiling. He was leaning against the blackboard, chucking a piece of chalk up in the air and catching it. 'But – yes – I have.'

Even Ms Smith, standing at the back of the room, chuckled about that.

After the lesson, we let Mr Burkett out of the class first, then we shouted down the corridor at him: 'WAN-KER! WAN-KER! Mr Burkett's a wanker!'

I asked Darius if he wanted to know a secret about Alexander. He said yeah.

'The thing is, he can't feel pain.'

'What do you mean?'

'Alexander can't feel any pain. When he says ow, he's taking the piss out of people who hit him.'

'Of course he can feel pain, you batty man.'

Robert Lester heard him say that, and turned to join in: 'What you say, batty man?'

'It's just that Alexander once told me he can't feel pain, so whenever he bumps into things – or if someone hits him – it doesn't make any difference. If you think about it, it makes sense: look at him.'

They looked at Alexander, and were unimpressed. Everyone knew he lived near by in a big, expensive house, but the most common name for him was Tramp. His hair was always a nasty mess, and he had terrible dandruff. To annoy Diego or Daniel,

Alexander would flop his hair about with one hand, over their books, causing a snowstorm. He'd say: 'Salt and shake!'

'Is that true, John?' asked Robert.

I said it was – but I said it smiling, so I could tell him later it was a joke, if he got nasty.

They told all the other bullies. Heading for Dr Bowes' French lesson, I passed Alexander in the playground. Martin Palmer and Mark Pye, of 2.9, were giving him dead arms. Whenever he complained, they said:

'Are you taking the piss?'

He said: 'No! What do you mean?'

'We know you can't feel no pain. So shut up.' And they hit him again.

'Owww! Argh! But I *can* feel pain – of course I can feel pain, why shouldn't I feel pain?' said Alexander. It was obvious they weren't the first people to try it on him this morning. He began to cry. I felt like running to rescue him, and be friends again. Instead, I just walked past.

Mr Raymond and Mr Bryant are trying to stop Robert being bad in class. They sat him next to Alexander. They thought Alexander would be a good influence. Alexander mumbles a lot, but most people like me can understand him easily. Robert didn't seem to understand his accent. Once Robert asked him what the teacher had just said, and Alexander tried to tell him quietly. Then suddenly Robert grabbed Alexander by his hair – which is pretty disgusting, when you think about it – and shouted at him:

'Speak clearly,' he said, 'or I'll kill you.'

Robert Lester took a handful of live locusts out of the tank while the teacher wasn't looking, and stuffed them down the back of Daniel's shirt.

'Oh, euh, aargh,' said Daniel, tearing his shirt off. He shook

125

out the locusts. Most of them were squashed dead. The girls laughed at Daniel, standing there topless. Robert spat on his naked back, silently.

'Robert – GET OFF!'

'Are you going to make me?'

'No, but PLEASE, leave me alone.'

Robert spat at him again, then offered him a handful of locusts to eat.

'Nyam these, you damn batty man,' he said. Some of them were still alive, wriggling their legs.

I know the rules. Always act harder than you really are. Never say please, or they spit on you twice. And if someone challenges you to a fight and you back down, you're under manners to them for ever. Or until you eventually fight them. Those are the rules, but I'm not much good at sticking to them. I'm better at inventing ideas for hard boys.

Later in the lesson, Robert got hold of Alexander's bag of liver-pâté sandwiches, without Alexander seeing. He opened up each sandwich in turn, and squashed a locust on to the pâté, sticking the second piece of bread back in place on top. Today, Alexander was going to eat locusts.

This was my chance to make up to him. When Robert was at the other side of the room, messing around with Gilbert, I said:

'Alexander!'

He looked at me suspiciously.

'What?'

'Don't eat your sandwiches, Robert Lester's put locusts in them.'

Alexander looked in the bag and opened a sandwich. He saw the locust, and scowled. 'John, you are a real wanker. Why did you tell him to do that?'

'I didn't – I really didn't – there was nothing I could do to stop him. You know what Robert's like. I only told you cause I thought I should stop you eating them.'

'Well, thanks a *lot*,' he added sarcastically. Diego and Daniel were sitting beside him. They looked at me as though I was a stranger, then looked away and started talking to each other.

I've been kicked out of the Scouts for being a troublemaker. Crispin was kicked out too. We told our parents it was because of a 'personality clash' with the new leader; like they have in football teams when a new manager arrives.

Kiss me, you wanker

Even after two years at secondary school, Rebecca Brewster didn't have any tits. Everyone else had *some*, but Rebecca had none at all.

Donna was pretty big all over, so she had the biggest tits. After Donna, Alison from Fox was in the lead (but she's the oldest in the class, so that's not surprising). Yemisi probably came next (so maybe black girls have an advantage). Then people like Melissa weren't doing badly, with Sharon and Ellen and Rosalind close behind, and people like Manmeet didn't have much more than Rebecca. Manmeet always covered up her whole body, cause she's from Pakistan, so you couldn't see *any* bumps under her clothes. But nobody's interested in Manmeet anyway. She thinks people will fancy her because she wears a long leather coat and gold chains, but I think not.

Manmeet fancies this boy in another tutor-set, a white boy called David Whittaker. He's the school New Romantic. He's got the lot: a silly fringe, a white suit and a permanent tan. Half the girls in the school fancy him, the rest think he's a dick. Personally, I think he's a dick, but he always seems quite friendly, so I suppose he's an all right dick.

Rebecca – who's the blondest in the class, and has a disgusting mole at the top of her cheek, near her eye – has less tits than anyone, but she still flirts a lot, with harder boys like Gilbert and Robert Lester. *They* quite like her, but the rest of us can see through her: Rebecca's a slapper.

In one History lesson, when the normal teacher was sick, Alexander told her it said in his textbook that Rebecca Brewster had the Flattest Chest of All Time. He said: 'Rebecca, does your chest actually go *inwards*? Is it concave?' Daniel, sitting next to Alexander, laughed.

The cover teacher told them to be quiet and get on with their work, then sat back at his desk to mark some exercise books. This cover teacher acted like he loved himself, wearing fancy clothes and a medallion, but he was going bald. We sometimes saw him on playground duty, and hid behind a wall to call out: 'Oy! Baldy!'

Rebecca replied: 'Alexander – is your fucking dandruff real, or do you sprinkle extra flour in your fucking hair before you come to school? Why don't you ever brush your hair, and buy some nice clothes, you fucking tramp?'

Darius, sitting at the desk behind Alexander and Daniel, silently gobbed on their backs to please Rebecca, looping the spit up with his tongue.

Desmond told Alexander he shouldn't dress like a tramp, unless his parents were Jewish, and wouldn't give him any money. (Last month, Desmond stole a pair of new Nike trainers from a boy in the year below. He threw his own ones away in the big bins behind the kitchens.)

Daniel shouted: 'Rebecca, your chest's so flat it looks as though you ran into a wall and crushed your tits. Your tits are like two fried eggs. You should put rolled-up socks in your bra. Or don't you have a bra? You should ask your mum to buy you a bra, everyone else's got one.'

Ellen, sitting next to Rebecca, told Dan to cut his disgusting big hair before he opened his mouth. 'And anyway, who cares what you fucking think? Nobody's ever going to fancy you, you wanker.'

Stephen Harris told Rebecca her mum was a whore, and so was she. Alexander laughed, and said Rebecca was the least successful hooker in history. He said he'd seen a sign for her in a phonebox in Queensway, with her telephone number, which said 'Flat-Chested Fucks a Speciality'.

The cover teacher was getting fed up, and said the whole class would be on detention if we didn't settle down and shut up. But they always say that.

Alexander told Ellen she should shave under her arms cause the sight of her hairy armpit made him feel sick: 'And it makes you look like a German.'

'Well fucking *everything* about you makes me fucking sick, Alexander.'

Donna told Alexander and Dan and Stephen to shut their mouths before she gave them licks. She wasn't exactly Rebecca's best friend, but she always took the girls' side if there was a girls-versus-boys argument.

Donna fancies Bug Eye. She told Ellen to tell him, and find out if he liked her back. But Donna's so big and ugly – and violent – that he can't possibly. He's scared of her, like everyone else is. Ellen told Donna he said he wasn't interested. She was furious.

'Jorge!' she shouted, while we waited for Dr Bowes to arrive for French. 'Come here and give me a kiss.'

'Nah, Donna, sorry man, but I don't really want to . . .'

'Come now? What you mean you don't want to, boy?'

'Nah, listen, Donna, man . . .'

'Don't give me none of your sayings, boy. Just come kiss me, before I lash you.'

Everyone in the class watched Bug Eye squirm. Darius pushed him forward, to the desk where Donna waited with her arms open. She lay him on the floor and sat on top, then banged his head on the floor, saying: 'You fancy me, don't you . . .'

But Dr Bowes arrived, so Bug Eye escaped with his life.

Afterwards, in the corridor, Donna grabbed Bug Eye and pushed him up against a wall, and said: 'Kiss me, you wanker, or I'll kill you.' He shut his eyes and kissed her softly. Everyone laughed like mad.

Donna winked at everyone, as though she was doing it for a joke. But nobody would mess around with Donna. She hit a teacher once, smack in the face. We thought she'd be expelled for sure, but she just got suspended.

Alison's old boyfriend, Sean, left school in spring, and ever since then she's started hanging out with people in the year above us. She's even going out with one of them, called Matthew Something-or-other. In class, Alison's joined Melissa and Rosalind's gang.

I expect Alison would still be going out with me, if I hadn't dumped her at Fox.

Cause her tits are the biggest, everyone's pretty sure Alison's already having periods. Gilbert told us that Rebecca Brewster told him Alison had a period before anyone else, in the first year. He was impressed when he found out I'd gone out with her at Fox, and he asked me if she'd been having periods then. I told him I didn't think she was.

I was the best person to ask.

On school journey this time round, we went to a youth hostel in Cornwall. The girls got the dormitory on the top floor, as usual. One afternoon, we escaped from some boring expedition to find shells on the beach – me and Gilbert and Bug Eye and the new boy who joined last month called Jason Cunningham – and decided to invade the girls' dormitory and find out if Alison had any Tampax.

Gilbert said we should check which girl had bloodstains on her bed.

Before we invaded, Gilbert grabbed this old red crab claw that was lying around in the kitchen. 'If she's got the curse, we have to leave a sign saying that we know she's got it.'

So he picked up the crab claw with a piece of kitchen paper,

131

and hid it inside his jacket. When we got to the girls' dormitory, Jason spotted a girl from David's class called Kate lying on her bed. She heard us coming in, and rolled over, looking half-asleep.

'It's all right,' said Gilbert, 'Alison and Ellen asked us to fetch something for them. Which one is Alison's bed?'

Kate pointed, then asked: 'Why didn't Alison come and get it herself?'

''Cause the teacher wouldn't let her leave the shell expedition.'

'What does she want you to fetch?'

'Her jumper.'

Jason Cunningham asked Kate why she was asleep.

'I wasn't asleep,' she smiled. 'I've got a stomach ache.'

'Oh.'

Without letting Kate see, Gilbert pulled back Alison's bedclothes, taking care in case there was some blood. There wasn't anything there, so he slipped in the crab claw, and pulled the sheet back. Bug Eye checked Ellen's bed, then picked up a jumper off the top of her bag. Gilbert took a jumper from Alison's bag too. Me and Jason just stood and helped.

'Well – hope your stomach ache gets better,' said Gilbert.

'Yeah,' said Jason.

As soon as we were outside, we laughed about the claw. 'Fucking excellent,' said Jason.

It was a shame Kate was in there, but she didn't spot us doing anything. Kate's quite pretty, actually.

We left the jumpers on the banisters outside the girls' dormitory, then went down to our dormitory to talk about what had happened, lying on our bunks.

'What shall we do now?' asked Jason. He started singing a porno song called 'Frigging in the Rigging'.

'Oy, Bug Eye?' asked Gilbert.

'Yeah?'

'Are you going to fuck Donna?'

'Nah, man, I don't even like her at all . . .'

'But she's got fucking huge tits. You could at least take a look at those first . . .'

'Nah, I'm not interested.'

Suddenly the warden's dog came in our dormitory. Jason said: 'Why don't we dress up the dog in someone's pyjamas?' It was a brilliant idea, but we had to think whose pyjamas were best. Jason said we couldn't use Alexander's cause the poor dog might catch something horrible.

'Yeah, it'd get dandruff,' said Bug Eye.

So we chose Kampol's, cause they were the cleanest and the most colourful. Jason lifted the dog so we could put its forelegs into the jacket. Then we buttoned it up under the dog's tummy. The dog still wagged its tail, enjoying the fancy dress. But the trousers were too long, and we didn't know where to put its tail, so we gave up.

Then we pushed the dog outside. After a few minutes we could see it trotting around on the lawn, but it got hot, so after a while it lay down under a tree.

Then we decided to raid everyone's bags. We mixed up everybody's things on purpose. Bug Eye took some of Darius' things and put them in Diego's bag. 'Darius will kill Diego when he finds it.'

Gilbert threw Daniel's things round the room, hanging his pants from the light and putting them in hard-to-reach places. Then he moved on to Ian's bag and did the same.

'Alexander's got a camera,' said Jason. 'Let's take some pictures.'

We raided Alexander's bag, throwing all his stuff on the floor, and ran downstairs after the dog. Jason took five pictures of it in Kampol's pyjama jacket. It looked happy to see us, jumping up and wagging its tail, and sniffing the camera. Afterwards, we took the camera back in the dormitory and took pictures of each other's dicks, so if Alexander's mum got the film developed she'd think he was a homo.

Jason Cunningham, who's a bit fat, has a tiny dick.

When Kampol found the dog, he went mad, shouting, 'Fucking hell, fucking hell!' with his Thai accent. Whenever he ran after the dog to get the pyjama jacket off, the dog ran away, thinking it was a game. After Kampol finally got the jacket off, he didn't complain to anyone, cause he was scared of Gilbert and Bug Eye. He refused to wear the jacket again, even after the teacher washed it for him twice. But he wore the trousers, because he didn't know we'd put them on the dog's back legs. They'd been all over the dog's hairy bum, and Kampol didn't even wash them.

When Darius discovered his things in Diego's bag, he nicked Diego's glasses and threatened to drop them out of the window. But he didn't, cause he knew it wasn't Diego's fault.

Rebecca told Gilbert when Alison found a crab in her bed she cried. That Kate must've told them who did it, cause the four of us had to wash up for the rest of the holiday.

Daniel didn't notice his pants were missing till the following morning, when he needed a new pair. He didn't have any clothes on, so he refused to climb up and get them off the light. He told the teacher, and the teacher made Bug Eye climb up.

That night, the boys held an unofficial disco in our dormitory. Before we packed, we were told to bring torches on school journey. Gow's got a brilliant one, his dad borrowed it from some builder in Shepherd's Bush. The beam's as strong as a car headlamp, and if you want it to, the light flashes on and off. We put it in the middle of the room and danced round it, but it didn't last long cause everyone started to bundle each other.

Most of the girls in our class say boys are *so* immature, but Rebecca and Ellen don't say that. Nor does Lisa St John. Lisa's this quite-new girl with buck teeth who has BO.

Lisa fancies everybody. Even her little sister in the first year fancies people. They must be a family of sex maniacs. Her little sister sent me a card with a drawing of a heart on the front. Inside, it said how much she loved me, but I don't even like Lisa, so why should I go out with her little sister? Anyway, it's illegal to go out with someone that young, I think. I mean to have sex.

I played a game of Catch once, around this block of posh apartments with security gates we'd leapt over, with Lisa and her little sister and boys like Jason Cunningham and John McGuire and Bug Eye and Samuel Thomas. When the girls were on it, the only boy they ever chased was me.

Lisa's sister gave me a little present. I unwrapped it and it was a tiny bottle of aftershave. I said thanks and everything, but I didn't want it. In class, Bug Eye and Jason asked me if I was going to fuck Lisa's little sister and I said: 'Of course not, I'm not interested.' Then I threw the bottle of aftershave in the bin so everyone could see me do it.

Melissa said that was really mean, to throw away a present.

I said: 'Well, I didn't *ask* her to give me it.'

The advantage of Lisa's younger sister though is that she doesn't have BO, or buck teeth. But maybe she'll get them when she's older.

Another new girl called Claire Miller has joined our class and she's the prettiest girl in our year by miles, I'd say. I sort of fancy her a bit, but not madly or anything.

I sat next to her once and tried to flirt with her. I was messing about and telling jokes about people, so she'd know who we all were.

I said she should avoid Alexander, because everyone spat on him, and anyway he had terrible dandruff. I told her Gilbert and Bug Eye and Jason were bullies, but even they weren't half as bad as the real nutters, like Justice and Robert Lester and

135

Darius. I told her I was one of the few people who could sit next to Justice and not get beaten up.

She asked who my best friends were, then.

I didn't really want to say Stephen Harris (too thick), or Kampol (too shy), or Gow or Ian (too boring, and Gow spits when he talks). So I said: 'Oh, my best friends are in some of the other tutor-sets, I'll show you them another time.'

Claire's got fantastic smooth dark brown hair which goes down to her shoulders. Straight down. And a *beautiful* smile.

(Her tits are about average for the class.)

I quite like her. Put it this way, I wouldn't mind going out with her. I can already imagine us walking home together after school, through the park. When I imagine it, I always sing the same song inside my head, again and again: 'It started with a kiss . . .' The way I see it, I'd tell Claire jokes about people in our year and help her avoid any trouble by telling her about how the school works. We'd buy each other sweets at lunch, and probably have a snog on a bench.

Lisa and Ellen drew up a list of boys they wouldn't mind fucking. It was in Ellen's French book. Gilbert saw it over her shoulder, and nicked it.

'Gilbert,' shouted Ellen, 'fucking give me that back or I'll kill you, I mean it.'

She sounded serious. Lisa was shouting too. They both got up and chased him round the class. The teacher stopped them, but Ellen said: 'Euurgh, sir, get your hands off me, sir, man.'

Dr Bowes told her to stop being silly and sit down.

'How can I work when Gilbert has got my book, sir?'

'Gilbert.'

'What, sir?' Gilbert was reading it and smiling.

'Have you got Ellen's book?'

'No, sir.'

'He *has*!' said Ellen and Lisa.

'Well give it back to them now.'

'All right, sir, just a second.'

'No – now!'

Gilbert handed it back and came back to the desk where he was sitting with Jason and Bug Eye and me and Stephen Harris. He told us about the list. The title was 'Boys We Wouldn't Mind Fucking'. On the left of the page was Ellen's list, and on the right was Lisa's. Gilbert said Bug Eye was top of both lists. Justice was next. Then there was a mixture of people. Gilbert said he was on both lists, but Jason wasn't on either of them. Jason's quite fat, which might be why. Also, he got a Mohican a few weeks ago, which makes him look odd. Gilbert said I was on Lisa's list.

But I'm not interested.

We all made fun of Ellen and Lisa, calling them slappers, and passing them notes saying they were whores.

Claire Miller is best friends with Ellen and Lisa. After I sat next to her that first time, I didn't get near her again for ages, but I always try to sit quite close.

I never sit down in class till I've seen where Claire's going, then I take a seat near by.

In Maths I sat next to her, with Jason opposite and Ellen next to him. I was so pleased, because only that morning I'd drawn a lucky tattoo on my arm before going to school. It had an anchor, and the words 'I love CM'. Of course, I rolled my sleeve down over it before getting to school.

Most of the lesson, the whole class acted out last night's episode of *The Young Ones*. Everyone wants to be Viv, because he's hardest. Gilbert appointed Daniel Murphy to act as Neil. Gilbert said: 'That's cause you're a smelly hippy, Dan.'

After we'd done the whole programme a couple of times over, the teacher told us to shut up, so Jason leant over the desk and said: 'Oy, Claire, John fancies you.'

I said I didn't, but Claire and Ellen started laughing anyway.

Claire said: 'Do you, John?'

I said no.

She said: 'Why, what's wrong with me?'

I went red, getting all hot under my coat which I hadn't taken off in case someone tampered with it, so I said: 'There's nothing wrong with you, but you're not my type.'

If only the others weren't so near, I'd have whispered to her to stop. I'd have said: 'It's true, I do love you.' If the others weren't there, I'd have told her how we could walk home together through the park, and about snogging on a bench. But I didn't say anything.

'Bollocks, John,' said Ellen, 'I've seen you watching her.'

'Fuck off, I don't.'

'Come on John,' said Jason, 'admit it. What's the big deal?'

Claire grabbed my hand under the desk, as if the others couldn't see. I wished she hadn't, because my hand was all sticky, and she'd think it was always like that. She said: 'John, will you go out with me?'

I went really red. I wish she hadn't done that. How could she make fun of someone who really did love her? This was true love, and she was going to spoil it.

'Fuck off, Claire,' I said. I tried to look like I was relaxed about it, but I was all red. I knew I was. All three of them were laughing at me. Probably everyone else in the class too, but I couldn't see because I was looking down at the floor to hide my embarrassment.

I looked up at Ellen: 'Well at least I never wrote a list of girls I'd like to fuck.'

'Fuck off, John, you weren't on *my* list.'

'Well you wouldn't be on my list either, with your hairy armpits.'

Then Claire said: 'John, have you ever had a wank?'

Oh, Claire. How could you? I went *really* red that time.

'No.'

But I had.

'Bollocks, John, you must of,' said Jason.

'Why – have you?'

'Of course.'

'What's the matter, John,' asked Ellen, 'not old enough? Can't you get a hard-on?'

'Of course, but I don't need to wank.'

They all laughed at me.

I hate them. I even hate Claire. She's a slapper.

Accessories

We watched *Gregory's Girl* in a cover lesson. At the end of the class, Justice noticed that the teachers had forgotten to lock the room. He tested the door, then grabbed Gow.

'Give me your bag.'

'Aw, come on, Justice – I can't, it's new, my mum only bought it at Easter . . .'

'Shut up and give me it, before I box you.'

Gow handed over the huge, black plastic Adidas bag. Justice unzipped it and turned it upside-down, so Gow's books and pens fell on the floor. So did the tennis ball he played footy with at break.

'Aw, Justice . . .'

'Shut up.'

Justice pushed Gow away, and told me to go with him and stand outside the classroom, to check that nobody was coming. After a couple of minutes, he hurried out and rushed down the stairs. Half-way down, he handed me the bag, which weighed a ton.

'Carry this for me.'

'But Justice, I can't – what if I get caught?'

'Shut up,' he said, and ran off. He missed the next couple of lessons. Sometimes he did that, bunking off and going to the park with some of the older black boys he hung round with, fourth- and fifth-years. I saw him again after lunch. He flopped down beside me with his eyes all red, and put his head in his hands on the desk. I gently nudged him, and said:

'What'm I supposed to do with this?'

'Jus hol on to it till the end of school an I'll take it from you then. Now leave me in peace.'

'Do you want those wallets as well? Should I put them in the bag?'

He sat up slowly and looked at me as though I was taking the piss.

'What wallets?'

'The ones I've been looking after for you.'

After thinking about it for a moment, he smiled and said: 'I don't want them. You can throw them away if you want.'

At break, I took an empty carrier bag to the locker, and filled it with wallets. Then I wedged Gow's bag inside. While everyone else played football, or smoked under the Sports block, I sneaked into Holland Park – the wild, foresty bit of it – and abandoned the carrier bag full of wallets deep inside one of the park bins.

Seeing me without his bag at the next lesson, Gow asked where it was. I told him I'd hidden it for Justice.

'What's he put in it? Did he nick something from school?'

I said I didn't know.

'Bollocks, John, you must know.'

I said I really didn't.

'Well, just make sure I get the bag back, that's all I'm saying.'

At the end of the last lesson, I told Justice he could come and get the bag from my locker. But he said he had some urgent business to attend to, and told me to carry the bag down Campden Hill towards the shops, and the bus stops in front of the Coronet Cinema. He'd collect it from me there.

I did what he said, and he jumped on a bus going west. The next day – I couldn't believe it – Gow got his bag back.

You know what? My old friend Carlos, from Fox, is in Desmond Mears's new class. Once after school Desmond told Carlos to follow him. They went into Holland Park, and Desmond took him to the wild bit, all covered in blackberry bushes and weeds. Under a bush was this white carrier bag. Desmond told Carlos to take it home and look after it.

Carlos didn't dare to argue, so he took it home. When his parents were out, he opened the bag, and it had another bag inside, and then another.

Inside the last bag was a machete with blood on it. Desmond still hasn't asked for it back.

The trials of Daniel

Daniel Murphy keeps trying to change his ways, so that people stop bullying him. He started wearing a long tweed coat, like the sort of thing country gentlemen wear (but Dan bought it from Kensington Market). He wears it all over the place, strolling about with his hands in the pockets.

He even sits in hot classrooms with it on. It's so long it dangles over the chair and flops on to the floor, so it's always dusty. Darius and Robert Lester walk on it on purpose.

He's just trying to be trendy, but nobody's going to let him get away with it. His big hair still needs sorting out.

One day at the beginning of Maths, Jason Cunningham was sitting next to John McGuire. They both stood up and pointed at Daniel when he walked in. Jason shouted: 'Oy, everyone, look at Dan and his sad coat. Look at the plum trying to be trendy.'

Another time, Dan decided he was going to be hard. He was standing outside History with his own friends, people like Alexander, Gow, Ian, Stephen Harris, Hanif and Diego, when all the hard boys turned up. They were up to something.

Suddenly Gilbert and Jason and Robert Lester shouted out: 'Steeeeam!'

They rushed at the softies, to steam them. 'Steaming' means attacking them and giving them dead arms. When you steam someone properly, outside school, you normally nick their money. But this was just a joke.

Diego and Hanif lifted up their briefcases to ward off the

punches. Alexander lifted up his carrier bag. Ian and Stephen just sneaked out of the way. But do you know what Daniel did? He *joined in* the steam. He squinted his eyes, in case anyone accidentally hit him, and charged at his own friends. He started punching Alexander, and shouting, 'Steam! Steam!'

Daniel can't punch properly. He punches like a spaz. He always squints, almost shutting his eyes, cause he's scared. And he lifts his arms up too high, as if he was trying to hit a giant. Anyone can just hit him in the tummy when he does that. Anyway, the point is, he looks really stupid, lashing out like that and shouting steam when he's supposed to be the victim himself.

Jason started laughing, and pointed at Dan again. He said: 'Ha ha! Look at the plum trying to be hard!'

Dan looked embarrassed, and stopped. He said: 'Fuck off, Jase, why shouldn't I do it too? What makes you so special?'

Jason punched Dan in the shoulder and told him not to call him Jase until he was specifically allowed to. 'Only my friends call me Jase, not plums.'

The other thing Dan did when he was trying to reform himself was ask questions in class. We were doing Science, and Mr Stewart was going on about muscles and bones and organs. Dan put his hand up, which he didn't normally do.

'Yes, Daniel?'

'Sir,' said Dan, all serious, waving his pen in his hand. 'Is the brain a muscle?'

'In your case, Daniel, it probably is.'

Gow said: 'John, did I tell ya I went to Epping Forest at the weekend?'

'No.'

'Yur, I went wiv Claire and Ellen. They asked me. But I was scared of going on my own wiv em, so I asked Dan as well. I tell ya, when we got there, we drank all this booze that Ellen'd bought somewhere. Ellen and Claire drank loads, but I only drank a bit, right? (Dan drank quite a lot, I tell ya.) On the bus ome, Ellen said, "Less get rid of Dan" – and I din really wanna, but I *did*, in the end. Anyhow. We sent Dan to the front of the bus, upstairs, and when the bus started going again, the three of us jumped off. But Dan guessed what was happening, and he rushed after us. The bus was going at about thirty, maybe forty mile an hour, but he jumped off, din he! He fell over and grazed his chin, so we like said sorry and all that. Then on the tube, Claire came over and sat on my lap, I couldn't believe it, I tell ya, I had a right hard-on! But the thing is, when we got to Dan's stop, Erws Cawt, he stood up and asked me if I was coming back with him. I gotta tell ya, John, I was too scared to stay with them girls on me own, cause there was no telling what they'd do now they was drunk, and the thing is, I felt a bit bad about Dan on the bus and all, so I pushed Claire off and went with Dan.'

'Brilliant,' I said, but I was gutted about Claire. 'What happened next?'

'Well the fing is, John, I was after your advice, cause now the girls aren't talking to me any more, they ain't even said hi. What should I do?'

Rebecca Brewster told Gilbert she'd given someone a blow job. She said it was a friend of her brother's, at a party in her house in Chelsea, when her parents were on holiday.

Rebecca's brother goes to a private school; I used to know him at Fox, his name's Nick. Anyway, you could see that Gilbert was impressed about the blow job.

Bug Eye said: 'So when's she going to give you one, Gil?'

Gilbert just smiled, with foxy eyes, trying to suggest she already had. But he never said anything.

I told Alexander and Daniel what Gilbert had told us. They told a load of their plum friends. Soon everyone knew about it. Even people like Mark Pye and Martin Palmer.

In the playground, everyone said: 'Oy, Rebecca, give us a blow job.'

She told them to fuck off.

In class, Daniel asked her if the boy had refused to have sex because she had such a flat chest. 'Did he want a blow job instead?'

Rebecca went over to Daniel's chair and hit him again and again around the head, then she started crying and ran out of the class. It was getting too much for her.

The very next day, Mr Bryant said that Rebecca had left the school because she was so upset by people teasing her. So we shouldn't pick on people, he said. He didn't tell us where she'd gone instead. I wonder if it was a private school. The one her brother Nick's at is just for boys.

A couple of weeks later, Ellen said she had to tell Gilbert something at break. They went down to the park together.

In the next lesson, Gilbert told Jason and Bug Eye. Then Jason told me: 'Rebecca tried to kill herself cause we made jokes about her flat tits. She took 150 aspirins. Her brother found her in her bedroom, with the music on loud. He was with the boy she gave a blow job to, they took her to hospital, Charing Cross. Then she had to have a stomach pump.'

I felt bad about Rebecca, but it was amazing news; I told Gow, Ian, Kampol and Stephen Harris.

Kampol didn't know what a blow job was, so we had to explain. The thing is, none of us really knew either. I told Kampol it's when a woman blows on your dick, cause that's what it sounds like.

Kampol said that was disgusting and Rebecca deserved to die.

In class, Ellen said: 'Oy, Daniel.'

'Yes?'

'Have you heard what Rebecca did, you bastard?'

'Um, yes.'

146

'Don't you feel guilty, you wanker?'

Daniel turned back to his plum friends without answering. I felt a bit sorry for him. It wasn't all his fault.

Out the window

I came up with another trick for Justice. Mr Burkett was covering the lesson because Ms Smith was sick. Justice called Stephen over.

'Stephen!' he said.

'Yes?'

'I've had an idea to scare Mr Burkett.'

'What is it?'

'You got to climb out the window and hold on to the frame, then I'll call Burkett and tell him you nearly fell out. He'll go crazy.'

We were in the Social Education class on the second floor of the West Block, looking over the park. 'But I'll get in trouble,' said Stephen.

'No you won't, we'll pretend it was an accident.'

Stephen didn't dare to say it just couldn't happen by accident; people don't just fall out of second-floor windows. He said he didn't feel like it very much.

Justice told him he had no choice.

'But Justice . . .'

'Just do it.'

So Stephen opened the window at the back of the room while me and Justice caused a diversion at the front by throwing things at each other. Mr Burkett told us to settle down.

Stephen was hanging out of the window and holding on to the frame with both hands. You couldn't see his face because it was below the bottom of the window. You could just see his arms, and the top of some trees in the park. Justice let him hang there for ages. Everyone in the whole class noticed except Mr Burkett.

Gilbert was sitting nearest Stephen. He stood up and looked out. Stephen must've said something to him, because Gilbert started to grab hold of him. Suddenly Mr Burkett noticed, but all he could see was Gilbert with somebody's arms outside the window. 'What the hell are you doing, Gilbert?'

'I'm trying to help Stephen get back in, sir.'

Mr Burkett was at the window in half a second, helping to pull.

'What the devil do you think you are doing, Stephen? That is the most dangerous stunt I've ever seen. Are you mad?'

'No, sir,' said Stephen, who was white as a sheet, but covered in sweat.

'Well what were you thinking of?'

'I don't know, sir.'

After that, Mr Burkett didn't say a word to anybody for three whole lessons.

Even Stephen Harris comes up with ideas sometimes. 'Do you want to faint?' he asked me.

I said, 'Why?'

'It's EX-cell-unt,' he explained. 'You get a real rush.'

'Go on then, show me.'

We were supposed to be doing an experiment with sodium, checking out what colour it burns with. I turned on the Bunsen burner so it looked like we were working, and put a tripod over it.

Stephen started gasping really fast. In, out, in, out. In, out. He was wheezing loudly, but the teacher was too far away to hear. Diego was sitting on the other side of the lab desk, doing the sodium test with Hanif. Both of them had Science goggles

149

over their real glasses. They watched Stephen through the double lenses. I told myself a Maths joke about their glasses: $4e \times 2 = 8e$, where e is eyes.

It was getting boring. Stephen was just wheezing in and out, in and out. Nothing was happening. But we still watched, because it was funny to see him breathe like that.

Then he stopped, and put one finger in his mouth to stop it, as if he was playing Pop Goes the Weasel. His face went bright red, his eyes went out of focus, and he fell over backwards.

As he fell he knocked over a couple of chairs, and a table scraped backwards across the floor, making a terrific noise. Mr Stewart came running over. 'What the hell is happening? Did he burn himself?'

'He just fainted, sir.'

Mr Stewart leant over and started slapping Stephen's cheek gently. He put his hand in a beaker of water and sprinkled his fingers over Stephen's face. Everyone in the class was standing round.

'What was he doing, John?'

'He started breathing fast on purpose, then stuck his finger in his mouth and fell over.'

'Fucking idiot.'

When Stephen woke up, Mr Stewart slapped him in the face really hard and told him never to do that again: 'You might die next time, you idiot.'

When Stephen climbed out of the second-floor window, he started a trend. Other classes heard of the stunt and sometimes some nutter did the same as Stephen.

When Justice got back from borstal, he heard about that. He decided to do something a little more flash.

(Justice goes to borstal sometimes, he told me. Every so often, he's away from school for weeks and then he comes back as if nothing has happened. I asked him where he'd been and he said he'd been in prison, grown-up prison. He said he was too big for borstal, they couldn't handle him. But when I asked a teacher, they said minors never get sent to adult prison, however big they are.)

So Justice had this idea, in English. Just like the room where Stephen climbed out of the window, our English class looked over the park from the second floor. We were left alone for a moment while Mr Wilson went to fetch additional textbooks from the office. Justice had about three minutes to get things done.

He told everyone to shut up, and sent Jason to keep a look-out.

'We're going to throw the furniture out of the window so when Mr Wilson comes back there's nothing left in here. Everybody carry your chair to the window.'

The girls didn't like the idea. Not sensible girls like Rosalind, Melissa and Alison; not even the sort who are usually ready for a laugh like Ellen and Lisa St John. Alison said: 'Oh come on, Justice, you can't do that, we'll all get in serious trouble.'

Rosalind said: 'You might break all the furniture. It might bounce when it gets to the bottom and break the windows on the ground-floor class.'

Ellen said: 'Come on, Justice, man . . .'

But he was looking angry. He charged round the room, tipping people out of their chairs. He pulled Hanif up out of his seat and swung him round by the coat and placed the chair in his hands.

'Carry that to the window – NOW!'

Hanif started towards the window, and Justice did the same to Daniel, Diego and Gow. Gilbert, meanwhile, laughed like a cartoon hyena but didn't lift a finger. Justice didn't seem to care about Gilbert.

Jason stuck his head into the class a couple of times to see what was happening. The second time he looked, there was a stockpile of chairs by the window, and Justice was ordering people to move the tables over too. Then he told Stephen Harris to start throwing all the furniture out. Stephen started slowly, one chair at a time. He watched it all the way down, and saw how it landed.

Each item dropped past two classes below us. But plenty of other classes could see what was happening if they happened to look out of the window.

Stephen speeded up. Bug Eye joined in. Each of them lifted two chairs at a time and just dropped them, no longer bothering to watch the fall. Within a minute, all the chairs had gone and the tables were piled high by the window.

Jason rushed in: 'Look out!' Everybody moved rapidly away from the window, so the whole class stood on the far side of the room, drifting.

Three teachers rushed in at once. One was a Maths teacher, so he probably had the classroom below us. 'What the hell do you all think you are doing?'

Mr Wilson trailed in immediately after the other teacher had spoken, heaving a pile of textbooks. His face dropped when he saw the upheaval in his class: a group of pupils shuffling about on one side of the room, and on the other, tables standing ready to jump from the open windows.

'Jesus,' he said.

The head of English rushed in after Mr Wilson. 'OK, who the hell is responsible for this?'

He walked up to Bug Eye, a known troublemaker, and asked again. Bug Eye said: 'Don't know, sir.'

The teacher asked Gilbert. 'Don't know, sir.'

Even when he asked the girls, they didn't grass. The whole class just stood there saying, 'Don't know, sir.'

Most of the chairs were irreparable. One had bounced back against the window of the ground-floor class, but not actually broken it. The whole class got a month's detention.

But that didn't stop us. After that month was over, we were

sitting in Mr Burkett's class waiting for him to come in. Claire Miller started smoking a cigarette out of the window. John McGuire spotted her: 'Oy, Claire, stop that or I'll grass yer ter the ead.'

'Fuck off John,' said Claire.

Donna said: 'Claire, borrow me your lighter a second.'

Claire passed the lighter to Donna, who rolled up a Social Education fact-sheet and pretended it was a cigarette. Then she lit the end of it.

Soon everybody – or at least the funny people – was tearing pages out of exercise books and even out of textbooks to make fake cigarettes. Stephen Harris was put on guard at the door. About ten of us were smoking these fake cigarettes, when John McGuire said: 'Let's make a proper bonfire.'

He took all the textbooks he could find, and put them in the middle of the room, with the pages open so they'd catch fire. He grabbed Alexander's exercise book, and Ian's, and tore them in half.

'Oh, John . . .' said Alexander, who was too scared to make trouble.

'Shut up, Alexander.'

Then Donna handed John the lighter and he lit the books. We all went back to our seats, leaving the pile burning in the middle of the room. Melissa said: 'I can't believe you've done that, we'll all be on detention again for weeks.'

Manmeet said: 'Oh God, my dad will kill me.' But I didn't see why – it wasn't *her* fault.

Still no sign of Mr Burkett. Ellen said: 'Let's make paper planes to throw at him when he comes in.'

We tore out more pages from our exercise books and made darts. Stephen Harris came back in, and rushed to a chair. 'He's coming!'

Then Stephen rushed back to the door and balanced the black-board rubber on top. When Burkett came in, it narrowly missed clunking him on the head. ('Ling!') We all threw our planes at once, with lots of them hitting him. 'Stop it,' he said, but he smiled as if to say he could take a joke. Then he saw the pile of burning books, and he went crazy.

Everybody was laughing, so Donna stood up and pretended to be really responsible. She shouted out: 'Seckle down!' But nobody shut up, so she pretended to be furious: '*Ras clat!* Oy! Everyone: SHUT. UP. I said seckle! Dintcha hear me? SECKLE DOWN!'

The whole class was on detention for another month, including Donna. Once or twice that day, on the tannoy, you could hear the headmaster asking all teachers who taught our class to meet in his office at the end of the day. He'd created a special task force to deal with us. It was like the Falklands Conflict.

Traditional fighting

At the end of the year, the fifth form went on a riot. It's a tradition. They're supposed to beat up the fourth-years to show who's boss, before the fourth-years become next year's fifth-years.

All day, while we were in lessons, we could hear them setting off fireworks, and bangers they'd most probably bought on school journey to France.

One boy punched Mr Lyndon in the face, and the rest went on the rampage, smashing all the windows they could reach. That was a Friday, after school. Most people didn't see much evidence, but I did because I gate-crashed a Scout meeting, coming back to school at six p.m. The windows of the gym were cracked, but the glass was reinforced with wire mesh. The covered glass walkway that leads to the gym was smashed too. The Scout leader chased me off when he spotted me.

The other thing they did, they set fire to this Maths teacher's car. They put a burning newspaper underneath, with paraffin on it. The whole thing was burnt through. I never had Mr Sharman for my teacher, but he's only small, and he's quiet. I don't think they wanted to get *him*, particularly, I reckon they would have set fire to anybody's car they could find.

A few weeks before, some grown-ups had come into the school one evening, after everyone had gone except a few teachers. Dr Rushworth asked them where they thought they were going, and they beat him up! They kicked him, and broke both his ankles. At assembly that week, he came on stage with crutches, and you could still see the bruises on his face. In his speech he said they were stupid people who probably didn't mean any harm but didn't understand what they were doing. He said they were probably high on drugs.

Everyone in the entire school thought he was brave, even people who don't like him. He does sound old-fashioned, though. Some people laughed when he said 'high on drugs'.

The kids below us have started to get lippy. One boy called Paul keeps shouting, 'Fatty!' at Mark Rooney. So when Rooney comes after him and knocks him around, Paul pretends to cry, with his face in his hands and his shoulders shaking. Then once Rooney's left him alone Paul pops his head up again and grins, whispering, 'Fatty!' under his breath for the rest of us to lip-read.

Paul's supposed to be rich: sometimes he comes in with £100 to spend on his friends. One afternoon he took a load of people to see *Return of the Jedi* when they should have been in class.

One lunchtime, we were playing footy with Kampol's tennis ball outside the Music department, just below the sign saying NO BALL GAMES, when Gilbert and Bug Eye ran through the gates looking worried. They raced past us, towards the East Block. Gilbert shouted:

'We've just had a barney with Cardinal Vaughan, just the two of us.'

They got into the East Block, by the door below Ms Edwards' old class, then disappeared. Ten minutes later, after Kampol and Gow had argued over a goal decision, and I'd scoffed my apple, a crowd of hard boys from our year came out of the same door, with Paul Grant and Desmond Mears quizzing Gilbert and Bug Eye as they walked.

Desmond saw the five of us playing Three-and-in, and he waved us over: 'Oy, come here.'

Kampol pocketed his tennis ball, and we carried over our bags.

'We're going to do Cardinal Vaughan,' said Desmond. 'Everyone has to be ready to fight.'

I counted our group. There were twenty-five boys, including me, Kampol, Gow, Ian and Stephen Harris. Most of them were harder than us. There were still a few people missing for a proper war party – Mark Rooney, Tony Forrester, Clifford. (Justice was away.)

We walked down the passageway towards the park. Gilbert and Bug Eye told Desmond and Paul Grant what had happened. They'd been smoking a fag in the park when seven or eight Cardinal Vaughan boys attacked them. 'Like, we hit em back a bit, Des,' said Bug Eye, 'but we dint have a chance. So we legged it.'

'Right, we gotta mash em hard,' said Paul.

Paul Grant was half black and half white, like Robert Lester and Donna. He had lighter skin than they did. His hair was amazing, for a blackish person: it was ginger! He wasn't very big, but he was very hard. Nobody knew exactly *how* hard, because he didn't fight much, but he had no fear. Once a pigeon flying overhead shat on his shoulder when he was smoking by the Sports block. The white and green slime started to dribble down the front of his jacket, so Paul grabbed a passing sixth-form plum and wiped the shit on to this plum's jacket. The plum never said a word to complain – and Paul was only a second-year. *That*'s how hard Paul was.

Gilbert said the hardest boy out of the Cardinal Vaughan gang had said Cardinal Vaughan could run us any time. That was the challenge. We had to prove we were harder than some poncy church school. We walked to the north end of the park, where Gilbert and Bug Eye had been attacked, but there wasn't any sign of the enemy. So we split up into groups of five. 'If you see anyone,' said Desmond, 'you gotta shout for reinforcements.'

Me and Kampol went with a boy called Barry and a hard boy in his class whose name, I think, was All-Rick. There was also this giant boy from the year below us, called Shelley. Everyone had to have someone hard in their group. But there wasn't any sign of Cardinal Vaughan. At the end of the lunch hour, we went back.

During afternoon break, we got word that Paul Grant was organizing a fight after school. He had talked to some friends in the year above us and they were all going down. All fighters had to go, and Gilbert told me I was included. No choice. We were meeting at the north exit, then we'd all walk down Holland Park Avenue to Cardinal Vaughan and fight them.

I escaped. I didn't want to be involved. I sneaked off through the south exit to High Street Ken. The next morning I thought Gilbert and Bug Eye would attack me for doing that, but they didn't. They were too busy telling everyone what had happened.

'Paul Grant's a nutter,' said Gilbert. 'He walked in front of us all the way there, with a baseball bat. He kept hitting it into his hand, *bang, bang.*'

When they reached Cardinal Vaughan, Paul Grant and that boy Shelley were stopped at the gate. 'This Cardinal Vaughan teacher told them he'd call the police unless we all went away,' said Bug Eye. 'But Paul just stood there sucking his teeth.'

About five minutes later a couple of police cars turned up and the coppers all told everyone to go home. 'We were itching for a barney with the coppers,' said John McGuire. In any case, nobody dared to leave, in case Paul Grant and Desmond and Tony Forrester and Rooney came after them.

Then our deputy head, Mr Lyndon, turned up and took a note of all the people who were there. He told them to disperse as well, and asked what had prompted the incident. Paul Grant pushed Gilbert and Bug Eye forward and said they'd been attacked by Cardinal Vaughan boys in *our* park. '"And we ain't taking that," Paul said,' said Bug Eye. 'Then he started pushing forwards again and a copper reached for his baseball bat, but Paul wouldn't let him have it, so there was this, like, scuffle, and the copper fell over. Paul kicked his helmet. So the other coppers came over and nicked the baseball bat and told him he was lucky they didn't nick im.'

Then Cardinal Vaughan's deputy head had come forward and said he was very sorry, to Gilbert and Bug Eye. He promised there'd be an inquiry into the incident in the park, and the boys involved would be punished. 'Then he said if everyone else went home, he'd take a description from me and Gil of the boys who attacked us in the park. He even said Cardinal Vaughan boys was banned for ever from going into our park.'

Vote Labour

I was walking into school on the day of the general election, and I was wearing my little Labour badge. Last time round, at Fox, Rosie Capel had come into school with a blue rosette and the Tories had won. She was the only person in our class that supported the Tories, even though Fox was quite a posh school. Everyone else was sad when the Tories won, because their parents were Labour or Liberal. Today I was wearing my badge so I'd bring luck to Labour like Rosie had brought luck to the Tories. It's a tiny enamel badge, oblong, with the Labour symbols on it.

As I was crossing High Street Ken, this bloke with a blue rosette stopped me on the traffic island. 'I see you are wearing a Labour badge. Did your parents put you up to that?'

'No, I believe in Labour myself.'

'Tell me, what do the symbols actually represent? I'm not sure I even know what they are.' He pointed with his biro at the badge. It was so high up my jacket, I could hardly see it without squinting, like when you look at the end of your nose. The symbols were upside-down, so I couldn't see them properly.

'Well, the fact is, I'm not sure what the symbols are,' I said.

'Well how can you wear the badge, then?' he said. He was smiling, but he was trying to wind me up. 'Should you really be wearing it if you don't understand it?'

'I do understand about nuclear disarmament and unemployment though.'

'Really. And I suppose you think the country should give up its nuclear arms. Do you think the Argentine junta would have taken us so seriously if we didn't have the weapons of last resort?'

I *could* have told him to fuck off and carried on crossing the road, but you know what – I recognized him from the papers. It was the morning of the general election, and here I was, talking to the actual Tory MP. So I didn't mind being a bit late. After all, you couldn't get a much better excuse.

'Well if they were so scared of British nukes why did they invade the Falklands in the first place? Why did they attack British ships and fight British soldiers if they were so scared?' I never said 'our' soldiers, because when they say that on the TV news, it's too partisan. I don't see why we should cheer when an Argentine soldier is killed, and cry for British soldiers. I'm a pacifist, I don't want any soldiers at all.

The Tory MP changed the subject. He looked at his watch and at all the crowds of grown-up voters walking past while he wasted time talking to me, just a kid. So he said: 'Aren't you late for school?'

'No. I should still be there on time.'

'But it's nearly twenty-past nine.'

'Registration isn't over till twenty-five past. I'll be on time. Anyway, it's important to discuss politics.'

'Which school are you at?'

I told him.

'Well I suppose you've been indoctrinated, then. Will they let you wear your badge all day there?'

I told him Rosie Capel had worn a Tory rosette at Fox.

'Good for her.'

'Then why shouldn't I wear my badge at school?'

'I'll tell you why. I think it is a crying shame for parents to send out their children with political badges on when the children don't understand what they represent. And you can tell your parents that from me.'

161

Then he tried to give me some pamphlets, which was a bloody cheek. I took them anyway. As I crossed, I thought about throwing them in the bin while he was watching, or tearing them up. But that would make him feel morally superior, so I just read them with a look on my face like I couldn't believe this rubbish.

I showed them to Ms Smith in Social Education, and told her what the MP had said. 'He's a patronizing so-and-so, isn't he,' she said.

Last week we'd carried out an opinion poll in class. In the papers, Labour was well behind in the opinion polls, but in our class nobody voted Tory. Only a couple of people, Alexander and Daniel, voted against Labour. They voted Social Democrat; they split the left vote.

Today Ms Smith sent us out to do more opinion polls. I paired up with Ian. We wrote a few questions on the sheet, then headed off towards High Street Ken. I hoped I would see the MP again, now that Ms Smith had explained the Labour symbols on my badge.

We stopped grown-ups here and there and asked them who they would like to win the election. We asked why they wanted that party to win. I wrote down all the answers. Most people said they were influenced by a party's position on unemployment, or taxes, or nuclear weapons.

We found Kensington Library, which was closed for the day. It had a giant sign outside: POLLING STATION. Usually they use primary schools; Fox was closed today. There were three women sitting on a bench outside the library, each of them with a rosette. We didn't have to ask who *they* were voting for! So we waited for normal voters coming in and out of the polling station. We asked a couple. One bloke wouldn't tell us. About five minutes after we talked to him, he came back with a copper.

The copper said: 'Are you asking people about their voting intentions?'

We said we were, for a school project. The copper pointed at my badge and said: 'Well that isn't very open-minded, is it? You can't do this any more, you've got to move away from here. It's actually against the law, what you're doing.'

He said he didn't mind us continuing, if we moved away from the polling station. He was nice about it, but when we walked off, Ian made an *oink* noise, and I said, 'Yeah, fucking pig.'

We had to be sure we asked a proper 'cross-section' of people. Around the town hall complex, there's a good mix. You have the posh people working inside the offices, wearing suits and parking their expensive cars down in the underground car park where we got nicked that time, and there's always a few janitors and people like that walking about. We asked a man up a ladder, cleaning the windows. We had to shout.

'Scuse me,' shouted Ian.

'What is it?' shouted the man.

'We're doing an opinion poll for our school project. Who do you want to win the general election?'

'Labour.'

'Why?'

'Are you going to quote me on this?'

'Nah.'

'Because our Tory MP is a posh cunt, son.'

'All right. Fanks.'

Upper School

What do you need for Oxford?

Towards the end of the third year, we had to choose our O-level subjects. English – including Language and Literature O levels – and Maths were compulsory. A special event was held after school to help us choose, with teachers sitting behind labelled desks, like market stalls. One desk said HELP. The teacher looked really bored, with his arms folded. He was going bald; and he had dark bags under his eyes.

I sat down in front of him.

'What can I do for you?'

'I don't really know what courses to choose.'

'The first thing to think about is what you want to do when you leave school.'

'I want to be a cartoonist. I can draw excellent caricatures.'

'Well I'm an Art teacher and I can tell you it's almost impossible to make a career as a cartoonist.'

I thought about that. 'But somebody has to do it – why shouldn't it be me?'

'Nobody says it won't, but the chances are stacked against you. You might want to make other plans, to avoid disappointment.'

'I only want to be a cartoonist.'

He sighed and shrugged his shoulders. If I'd gone, he wouldn't have cared, he wouldn't have called me back. But I wanted more help, so I stayed where I was. He said: 'Put it this way, apart from Art, which lessons do you most enjoy?'

'I don't enjoy any *more* than others. Everyone messes about all the time and the work's easy. It's boring. Some are a *total* waste of time.'

'Which ones?'

I told him: Needlework, Home Economics, Design and Technology, Geography, History . . .

'History?'

'Yeah, we never do the sort of history I like, *English* history.'

'Do you like languages?'

'Yes, I'm pretty fluent at French.'

'Why don't you do some other languages?'

I didn't say anything, I wasn't convinced.

'What about Science, do you like that? You can do more than one science now, if you want. You could choose Physics, Chemistry or Biology . . .'

A teacher at Fox once gave me a book of chemistry. I knew the order of chemicals up to number 25 on the periodic table, but we *still* hadn't studied that. It was like learning the order of kings and queens – wasted knowledge. 'Would we do the periodic table in Chemistry?'

'You'd better ask the Chemistry teacher over there, but I would expect so, yes. Do you want to carry on after O levels and do A levels?'

I'd never thought about it. My parents had gone to Oxford, but for me, we never planned that far ahead. I said: 'Do you need A levels to go to Oxford?'

'Err – *yes*.'

I went round the room asking teachers about their subjects. I ignored the stupid women on Home Economics. The only people talking to them were Asian girls who wanted to be good wives. I walked past Mr Makin on Drama. Everyone said he was a poof, and Drama was a waste of time even though it was brilliant fun. My dad's an actor and *he* never did it for O level. As I passed Mr Makin's desk, I heard him say: 'Well, you can't actually take

168

it to *O level*, but if you get a grade 1 in your CSE that counts as the same.'

Some people's parents turned up. One boy looked really uncomfortable because his dad was dressed like a total ponce, with a cravat and white shoes. I felt sorry for him, because he was bound to be given a load of abuse the next day, about his dad being a bender and all.

I decided to do Latin. I don't know who teaches it cause there wasn't a separate Latin table – but it sounds flash. I'm carrying on with French too, cause the O level will be easy.

And I'm doing Chemistry, not Biology or Physics. I nearly went for Drama after all. It's either Drama or Music or Sport – you can only do one of them cause of a timetable clash. In the end I went for Sport, cause most boys are doing that. Naturally, I'm doing Art. At the end of the fifth year, if I get all of them, I'll have *seven* O levels!

But Jason Cunningham told me I could forget going to Oxford: 'You're not good enough at Sport.'

Nobody else chose Latin, so they cancelled it. I'm doing German instead.

Mr Bryant said: 'The headmaster was going to take the Latin class, but you're the only one who chose it. He says he's willing to give you the textbooks and teach you at lunchtimes and after school – if that's what you want.'

Brilliant. I'd be the only boy in the school who could talk Latin. What a triumph. *Quo vadis? Veni, vidi, vici*. I could explain all the jokes in *Asterix*.

I knocked on Dr Rushworth's door at lunch, and he said, 'Enter.'

'Hello, I'm John-Paul. I've come about the Latin.'

'Hello, John-Paul. Take a seat over there,' he said with his squeaky voice, gesturing towards a line of easy chairs with their backs to the window. Outside the window these two third-years were tugging at another boy's bag. One of the third-years was that nutter, Shelley. They didn't know we could see them because Dr Rushworth had net curtains in his room. Dr Rushworth banged on the window and shouted: 'Go on, leave him alone.' When he shouts, his voice squeaks so hard you think his throat might collapse. He's got a high voice, cause he isn't very big.

I sat in a chair, like he said, and sank right down. Dr Rushworth pulled a couple of textbooks off the top of a shelf and blew the dust off them. He's so short, I don't reckon he could reach the top shelf without standing on a chair. He gave me the first book, *Path to Latin*.

Then he wanted to know why I'd chosen Latin. I said it was cause I was good at languages.

'Which ones?'

'Well, just French at the moment, but I pick up other things easily.'

He asked me in French if I was taking it for O level. I said, '*Oui*,' and added that I was doing German too, now that the official Latin classes had been dropped.

'You've got a good accent,' he said. 'But why *Latin*?'

I said I wasn't sure, but I knew a lot of people at other schools studied it, at schools where they *paid* for their lessons, so there must be a reason.

He liked that. He told me a load of stuff about how Latin would always be useful afterwards when I learnt other languages, especially Italian, Portuguese, Spanish and even Romanian. 'What's more, you'll be able to sample the great classic authors in their original tongue, you'll be in touch with ancient civilizations.'

I said that sounded a good idea, but I don't think I'll be learning Romanian.

So he led me through the first couple of exercises in the book, and told me to ask my tutor for a new exercise book. 'Come back in a week or so when you've done the first chapter.' Then as I was leaving he shoved a book by Julius Caesar into my hand, but I haven't a clue what it's about, because it's *entirely* in Latin. Not even an English introduction.

The whole lesson lasted just fifteen minutes. I found Gow and Ian playing footy in the North Playground, and said: 'Sorry I'm late, I've just had my first Latin lesson with Dr Rushworth.' Ian was impressed, he stopped playing for a second, so Gow ran round him and popped the ball in the goal.

Sport was a terrible choice. You don't get an O level at the end, and none of the girls I fancy does Sport. The only people who do it are the nutty boys, the very hardest in my year.

Out of all the Sport options, I thought rowing sounded civilized. But it's terrible: the other people in rowing are dangerous. Not a single normal, safe person, like Kampol, for example (he's doing badminton). I've got Mark Rooney in my squad, Bug Eye, Justice (when he's not in borstal), Andrew Smith, All-Rick, Mark Pye (who's had trials for West Ham United), and this tall boy they call Geezer.

Geezer wears crocodile shoes, and he's got a gold tooth. When he gets changed, you can see the muscles on his tummy, in horizontal rows. And he can do this trick where his shoulder blades come right out of his back, as if they were growing into wings. He told me he's a pimp, told me I could fuck his big sister if I wanted, if I paid the right charge, but I don't believe it. He's only fourteen.

To reach the river, we have to travel on a coach from Holland Park to Barn Elms, all the way to Hammersmith and across the river, which means putting up with that lot for half an hour. Rooney and All-Rick slashed the back seat, once, with flick-knives from France (we all got detentions). Another time, they pissed in a Coke can and tried to make Bug Eye drink it. They're always playing punching games. When you finally get to the sports ground, it's freezing cold cause winter's on the way, then you sit in the training room for two hours. It's just a room with a fake boat screwed to the floor, with deep water channels about three yards wide on each side. You sit on the fake boat and practise your strokes with real oars, so you can all row in sync. You have to get the blade in the water channel at just the right angle and take it out again at the right angle – then do it all over again, for years.

So we sit there practising in this room in a fake boat, totally *freezing*, while the teacher shouts at us through a loud-hailer even though we could hear him if he whispered. Then he goes away and leaves us with a tape recorder of him pretending to be a cox. We're all rowing backwards and forwards with the tape going 'Stroke!'

After we'd done a few yards, Rooney (who sits at the front) turned round and punched Bug Eye right in the chest. 'Pass it on.' So Bug Eye punched the next guy in the chest really hard, and he passed it on, till it got to me. The first time, Geezer turned round and punched me right in the chest, so I could hardly breathe, and my eyes watered. 'Pass it on,' he laughed.

I turned round and hit Mark Pye in the chest, but I didn't dare do it hard. 'Pass it on,' I said. But I should have done it properly, cause he saw the fear in my eye. He slapped me in the face and said: 'Fuck off, Curly-Bollocks.' Everyone else laughed, and we carried on rowing.

After we'd done our training, we went on the river, literally opposite Craven Cottage, where Fulham play. The first day, we're rolling about on the waves, waiting to get going, and the teacher tells us this is a prime spot for dead bodies washing up, when people have drowned, people who jump off Hammersmith Bridge. He said we should keep our eyes open cause there might be a reward.

Rooney shouted out: 'Fucking *yeah*, sir – d'you think we might see some dead cunts?' The teacher told Rooney to watch his language and get on with his rowing. I thought I might faint if I saw a dead body. I could imagine it now, looking down to my side at the cold water rippling past us. I pictured some green face bobbing up suddenly and making me scream.

After that, I couldn't stop imagining drowned bodies. Nearly every other stroke, my blade glanced off some solid object floating by. I looked down my oar to see if it was a body, but it was usually just some cardboard box.

I hate rowing. It's cold all the time.

That boy I thought was called All-Rick is called Ulrich. He's in my German class; his mum's German, his dad's Turkish. The other people are from classes I've never been mixed up with before. That's the beauty of O level, the whole fourth year is totally mixed up. If you play your cards right, you get to be in all the classes with the best girls.

Quite a lot of posh girls do Drama, Daniel told me. It's *civilized*. He chose Drama instead of Sport (cause, let's face it, he's crap at Sport), and now he's one of just six boys in the Drama class. You know how many girls there are? *Twenty-three*. And that includes a sexy girl who used to be at a private school, called Kate (she's in my French class), two other newish girls called Kylie and Naimh, Alison, and a girl who was at Fox called Julia.

I asked the head of year if I could change from Sport to Drama. Guess what: he said OK! When I told Geezer I was giving up rowing, he called me a soft pussy, but I pointed out that I'd have all those girls in my class so he smiled at me as though I was a sex maniac. Ulrich laughed and said good luck. And anyway, I pointed out that even Paul Grant doesn't do Sport: he does Music, he plays the bass.

Ulrich fancies Yvonne and Melina in our German class. Apart from them, there's just two people doing German, a plum called Aaron, with glasses, and a Jordanian boy called Aimann.

173

Aaron's a good friend of Carlos, who got rid of Desmond's machete. They play Dungeons and Dragons together. Aimann taught me how to say 'arsehole' in German: '*Arschloch*'. I tried it on the teacher. He was quite impressed. He's the kind of teacher that's young enough not to be pompous. In fact, he thinks he's still pretty young, like he could hang out with us if he wanted. He made a joke, though, about how old he's getting. He said: 'I'm at the age when you're pleased if you get a spot on your chin!'

Apart from Sport, I chose pretty good classes. I only see the nutters at registration, and in compulsory lessons like English and Maths. Nutters all seem to choose Design and Technology, and Sport – cause if you are a nutter, you probably aren't that academic, let's face it.

Cover teachers

All our teachers are sick these days, or on strike. We're always getting cover teachers. Sometimes Captain Caveman, sometimes someone else. We even get a few *real* cover teachers, fresh recruits. One of them who comes quite a lot is called Mr Singh. He's a Sikh, so he wears a turban. He covered History once. I was bored so I asked why he wore a turban. You could see it wound him up, he probably thought I was going to be racist, so I pretended to be fascinated by everything about Sikhs.

'There are lots of Asians here, sir,' I said, 'but not that many Sikhs.'

'That's right.'

'There's one boy in the second year, sir. He doesn't wear a turban but a sort of hanky tied round a small lump on top of his head.'

Mr Singh started to explain. Something about how Sikhs weren't supposed to cut their hair.

'Why, sir?' asked Yemisi. 'I think turbans look stupid, sir. No offence, though.'

'Well, it's so that God can lift us up by our hair.'

He had a silver bracelet on his arm. 'What's that for, sir?'

'That is a reminder that we love peace. Whenever a Sikh is about to strike a violent blow, he sees the bracelet on his arm and it reminds him not to be violent.'

A couple of weeks later, I told our usual History teacher and he said: 'Well that's the first time I've heard the Sikhs described as a peace-loving people.'

Another time, we had a posh woman covering our lesson. She didn't have a clue. She couldn't even get the class to be quiet at the *beginning*. It was Maths, so we asked her some tricky Maths questions. She wasn't a Maths teacher.

'Doesn't it explain in your book?'

'No, miss, I can't see any answers anywhere,' said Ellen. But the truth is, our Maths books are a piece of piss, because they've got all the answers at the back, if you know where to look.

Gilbert took his book up to the front of the class and showed her. Everyone went quiet for a minute while the teacher tried to work it out. She had deep frown lines on her head.

We took the batteries out of our calculators, me and Gow and Stephen Harris. We told the teacher the calculators weren't working, so she said to borrow someone else's.

Then Peter Davies did the same trick, and before you knew it there was an epidemic of faulty calculators. The teacher thought we were joking, till she tested a couple and found they didn't work. 'Well, I'm very sorry,' she said, 'there's nothing I can do.' So we put the batteries back.

Then John McGuire started to fight Jason Cunningham. Nobody knew how it started. The teacher put down Gilbert's book, so he rolled his eyes at the ceiling and sighed as if he was really upset not to get the answer to the Maths problem. I couldn't help laughing. I'm still a little scared of Gilbert, but he's very funny sometimes.

As soon as the teacher got to the back of the class, Jason and John stopped fighting, and laughed. It was only a joke fight. The teacher started to head back to the front, but as she was turning Donna launched the blackboard rubber towards Diego. Peter Davies intercepted it and threw it at Alexander, clonking him on the forehead.

'Ling!'

Alexander stuck his hand up in the air to tell the teacher. Everyone was watching except the posh cover teacher, who had stuck her face in Gilbert's exercise book again. She was frowning. She wore a long string of beads which curled up on the table below her chin as she read the instructions. She was wearing a black polo-neck top and a tweed skirt. She looked like a photo of some woman writer from the 1930s.

Alexander still had his hand up, but the teacher wasn't looking. 'Miss . . .' he said.

She didn't look up. 'Just a minute, I'm trying to work this out.'

Gilbert was standing over her, and everyone watched as he pretended she smelt, by waving his hand by his nose and frowning.

'Miss . . .' said Alexander.

'Look, for heaven's sake, have some patience . . .' she said.

Peter Davies slapped Alexander and instructed him to put down his hand. Alexander looked determined, and stuck it higher and higher. Peter started to spit in Alexander's face.

'Miss, please tell Peter not to spit in my face,' pleaded Alexander.

She looked up and told Peter to return to his seat, which he did. Alexander put his hand down.

I tore a page out of the back of my exercise book and wrote on it. I handed it to Peter with a bit of Sellotape. It said: 'Spit on me.'

'Go over to Alexander and pat him on the back to say sorry, and while you're doing it, stick this on his coat.'

Peter liked the idea. Alexander didn't trust him at all, but never guessed about the note. Everyone in the class could see it except Alexander and his friends.

Stephen Harris tore a page out of his book and handed it to me. 'Write "I have a big . . ." on there,' he said. 'And leave a little space at the end.'

'Why?'

'Go on, just do it!'

I wrote what he asked, then handed it back. He drew a picture of a dick on it, then attached a sliver of Sellotape and patted it on to Ian's back. Ian spotted it at once, and pulled it off. Soon everybody was doing them.

Jason Cunningham came over to my desk and dared me to do one. I said all right.

I tore another page out, and wrote 'I am the biggest lesbian in the school. Girls kiss me quick.' Then I attached the Sellotape and stuck it temporarily on my leg so nobody would see me carry it. I put up my hand and asked the teacher really politely if I could go up and do some diagrams on the board.

'Do you really have to?'

'Well our normal teacher lets us . . .'

'What do you want to do?'

'Just draw a few shapes and label them, like pentagons and hexagons.'

'Well all right, but why you? Does everyone have a go?'

'Sometimes, miss, but I usually go first.'

Jason was watching me carefully. Gilbert was still standing next to the teacher, who'd been studying his textbook for about ten minutes, and he was getting bored.

I went behind the teacher and drew a couple of diagrams so she'd forget about me. One of them was a diagram of a willy, like Stephen had drawn. I labelled it DICKAGON, then when everyone laughed and the teacher looked up, I quickly rubbed it off.

'What are you doing?' the teacher asked.

'Nothing at all, don't you worry, miss,' I calmly explained, patting the label on her back as though I was just reassuring her. She thought that was a bit strange, but she didn't guess about the label.

I was sweating!

Then I said I'd done my bit and went back to my chair. She looked at the board and saw a few shapes and said: 'Well, thank you very much. Does anyone else have anything they'd like to do on the board?'

Loads of boys stuck up their hands. She let them come up in turns. Everyone drew silly pictures behind her back. Jason even managed to play Hangman. He drew the missing letters and we whispered them at him. Gilbert left the teacher with his book and sat down to join in. Jason had nearly finished the hangman's noose and the body when the teacher turned around and caught him. The word on the board was _ASTUR_AT_N.

'Look, I trusted you to get on, what the hell do you think you are doing?' she shouted.

'Sorry, miss,' said Jason, but he was smirking because she had the sign on her back, pointing at the rest of the class.

'You think it's funny, do you? Well, we'll see about that. Do you actually want a detention?'

'No, miss.'

She sent him back to his seat, and the teacher began wiping off the hangman. Melissa put her hand up and said: 'Miss . . .'

'What is it now?'

'You've got a sign stuck on your back.'

The teacher put her hand over her shoulder and reached for it. That didn't work, so she put the other hand around the back and reached up. She pulled the sign off, then looked straight at me, furious. She'd worked it out fast.

'Right, the rest of you keep quiet, and you – come with me.'

I followed her into the class next door which had eight sixth-formers in it and the head of Maths. The cover teacher asked the head of Maths to keep an eye on me for the rest of the lesson. The sixth-formers pretended not to look at me, but you could tell they wondered what I'd done. I slouched in my chair and stared at the posters on the wall ahead of me. One said that you should always avoid walking behind women at night, in case you scared them. I couldn't work out why it was in a *Maths* class.

I don't know about at night, but Samuel Thomas scares women in the daytime, and old men. He walks towards them on the pavement and, just when they're passing, he swings his hand right out so they think he's going to thump them – but all he does is, he looks at his watch!

I rocked backwards and forwards on the chair, until the end of the lesson. Then the cover teacher came back for me, and marched me to Mr Raymond's office.

Mr Raymond put me on report. Each lesson, I must get the teacher to describe my behaviour and my work. At the end of the day, I must take the report to my parents and one of them must sign it, before I took the finished report back to Mr Raymond. This was to continue for three weeks.

'But how do I explain this to my parents?' I asked him.

'You might consider telling them what you did to your teacher today.'

Walking alone, head down, to collect Crispin from Fox, I couldn't stop my face turning red at the very thought. All the way on the 28 bus, I didn't say a word to him.

Mothers

Diego invited me round to his house one lunchtime to eat a real Spanish omelette. He promised this would be better than any omelette I'd ever eaten in my life.

Diego lives above a kebab shop, on the top floor, half a mile up Ladbroke Grove. When we got to the top, we were sweating from walking so fast up and down the hill, and up all those stairs.

He's been in this flat for at least two years, but it looks as though they just moved in. I'm not sure if Diego's got a dad – he usually mentions only his mum. Perhaps his dad was killed in Spain, murdered by Franco.

In the corner of the living room were three suitcases. Diego went over to shut them, but before he did I noticed they were full of clothes, like a portable chest of drawers. Spilling out of the first case he shut was a white bra.

There was no sofa, just three chairs around a table, and a single bed in the corner opposite the suitcases. Diego said, 'Make you-self at home,' but I wasn't sure if this was the living room or his mum's bedroom, so I didn't sit down. I said: 'I need to go to the toilet first, if that's all right.' Diego said he'd give me a tour.

First we passed the little kitchen, which looked over the main road. Then he showed me his own bedroom, which was tiny. There were no pictures on the wall, just one high window which showed the clouds going past way overhead. Like in the other

181

room, a suitcase spilled over with clothes. Taking another couple of steps, we reached the loo. Diego showed me in, then pulled the door shut after me, and I heard him stepping back into the kitchen. I looked for a lock on the door, but there wasn't one, so I decided to stick at having a piss, just in case.

Turning round, I saw the bath and had a big surprise. A giant leg of meat was hanging over it, from a hook in the ceiling. Two feet away from the meat, but hanging over the bath by another hook, was this budgie cage. The budgie flew about, going *cheep*, while I pissed.

I went into the kitchen where Diego was chopping some onions. There was a photo of Diego on the fridge. The only picture in the whole flat. I asked if I could do anything and he gave me three potatoes to peel. While I did that, he fried the onions. Then he took the peeled potatoes and chopped them into tiny bits, which he threw into the frying pan with the onion. Going to the fridge, he took four eggs from a box. He cracked the eggs into a jug that stood on the sink, then added some water, some salt and pepper, and whisked it all together. He gave me a commentary as he was doing it. 'Now you take the eggs . . . now you take a jug . . . now you take some salt . . . now you take some pepper.'

He was smiling all the time, proud to be able to cook for me. I was happy that he was proud. We both smiled a lot. When he'd finished cooking, we had five minutes to scoff the Spanish omelette, which Diego said was called *tortilla con patatas*. Then we rushed back up Ladbroke Grove for registration.

That nutter in the year below me, Shelley, was half black, half white. Everyone used to call that 'half-caste', but in the first year my Geography teacher told us that's rude. In Brazil, she said, people like that are called 'mulatto'. Or you can call them 'mixed-race'. Shelley was hard, but he wasn't much good at football. In fact, come to think of it, there aren't that many

182

mulatto people who are good at football. Robert Lester's crap, always mucking around in a match and spitting at you if you get past him, or holding you in an arm lock.

But there *was* a mixed-race girl two years older than me, she got into the *boy*'s school team for football. Her brother James is in my year, he's a really nice guy, he's about the nicest person I know who's (sort of) black.

Anyway, this boy Shelley used to take dope even in the second year, I heard. I wasn't all that surprised when someone told me he'd been suspended for smoking in the South Playground. (Only *cigarettes*.) That was a couple of months ago. Then one day in Art, Captain Caveman told us Shelley was killed. It happened at the weekend, on the Underground. Captain Caveman looked shocked, cause she'd only just been told herself. She knew him cause he used to be in her class.

Shelley was on acid, and someone dared him to walk all the way down the tracks from Notting Hill Gate to High Street Ken. He didn't make it.

Captain Caveman said that was terribly sad, cause he was such a lively boy. 'Yeah, all right,' she said, 'he *could* be a trouble-maker, and disruptive, but he always livened up the class. He was good-humoured, he never did anything *malicious*.'

Then she actually started crying. Melissa put her arm round Captain Caveman to console her. Most of us were embarrassed, but would have done the same if we weren't. Captain Caveman's all right, really: her stepson's one of the blokes in Madness (but not Suggs).

When I was young, Mum used to warn me about leaning out of high windows in case I fell, cause I'd end up as a smear of strawberry jam on the pavement. On the tube, too, Mum always warned us to stand right back – unless we wanted to finish up as strawberry jam on the tracks. I stopped painting, I couldn't get the thought out of my head: that boy Shelley was nothing more than strawberry jam.

I never even *liked* Shelley; he was so boisterous, I found him too threatening. I tended to avoid passing by him in corridors in case he played some trick on me, or punched me. You can never be too careful.

The thing that bothered me was: Shelley's mum. Captain Caveman said he didn't have a dad, or any sisters and brothers. Shelley was fourteen when he died, so his mum must be thirty at the very least. She could be forty. She might never have any more children. In one afternoon she went from having a small family to no family at all. Tragic. I was in a sad mood for days, really. I didn't make any jokes at all. Everywhere I went, I had this film playing in my head, of Shelley's mum standing alone over his coffin, and putting a single flower on top of it. I could visualize his body inside, so mangled after they'd scraped it up that the undertakers took pity on her and refused to let her look at it. In this film, Shelley's mum never stopped crying, so one of the undertakers sympathized with her and patted her on the shoulder. This undertaker, he had tears in his eyes.

The thing is, even though I could see this clearly in my mind, I couldn't tell you if Shelley's mother was black or white.

I'm so sentimental. You know what I was *really* thinking? I was imagining that Shelley's mum was my mum, that the body in the coffin was me. Somehow the rest of my family had been wiped out in some freak accident – like in Roald Dahl books – and I was the last one left. Then I died and Mum was left with no family at all, standing crying over my coffin and putting a single flower on top of it.

Teachers who muck about

Our O-level Chemistry teacher has a withered hand; he reminds me of Laurence Olivier in *Richard III*, one of my dad's favourite films. His name is Mr Watson. No offence, but he looks like a pervert, the kind you see on telly – cause as well as the floppy hand he's got a really old-fashioned, 1970s haircut, with side-burns, and his skin is all pale as though his mum never gave him any fresh fruit and vegetables.

But he's quite funny. In fact, he's mad. He loves blowing up hydrogen and oxygen, burning phosphorus in a jar, and mixing sugar with sulphuric acid to make carbon. That carbon trick is excellent, Mr Watson says it looks like 'a great black turd rising out of the beaker'.

One day he brought in a real bullet, and bashed it on the worktop with a hammer. He made everyone swear to secrecy, cause he wasn't meant to do it. Then he put the squashed bullet on a tripod and heated it up with a Bunsen burner. You know what? It exploded and a piece of shrapnel went flying at Daniel. It went right through his arm, but not that deep. There was blood all over the place. That made old Watson look worried. He told Dan to go to the infirmary, but first he made him swear not to say what had happened. Paul Grant (who's in my Chemistry group) was in stitches about it, if you see what I mean.

I reckon that might be how Watson did his withered hand. Maybe some teacher did the bullet trick to *him* when he was young. Maybe now he's living in a timewarp – with his sideburns and everything – trying to remind himself of the old days, when his hand was all right. Maybe he's seeking revenge on the youth of today, trying to inflict the same punishment on one of us. I told Dan that might be why he did it; Dan wasn't sure.

Stephen Harris told me he knows the recipe for gunpowder, or TNT or something. He said the Army Cadets handed it out every week. He said it's got manure in it – really!

After Mrs Arrowseed left, our new English teacher was Mr Wilson. He wears denim shirts and John Lennon specs. He's always going on about rock 'n' roll (Bruce Springsteen and stuff), but he's terrible at discipline. He stands at the front and whines at the class if we misbehave. But sometimes he does brilliant classes which are really funny. One was about similes and metaphor. He explained which is which. Then we had to invent stories about each other that were based on simile and metaphor. Alexander's story was hilarious. He said Justice was harder than the iceberg that sank the *Titanic*, Yemisi's voice was as musical as a lawnmower, Stephen Harris was more brilliant than a lump of clay. Everybody else started writing about Alexander in revenge. Nearly everybody stole my idea about his dandruff being worse than a blizzard.

Another time, Mr Wilson came into the class and said: 'What is it with all these tough black boys?'

I couldn't believe he said it. I thought he'd be sacked in about ten minutes.

Donna and Peter and Robert Lester and Darius all leapt up and screamed at him. 'What you saying about black boys, sir, man?' asked Robert.

'Calm down, all of you, and sit down. I'll tell you what I mean.' For a teacher who's usually so nervous about the class misbehaving, he looked very calm.

'The thing is, whenever you see the *really* tough black boys, the ones who win at Sports Day, the ones who are always being reported to the head for fighting – and you can all guess who I mean – they have this funny walk.'

We waited to hear more.

'They walk as if one leg is longer than the other. I don't understand, it's a ridiculous limp.'

Peter sucked his teeth a lot. Donna got up and said: 'I'm reporting you for racial discrimination, sir.'

Mr Wilson just got up and walked to the door, doing the walk with one leg longer than the other. One slow stride, then one short, high jerk. He did it perfectly, so everybody recognized what he was talking about: a black man's walk. Even Peter was laughing his head off by the time Mr Wilson got to the door. Then when he got there, Mr Wilson sucked his teeth: 'Tsssk.' We banged our tables in applause.

My old French teacher Dr Bowes is much better now, in O level. He doesn't come in the class *expecting* trouble. He even smiles a fair bit. He acts as though he's forgotten all the trouble I used to cause. It's a real breakthrough.

You know what he did one day? He brought a guitar into class – to sing a song!

'It's one of my favourite songs,' he said. 'It's called "La Mer", it's by a man called Charles Trenet. Has anybody heard of him?' Nobody had, so he asked if we'd heard of *any* French singers. I said I'd heard of Charles Aznavour, and Maurice Chevalier, but I was only showing off.

Anyway, that song 'La Mer', it lasted five whole minutes. Dr Bowes put his foot on a footstool, then fired away. When he hit the high notes, his eyebrows went up. He was brilliant, I'm telling you. I actually *hated* him before O level, but I was so impressed by that singing in front of us, I forgave him. I'm serious, I wanted to shake his hand afterwards, but that wouldn't have been cool. So at the end, we gave old Dr Bowes a massive round of applause; some of us even cheered. We were so loud, the teacher next door came rushing in, as Dr Bowes was putting away his guitar.

During the rest of the lesson, you could see Dr Bowes was pleased, because he had these faint red circles on his cheeks.

I sit next to that new girl Kate from private school. You can tell she's quite posh cause she's got this shirt with lacy bits. She's got a round face and blondish hair in a Sloaney haircut, but I'm sure she isn't a Sloane. I heard somewhere that Sloanes were a nasty piece of work.

There's a fashion going round for doing things with Bic biros. Everyone's doing it. Jason started it; he pulled the rubbery bit out of the plastic tube, and flicked it at Daniel, whipping his cheek. Then Jason actually bit off the metal bit, the nib, and he was left with this rubber tube, half full of ink.

He tried blowing the ink out, but it wouldn't come out, however hard he tried. It started to hurt his ears, he was blowing so much.

Then he had a brainwave. He waited till Mr Watson was giving some demonstration, in Chemistry, then Jason just slipped the tube into the pocket of his lab coat. For the rest of the lesson, you could see this little patch of blue ink expanding everywhere. I don't think Watson ever washes his jacket, cause the stain is still there.

The other trick was Gilbert's idea. He noticed that Mr Wilson always sucks his pen, when he's thinking. So Gilbert said to Ellen: 'Oy, Ellen, have you seen how Mr Wilson's always sucking his pen?'

'Yeah?' Ellen was smiling, cause I think she fancies Gilbert.

'Well why don't you nick his pen and put it up your fanny?'

So that's what she did. Stephen Harris went on manoeuvres to capture the pen. Mr Wilson was marking someone's homework, so he was using a red pen instead. Stephen swiped the pen and passed it to Jason, who passed it to Gilbert, who passed it to Kampol – but Kampol didn't know what was going on, so Gilbert had to get it back again, and pass it to Ellen himself.

She was sitting at the back of the class, wearing a skirt. She turned to face the wall and looked like she was doing it with the pen. Jason whispered: 'Oy, that's enough, it isn't a fucking vibrator!' Ellen told him to fuck off, then turned back round, holding the pen by her fingertips. She put it on the front of her desk, but nobody would touch it, so she had to take it to Mr Wilson herself.

She walked over to his desk and sneakily put the pen down: 'Sir, can I go to the toilet?'

'Must you go now? Can't you wait till the end of the lesson? It's only ten more minutes.'

'Oh, all right, sir.' And she went back to her desk, having delivered the radioactive pen.

The whole class watched closely. Mr Wilson pushed his chair back, picked up some chalk, and wrote something on the board for homework. Then he picked up a pile of exercise books and handed them back to everyone. Jason opened his, and saw some corrections. 'Sir, what does this say, I can't read it properly.' Mr Wilson went over and read it out to him. Jason said: 'Sir, can you write it out again for me, so next time I read it I can understand – for when I do my revision, sir.' Mr Wilson reached for Jason's pen, but Jason snatched it and said: 'Can't you use *your* pen, sir?' Mr Wilson said: 'Don't be silly,' and snatched Jason's pen. He wrote his comments out in Jason's book. Jason said: 'Thanks a lot, sir, that's much clearer.' Then Mr Wilson carried on handing out the books.

At the end of the lesson, as we were leaving, Mr Wilson stood behind his desk and said: 'Thanks for behaving so well today, class.' Then he popped the pen in his mouth, so we all killed ourselves. He couldn't understand it.

*   *   *

In O level, you can show off without being called a boffin. If someone attacks you, you say: 'Look, we've got exams next year, I might as well *try* and pass them.'

In Maths, I asked the teacher all about sundials.

'Sir?' I said.

'Yes, what is it?'

'Sir, you know sundials, right?'

'Yes . . .'

'Well, in winter, there's less daylight, right, cause the sun whizzes over more quickly from east to west, so does that mean the hours on a sundial are longer in summer than in winter? And the other thing is, sir, if you can only tell the time with a sundial, then how do you know what time it is at night? In the old days, they might not have noticed that winter nights were longer than summer nights, because there was no way to measure it.'

'That's a very good point. I think you should ask your History teacher.'

'But isn't it a Maths question, sir? I don't do History.'

'If it is a Maths question, you certainly don't have to worry about it for O level. That's more like an A-level question.'

'Really, sir?'

It was too much for Donna: 'Oy, John, stop fucking showing off, you batty man.'

I did the same in English. I said to Mr Wilson: 'Sir, you know adjectives, right?'

'Yes.'

'Well, who spotted that they were all the same? What I mean is, someone must of sat down, and said: "Look at all these words, like 'green' and 'big' and 'smelly'." They must of sat down and thought: These words are all the same.'

Stephen Harris laughed when I said smelly.

'Yes.'

'But if you think about it, adjectives aren't all the same at all.

190

If you think of a word like "smelly", it's completely different from a word like "fast". It doesn't make you think of the same thing at all.'

'Yes.'

'And until they came up with these names for words, like "adjective" and "noun" and stuff, people wouldn't ever have guessed which words were all the same as each other. Cause some people might think that words like "green" and "leaf" belonged in the same group, and words like "yellow" and "banana" in another group – but in fact one is an adjective, and the other is a noun!'

'Yes, that's true . . .'

'So what I mean is, the person who invented those terms, adjective and noun, must have been a bloody genius. Does anybody know who it was? There should be statues up for the man who discovered adjectives; there should be like a blue plaque on his house.'

'Well . . .'

'Or is it some Ancient Greek, or some unknown inventor like the man who invented the wheel?'

Alison said: 'How do you know it was a man?'

'Cause in those days,' I said, 'nobody would of listened to women.'

Gilbert put up his hand. 'Sir.'

'Yes, Gilbert?'

'Sir, is "fucking" an adjective?'

'Well it behaves a bit like one, but actually it's the present participle of the verb "to fuck".'

Yemisi put her hand up and said: 'Sir, you are terrible, man. I can't believe you just said that. I'm telling my mum, sir.'

Sexy girls

Our Drama teacher is supposed to be a poof, but he's really nice all the same. Nobody knows for sure if he's a poof, but he does wear big, colourful specs. Anyway, you aren't supposed to care if someone's a poof, cause it doesn't mean they're going to fancy *you*, necessarily. And you can always say no thanks, if they try anything. My dad was very *reasonable* about it when I was on report, that time, after I stuck the lesbian sticker on that cover teacher. He said: 'You should never make fun of somebody's sexuality.' I thought I was going to laugh when he said it, but I didn't. So nowadays I don't care if someone's a poof.

As soon as I joined the Drama class, I had to take over this role in a play, from some boy who'd just left the class. I couldn't believe any boy in his right mind would leave a class so full of sexy girls, but the thing is that the boy was Jeremy Simons, who was actually *another* poof (Dan told me). So it didn't bother him, leaving the girls behind.

Nobody in the class had liked Jeremy much, so when they were inventing this play, they devised a scene where he got a raw egg on his head. I think that might have been why he left the Drama class. I had to take over, I had to act the raw-egg scene. I was supposed to be some king, sitting next to the queen, who's Yvonne from my German class. And I'm supposed to think my court jester is hilarious, so I laugh and laugh and laugh. But Yvonne isn't supposed to think the court jester is very funny, so she breaks this egg on my head and then *she* laughs.

The play was part of our coursework, so it goes towards our final result. We have to perform it down the road – at Fox! Then the examiner gives us part of our final CSE result. I did it quite well, but I had to act for the second half of the play with all this egg running down my head, which was a bit disgusting.

We held a post-mortem the next lesson. Everyone in the class sat in a big circle. Mr Makin asked how we'd enjoyed it, did we have any problems. It was terrible. I became really shy, sitting there, with all those sexy girls, I became like Kampol or something. He said: 'John, how did you think it went?'

'All right.'

'Did you have any problems?'

I went bright red. I didn't have any problems, honest, but I was so embarrassed. The more I thought about how embarrassed I was, the more embarrassed I was. I was looking at the carpet, and I couldn't help it, but my mouth kept filling up with saliva so I had to keep swallowing, like I was scared. And all the time, the sexy girls were watching, like Kylie, and Kate, and Julia. They sat quietly waiting for me to say something.

'Well,' I said, still thinking what to say, 'it was a bit difficult acting with egg on my head.'

'Yes, I'm sure it was!' Mr Makin laughed. 'But was there anything else? How did you feel performing in front of all those people . . .'

The thing is, I'd been perfectly all right acting in front of the Fox kids. The whole school was sitting there watching the play, on the floor in the assembly hall, and I'd played the king perfectly. But now, sitting in front of my Drama group, I was uncomfortable as hell. I was staring at the carpet and swallowing like a maniac, wishing I'd stayed in Sport. The thing about nutters is, at least I know now how to behave with them. You muck about, you come up with good tricks to play on people,

193

you throw insults. The Drama group's different, girls don't go in for that sort of thing.

After waiting for me to say something, and watching me go red and swallow all the time, Mr Makin said: 'Are you feeling a little shy?'

Fuck.

'No,' I said, and gulped some more. I looked round to see if everyone was watching me. They were, but some of them looked away, to make me feel more comfortable. I didn't look closely – just glanced – but I think Naimh was staring at her hands, pretending she wasn't watching.

When the lesson ended, and everyone started to leave the classroom, Mr Makin stood by the door and intercepted me. He put his arms round me; he hugged me. I was astonished, I just stood there with my arms hanging down, taller than him. He said: 'John, listen, you're doing *so much* better, now, than when you started. *Well done.*' He said it quietly, under his breath so nobody would hear, but the thing is, everybody was staring at us.

In our mock O-level exams, Stephen Harris failed every one, but he can't read, so it's not surprising. He goes to special reading classes, but we try not to wind him up too much. You can't go round calling your friends thick.

Gow didn't do so badly – he didn't do well either – but he's already decided it doesn't matter. 'I got a job dahn the market. Me old man's fixed it up for me.' He says Mark Rooney's going to work there too, which sounds terrible. If it doesn't work out, Gow says he can always win a fair bit on the horses.

I got an A grade in every single mock. *And* I hardly ever do any homework. The other clever people are Kylie Sterling and Julia Myerson. Julia's Mr Makin's favourite in Drama, and she got good grades in other subjects too. She's already decided to study Drama at university, but I don't even know what to do for A level. I don't know what Alexander's doing, cause I don't talk to him any more, but I heard him say he might go somewhere else for A levels. Daniel will stay, cause his mum thinks he's really clever, even though most of his mock exams were Ds.

Ian and Kampol are leaving this year too. I'm not going to have any friends left. But the truth is, I'm getting bored of them anyway. Take Kampol. He's so shy, he's dull. He never talks to *anyone*, not a word, unless it's someone who plays football with him. Then he gets a bit more cocky. He supports Nottingham Forest; he thinks he's Gary Birtles. He dribbles a tennis ball across the concrete saying 'Birtoll, Birtoll.'

It's embarrassing. Once, in Drama, Julia Myerson was flirting with me and she said: 'You're a real mystery. Where have you been all these years? Who do you hang around with?'

I couldn't tell her. I said, 'Oh, you know, various people,' and looked away. She said: 'You're really sweet.' Kylie always says I'm sweet too, and Naimh.

I like it when they say that, but it's a bit condescending. It's like 'Boys are *so* immature.' Why can't they say I'm sexy?

Our *actual* CSE exam in Drama was about masturbation. It was this idea we'd fleshed out in class. It went like this: the government has decided to ban masturbation, but doesn't like to use the word 'masturbation' – and certainly not 'wanking' – so they called it 'DIY' instead. The play was set in a quiet English village with post office and pub and barber shop (I was the barber); and it was about this massive misunderstanding. A government inspector, played by Alison, turns up and tells everyone not to do any more DIY. Give it up straight away, or else. The village is furious, cause that means no more loft conversions and stuff. So before you know it, we end up killing Alison.

We had to perform the play before Easter, in the fifth year, for three days running, in front of pupils and parents, and the

195

examiner. Everyone was bricking it. This other boy, Sean West, said he could get hold of some dope. Everybody was excited, except me. To be perfectly honest I wasn't 100 per cent sure what dope was, but I thought it was a bad idea to get mixed up in drugs. When he asked me to chip in, I said: 'No thanks, I don't take it very often these days.'

The performance began at six-thirty p.m. They took drugs at five-thirty. Sean went on stage, behind the closed curtains, calling people up to join him one by one. They lined up on the left, then came out a few seconds later on the right. Whatever they did – smoke dragons on silver foil, inject it up their arm, snort it up their nose – they certainly did it fast. The queue disappeared in no time. Afterwards, they shuffled out on the other side of the stage, looking terrible. I sat in the stalls, pretending it was funny whenever someone came offstage. Daniel told me I should try some: 'It's really heavy shit, man.' But I said I didn't need to because I'd had some – loads of times – at a friend's house.

I was worried everyone might collapse when the play got going, but the play went fine. After the second night, walking with a big group through the park, towards the bus stop, Naimh took my arm and told me there'd be a big party the next night, and everyone was going to get *paralytic*. 'Even you,' she said.

God, I love Naimh; she's prettier than Julia or Kylie, although it's close. I hope I go out with her, but I'd be happy with either of the others. (Kylie's cleverer.) Naimh doesn't even live far from me, which helps.

Anyway, the next night, at half-past four, I was sent with this girl June to get loads of booze from the off-licence. I'm really tall, and June looks old for her age, so us two had the best chance of getting it, and not being spotted as under-age. We bought tons.

When we got back, the others were getting changed already. There was only one changing room, for boys *and* girls. We walked in, carrying these boxes, and the first thing I saw was Kylie walking around in her bra. I couldn't believe it. I tried not to look, but I couldn't stop gulping again – like you do, when you're embarrassed. Then when June started getting changed, she took her shirt off *right in front of me*, and I couldn't miss it. I looked at her bra for a fraction of a second, then looked away, but she'd seen me looking, and so did Naimh. June said: 'Enjoying the show, darling?'

I went red again, but tried to pretend it was no big deal, like I'd seen a million bras.

I couldn't wait for the party afterwards, but I didn't want to get off my head, I might not enjoy it. I might do something stupid. So when the curtain had gone down, when the audience had left and everybody had got changed, I sat in the loo wondering what I should do. I sat there for nearly an hour, so when I went back, everyone had already drunk a can or two of beer. Before I joined them, in the main hall, I sat down among a few empty cans backstage, and opened a drink for myself. I took a swig, and June appeared. She was on the way to the loo. She said: 'Hello. What are you doing *here*? Where have you been?'

You know what I said? I didn't plan to say it, but I said: 'I've been sitting here drinking a load of beers. Look,' I said, pointing at the empty cans beside me, 'I've already had a load.'

'What – you've drunk all that?!'

'No, not *all* of it, but I've already lost count.' I was putting it on a bit, pretending to be lagered.

'Why don't you join the rest of us?'

Maybe I was drunk already on one swig, but the next thing I said was: 'Cause I want to snog you.'

So June sat down next to me and we had a snog. She put her tongue in my mouth. I couldn't believe that would be nice, but it jolly well was. Then June got up, and put out her hand to help me up. She said: 'You're so sweet,' and took me through

197

to where the others were. She sat me next to Kylie, then she went to the loo.

When June got back, I was snogging Kylie. Then Julia came over and I snogged her too. *And* Naimh. They all thought it was funny, and kept saying how sweet it was I'd drunk all those beers on my own – so I had to keep up the pretence, slurring the odd word. I was getting good at this. If you ask someone for a snog, they do it. I asked Yvonne, my queen in the eggy play, and *she* snogged me. I asked another girl too, Kitsa. I snogged *six* girls in one night. This is the nicest thing that ever happened to anyone at school.

I didn't ask Alison for a snog, cause I'd done it before, at Fox (without tongues). I didn't want her to think I was desperate. As for that girl from private school, Kate, I didn't ask her cause she's going out with a boy who's twenty. None of the other boys in my class got a snog, not even cool Sean with his drugs. Even Mr Makin was impressed, which shows how nice some homos can be.

Naimh took me home on the 28 bus, and we snogged without pausing for seven stops.

On the grass

Sometimes Gilbert joins in with our footy games. He's not as tough as he used to be, but he's still the best player in the class, cause he can dribble the ball past loads of people and he's hard to tackle.

If he isn't playing football, he usually goes to the park with a load of hippy boys from other classes. I don't know how they became friends, maybe they're in his O-level classes. There is a boy called Ollie from 5.1, and Simon and Charlton from 5.2, and Ashley and Manuel and Andreas from 5.6 – and some others. They all bring racing bikes to school, they wheel the bikes everywhere.

One day Gilbert asked me if I wanted to go to the park with him and the hippies. I knew he was up to something, but when I looked suspicious, he turned his hands up like an honest geezer, and said, '*What*?!!' So I followed him. I had French after break but that can be a real waste of time, I'm well ahead of the others.

In the park, we chose a spot on the big lawn, near the back of the Commonwealth Institute, miles away from anybody. Manuel took a bag of leaves out of his denim jacket, and a box of cigarettes. He sat cross-legged on the grass, with the rest of them reclining like Roman emperors. I crossed my legs like at primary school, but leant far back on my hands to show I was really relaxed.

'So, John, I heard you got off with a lot of girls the other day . . .' said Manuel.

'Did you fuck any?' asked Andreas.

'Nah.'

Simon moved closer to Manuel, and started smiling. Manuel was sticking some cigarette papers together, then he licked the side of a proper cigarette and tore off the wet strip. It was like peeling a short white banana. He poured the tobacco into the cigarette papers. Everyone watched.

One thing bothered me: what's the point of destroying a ready-made cigarette, just to roll up another? Then, as Manuel took some of the herbs and poured them into the tobacco, someone said:

'Nice-looking dope.'

Dope! So this was it. I could watch closely as they all got stoned. I prepared myself. They might pass out, or their eyes might roll around wildly, they might throw up, or die of an overdose. That's why we were so far from anyone else, so they could have a fit in private. I wondered what I was doing here. Stephen Harris and Kampol, I knew, would be kicking a tennis ball in the corner of the South Playground, and shouting Birtoll.

Manuel's joint used the tobacco from two and a half cigarettes. It was as long as a Bic biro. He lit it, making the paper at the end flare up. He gasped at it to keep it alight, as if he had asthma. Nobody said anything, or asked if he was all right.

He passed it to Ollie on his left. After Ollie had taken several puffs, Gilbert started to growl: 'Come on Ollie, man, you hog . . .'

Ollie calmly passed it left to Ashley, who passed it on to Andreas, and then it reached Gilbert, who was propped on his elbows to my right. The whole circle had gone quiet, and watched carefully as the joint flared in Gilbert's mouth. As he breathed deeply, he moved his elbows out to the side, lying flat on the grass.

'Your turn, John,' said Gilbert.

I said I wasn't too sure. 'I don't want to be addicted. I can't afford it.'

Everybody laughed, their eyelids hooded.

'Hold him down,' Gilbert ordered, slowly rising.

Manuel and Ollie grabbed me by the shoulders, pinning me down; Andreas and Simon took my feet.

'Just breathe in. *Deep*. Breathe hard,' Gilbert explained. 'I'll do it up your nose, cause you'll cough if it's in your mouth.'

He turned the joint back to front – placing the lighted end inside his mouth! – then moved over my face. With his eyes, he signalled that I should breathe in, then he blew out the precious smoke.

After a few breaths, they let me go, and I sat up – preparing myself. I was ready for a carnival of bright visions.

'I don't think it's worked,' I said. I was pleased I wasn't seeing things. I pointed at all the bikes lying on their sides: 'Somebody's murdered your bikes.'

Manuel took the package out of his leather jacket and rolled another, but said I didn't need any more. I promised I wasn't seeing anything, which made everyone laugh again.

After the second one, everybody staggered up and clambered on to their racing bikes. Manuel offered me a lift. I climbed on to the saddle, and grabbed the belt loops at the sides of his black jeans, bending my legs up behind me to keep them out of the way of the pedals. We wobbled back up the hill to school. I was half an hour late for French; Ms Avis wanted to know why.

'Sorry, I had to go and see the, uh, Dr Rushworth,' I told her.

Everybody looked at me, then when I'd sat down they carried on reading out from their exercise books. I laid my head on the desk and went to sleep. I got back together with the hippies at lunchtime, and smoked another joint.

Ms Avis put me on report for sleeping in class. The next day she wrote 'John-Paul is very good at French, but he should try harder.' She wrote it in pencil, so I rubbed out the last five words.

Gow stands firm

Mark Rooney grabbed Jeremy Simons by the collar and told him to take off his jacket. It was a silver jacket, and Jeremy squealed: 'Please – just leave me alone – don't hurt me – please . . .'

Mark asked Jeremy why he didn't wear a proper jacket, like a Fila tracksuit, or at least Adidas. 'Is it cause you're such a fucking poof? Eh, poof?'

'Oh, Mark – please – please – Mark, please don't hurt me,' said Jeremy.

'Eh, poof?'

'I'm not a poof,' said Jeremy, so Rooney slapped him down.

Then Rooney went round every boy in the room and told them to gob on Jeremy's jacket. The thing is, although Jeremy didn't do anybody any harm, everyone thinks he's a real poof, so they hate him. Gilbert gobbed first, then John McGuire, then Bug Eye.

There was a small pool of gob in the middle of the jacket, with a bit of greeny in it from Bug Eye's cold.

Then Stephen Harris said to Rooney: 'Yeah, get the silly fucking poofter, Mark,' and gobbed. 'He's probably got the Gay Plague.'

Mark appreciated his support, and gave Stephen a friendly little slap on the cheek, not too hard. 'Cheers, mate.'

Then I gobbed on the jacket, then Ian.

But Gow wouldn't gob on it. He'd been to primary school

with Jeremy, so they were sort of old friends, in a way (but Gow's not a poof).

'Nah, I ain't gobbing on it.'

Mark said: 'Gob on it, you little cunt, or I'll slap ya.'

'Nah, you can slap me if you like, but I ain't spittin on the jacket. What's he done to you, eh, Mark? Leave im alone.'

Rooney slapped Gow, but still Gow wouldn't gob on it. Rooney slapped him loads of times. Jeremy (who was crying by now, of course) pretended he wasn't watching, but he did watch. He watched Gow taking slaps cause of his poofy silver jacket.

Then Mark pushed Gow right off his chair, and moved on to Jason Cunningham, who did gob on the jacket.

Revolution

We were in the Art class, painting a selection of pots and houseplants, when the tannoy suddenly switched on, making a humming noise, and it was Bob Marley, singing 'No Woman, No Cry'. Someone was playing it over the tannoy.

Then there was a voice, and it sounded like Paul Grant. 'Yeah, listen up . . .' Then the tannoy went silent for a second. We all looked at each other, smiling across the pots and plants, not sure what was going on.

'Listen up,' the voice said. 'This school is *ras clat* – too damn racialist, and we gonna listen up to some roots reggae.' Then Bob Marley started again. Paul must have taken the school secretary hostage.

Then it started again – Desmond's voice this time, with plenty of laughing in the background. 'Yeah, listen everybody, man, this place is fuckin racialist and we need to discuss the issue NOW!' They laughed when he said 'fuckin'.

Paul Grant again: 'So what we sayin is, right, you must stop what you're doing, and put down yo pens, and come into the hall for a special assembly.' More laughter, then more Bob Marley. Finally Dr Rushworth's squeaky voice: 'Hello. This is Dr Rushworth. Please would all classes *calmly* stop what they are doing, and meet in the main hall in five minutes.'

In the corridor I met James, that mixed-race boy I was talking about whose big sister was in the school team. He was laughing. He said: 'You know what's happening?'

'No.'

'I heard Paul and Desmond planning this at lunchtime.'

'What did they do?'

'They invaded the head's office and put on a Bob Marley record. It's a revolution, to stamp out racialism in the school.'

In the hall, Paul Grant and Desmond stood on the stage, with Mark Rooney next to them. Dr Rushworth was trying to get a microphone from Paul, but Paul was lecturing everybody. He said the school librarian wanted to cancel a subscription for a black magazine because pupils kept nicking back issues. But Paul said the librarian was racialist, he said there was no need to cancel the subscription because the magazine was *free*.

'There's too much racialism in this place,' he said. 'The black geezers don't get a fair chance. None of the teachers gives you no chance.' He turned and looked at Dr Rushworth. 'What kind of damn school is this, if it don't give nobody a fair chance if they're black?'

Dr Rushworth tried to answer, but Paul didn't give him the microphone. So Dr Rushworth was squeaking away – you could scarcely make out what he was saying – until Desmond snatched the microphone from Paul and started talking over Dr Rushworth.

'The thing is, right, no matter what Rushworth say bout us black geezers having as much chance as the rest, it ain't true. It's time we had a revolution, and there shouldn't be no more preference for the white geezers.'

Dr Rushworth kept buzzing around them, trying to get the microphone, but he didn't try *too* hard, cause they looked fired up, as if they'd smack him if he tried. So they carried on saying the same things, again and again.

I said to James: 'But James, seriously, would *you* say this place is racialist? I don't think it is. There must be loads worse . . .'

'The thing is, *you* might not think it is, but that's cause you're

205

white, innit? If *you* put up with all the comments, you'd know different.'

'But nobody would dare make any comments. If anyone was racialist in my class, they'd get their head kicked in. Cause – no offence, but all the hardest people are black.'

'Nah, sorry John, I ain't saying you're racialist yourself, but you're living in cloud-cuckoo land. You never noticed how many white geezers are skinheads? You never thought bout what they say to us when we're on our own? Dontcha unnerstan why us black geezers hang about together and ting? It's cause we'd get abuse, and shit.'

'Well, that might be true, but sometimes – no offence – it's black guys who're most racialist, specially about Asians . . .'

'Well, I'm not sure if I agree with you there, John.'

'All right, but what about this: why is *Rooney* up there with them. He's a racialist bastard, he's the worst of the lot.'

James couldn't help agreeing with that. Apart from calling Ian a Paki all the time, Rooney used to say Chinky to this boy in our Chemistry class. 'Why don't you go back to China?' he used to say, and slap the boy about. But the thing is, that boy wasn't Chinese at all, he was from Cambodia; he'd won a prize, against people from schools all over Britain, for this essay he'd written about escaping from Cambodia in a boat with his mum.

'Yeah, that's true,' he said, then we carried on watching. I was amazed by what James'd said, I didn't think there was any racialism here at all, apart from a couple of thick people like Stephen Harris.

After twenty minutes, Paul and Desmond got bored. They gave Dr Rushworth the microphone, and he started to answer some of their points, but they didn't bother staying to listen. They jumped off the front of the stage and walked out of the hall. Mark Rooney followed them. Dr Rushworth said: 'Well, school, I hope you have taken account of what they said, and will think carefully about prejudice in the future. Perhaps we can all go back to our classes now.'

As we walked back, there was more Bob Marley on the tannoy – but they were only messing about, cause it stopped after three seconds.

I know where you live

In the old days, I used to sit down and watch children's television together with Crispin and my dad. We'd make a pot of tea and buy some cakes or biscuits, then watch stuff like *Rentaghost*, *Blue Peter*, *Blockbusters* and *Murphy's Mob*, and the five-minute cartoons at the end like *Rhubarb and Custard*; then my dad got all carried away by the News. But nowadays, I'm always smoking dope in the park with the hippy gang, so when I get home I need sleep. Nowadays, I just sneak into the house and take myself upstairs for a nap.

Once, when everybody was out, I wedged a heavy box of football programmes against the bedroom door and took out this doobie Manuel had rolled for me 'in case of emergencies'. I knelt by the window, crouching down to stop any nosy neighbours from seeing me smoke, and stared over the window-sill at the council blocks opposite, watching people walk along the elevated passageways, wondering about their lives, wondering if any of them were dope dealers. Then I lay on the floor and watched the ceiling.

I didn't have any Led Zeppelin, or reggae, or ZZ Top, which Mans told me was the best thing for listening to when you're sparking up, but I found one of my mum's tapes of Joan Armatrading, one of the ones with a slight reggae beat, and put it on full volume.

I borrowed this record from Naimh, by a band called the Smiths; the album's just called *The Smiths*. It used to hang in the window of the record department at W. H. Smith in High Street Ken, as though it was an advertisement for the shop itself. But Naimh told me W. H. Smith has banned it cause one of the songs is about the Moors Murderers.

After Naimh lent me that record, I held on to it for ages, always pretending I'd forgotten to bring it into school, so I could hold on to it for longer. It reminds me of Naimh, and the lyrics are exactly about someone like me, in the same boat. I taped it, of course, so when I eventually gave it back I could still listen and remind myself of her.

Most nights after dinner I go out for a walk with my headset, listening to the Smiths. I always walk towards Naimh's mum's flat, so that I might bump into her by accident. I carry a box of cigarettes so if I meet her I can pretend I'd just popped out to buy some – but I don't really like smoking fags, they taste terrible and they're too expensive.

Usually I hang around the corner shop staring up at Naimh's windows for about ten or fifteen minutes, but I haven't bumped into her yet. She lives with this woman she calls her mum but in fact she's her stepmum. Her real mum ran away when she was young, and her dad's never at home, so it's a good thing this kind woman has brought her up.

One night on my way back home this tramp stopped me at the local recreation ground. He was sitting on a bench, watching the traffic, sipping out of this bottle of meths. He asked me if I was still at school and if I had a girlfriend. I said I did; I told him her name was Naimh. He said, 'That's a nice name, an Irish girl is it?'

'Her dad's Irish.'

Then he said: 'Do you like football, son?'

'Yeah, I support Fulham.'

'Oh yeah? Well I used to play for Rangers, do yer recognize me?'

'What, QPR or Glasgow Rangers?'

'QPR, local team, sonny.'

He told me his name, said he played in the late 1960s. I told him I'd heard of him from my friends who were QPR fans (although I hadn't). He asked if I had anything to write with. I had a pen in my pocket, from school, but I didn't have any paper except the back of the packet of fags. He said he was willing to give me his autograph, so I handed it over and said thanks.

When I got home, I washed the pen.

I know where other people live, but I keep my own address secret. I don't want anyone coming round and accidentally telling my parents I smoke dope and bunk off. Anyway, they might make fun of my parents later, or even at the time – you never know. It's safer this way.

If they wanted to, they could use their brains and look up my name in the phone book, like I looked up Alexander's (I was amazed, his dad is a knight, it says so in the book, Sir Timothy), but nobody really uses their brains all that much.

We were sitting in the park one time, hiding by some trees in case a teacher came to spy on skivers, and Ashley showed us this dirty homo porn mag. Inside it were blokes whose dicks were really long and bendy. It was gross. We all bundled Ashley for being a dirty homo, which made everyone laugh, so we needed another doobie to get over it.

After we'd smoked that, Ollie said: 'Why not post the magazine to Jeremy Simons' house?'

'Yeah,' said Gilbert, 'to tip off his mum.'

He took out this pen and wrote a message on the cover. It said 'Oy Jeremy you dirty homo bastard wank on this.' Everyone laughed.

'Who knows where he lives?' asked Ashley.

Even if anybody did know, we didn't want to admit it. I said, 'We can ask Gow, he knows him from primary school, but he might not tell us cause Gow thinks Jeremy's all right. We could always look him up in the phone book.'

Everyone said that was brilliant; Mans said I was a genius.

If other people get hold of your address it's murder. Bug Eye told me about this time when he was trying to hang around with hard people like Rooney and Desmond and Paul Grant. They all came round to his place, on this estate, while his mum was at work. He tried to make them watch telly but there wasn't anything good on, so they went all over the flat, in his room and his sister's room and his mum's room, and you know what they did? They nicked all his Filas and Nike gear and even his moon-boots. They even nicked his mum's perfume. From right under his nose, and he couldn't tell the police or everyone would kill him.

There was a worse time than that, too. Once Gilbert and Mans were bunking off in the afternoon, playing pool in Ken Market. There's this little room at the back, by the pool tables, right, and while they were playing this big black guy, looking really angry, came past them with a gun. They couldn't believe it, but he pushed into the back room and shut the door after him, and then wouldn't you know it there's this massive bang, the sound of his gun, and he rushed out and left. Gilbert and Mans were about to leave too, but somehow the police were in the area and stopped everybody from leaving. It turned out that the guy hadn't killed anyone, he'd shot a blank, but the coppers wanted to nick him. So they took Gil's name and address after asking him what he'd seen. Anyway, the point is, about three weeks later we were sitting around smoking in Gil's bedroom (his mum doesn't mind, so long as it's only dope) when the doorbell rang and his sister called out, 'Oy, Gil, s'for you,' so he went to see who it was. You know what? It was Justice, he'd found out Gil's address and come to give him a warning from the black mafia (that's what Gil told us), he said Gil had better not give no evidence or there might be some trouble. You could see

211

Gilbert was scared, even though he pretended not to be. His fingers were shaking when he rolled a spliff.

So you see, the last thing you want is for other people to know where you live.

I did tell Naimh, though. She writes me these cards sometimes, stupid cards with jokes on them; nothing about love or anything. She puts nicknames on the envelope, which is a bit embarrassing if I don't find them first. But once – it was amazing – she put 'Jomps', which is my family's nickname for me (but not in public). Maybe Naimh's destined to be in my family one day.

The other person from school who wrote to our house was Dr Rushworth. He gave me a bad report for Latin, you see, for not trying hard enough, and my dad thought that was unfair. So my dad wrote back to Dr Rushworth defending me, and Dr Rushworth wrote back *again* to say thanks for the letter and maybe he'd been a little harsh but he really believed I could do better if I tried.

I felt bad about that, because the truth is I *haven't* worked all that hard; after all, when you've got to smoke a lot of weed you can't put much effort into your work, so I *have* been a bit lazy. But I'm not even taking an exam in Latin anyway so why should I work harder?

Leaving parties

All the cool people were going to this party on Stephen Harris's estate; some friend of Bug Eye who lived there had hired a hall and a sound system one Saturday evening. I turned up with the hippies – Gil, Mans, Simon, Ollie, Ashley, this Greek boy Andreas, and Ashley's brother Tristan. We went by bus from Gil's house: we couldn't cycle cause we'd agreed everyone had to get off their heads.

Me and Gilbert went to this barber shop called Oscar's, beforehand, to get our hair cut in a flat-top. Oscar is supposed to be an expert at doing flat-tops: Jason told us, and he should know because he's always getting weird haircuts. To keep your flat-top properly, Oscar told me, you have to use hairspray. I'm not sure if I can be bothered with that, but he did it for me this time.

Naimh was at the party with Kylie and Julia and June, so I made my way over and hung around with them. I'm glad I did, cause the hippies were all taking acid and I don't really want to get involved with that; I mean, dope's one thing, it's supposed to be less dangerous than alcohol, but acid's what killed Shelley.

The girls said my flat-top was cool. I told them about Oscar's in Barons Court. 'He's lethal, he really knows what he's doing.'

Towards the back of the room, not far from me and Julia, Desmond sat down next to Ellen and her friend Becky, and told Becky to sit on his lap. She didn't really have much choice, so she did what he said. I was watching closely, cause I'd heard

213

Desmond in the toilets, telling Paul Grant he was going to fuck someone tonight; but I couldn't actually hear what he was saying to Becky cause the music was too loud. Desmond was making pleading faces, and he kept sticking his hands out with upturned palms, like the market traders do in Portobello Road, to show how honest they are. Becky kept saying no (I could lip-read that much), but after about fifteen minutes they got up and Desmond more or less dragged her outside. They were away for ages.

When they came back, Desmond looked pissed off, and started pushing a few people around; but Becky was crying. I tried to work out from the way they were behaving whether Desmond had fucked her. If he did, why was he so pissed off? But if he didn't, why was she crying? In the end I decided he must have tried – which would upset her – but she prevented it, which upset him.

Boys in Desmond's gang do that sort of thing a lot. Bug Eye went off into the sixth-form gardens once, with this girl Lola that used to go out with Ashley. She'd drunk too much in the pub at lunch. Everyone applauded as Bug Eye dragged her into the bushes, but later she told Ashley that Bug Eye had fucked her, even though she didn't want him to. Ashley went after Bug Eye with a bike chain, and they had a little fight in Airlie Gardens – but it was broken up before anyone was injured.

Julia and me smoked a joint together, which was strange, cause I'd never done that before, smoked with just one girl. Usually when I smoke it's with the hippies being all raucous, maybe bundling each other, and making nasty jokes about girls and things, so this time it was civilized. It felt intimate, both of us putting our lips in the same place on the roach, and when we passed the joint from one to another, I felt her hand glancing against mine; I prolonged the feeling by acting more sleepy than I really was, moving my hands in slow motion. I wondered whether I would snog Julia again, but we didn't.

Instead, we talked about the miners' strike. Julia and Kylie sometimes do collections, with a yellow bucket, for the miners' families.

At half-past two, we phoned for loads of cabs. We stood outside waiting for them. I put my head down on my folded arms, on top of someone's front wall, wasted by all the dope and booze. I nearly went to sleep, but not quite.

With my head down, I heard Desmond saying to Naimh that he wanted to snog her. She said: 'It would be nice, Desmond, but I can't because I'm going out with someone right now.'

He said: 'Who's that then?'

She isn't really going out with anyone, although Julia told me Naimh fancies a guy in the year above us. She said to Desmond: 'With him, with John.'

I still had my head down, but I heard that clearly. I smiled into the bend of my elbow, delighted.

Desmond said: 'Why d'you want to go out with that cunt?'

'I just do.'

'Well look, he's asleep, there's no need for him to know if we just have a frenchie.'

'*Des*mond . . . !'

'Come on, come around the corner and he won't see.'

Naimh said no-oo-oo, as though Desmond was dragging her. Kylie, who was waiting near by, said, 'Come on, Desmond, you can see she doesn't want to go with you.'

He said: 'Fuck off, bitch.'

Naimh shouted out 'John, John. JOHN-PAUL.'

'Don't call out, or I'll mash him,' said Desmond.

I was too scared to intervene, I kept my head down in my arms, as though I'd passed out. Naimh called again, and Kylie called too, but still I kept my head down.

Somehow Naimh pulled away from him, she came over and grabbed my coat, she tugged it angrily. I lifted my head and opened my eyes to see her glaring at me, tearful. She'd been

215

saved by the arrival of a taxi. I looked round; Desmond had gone.

Kylie put her arm round Naimh, helped her into the cab. I stood wondering what to do with my hands. Inside, Kylie kept hugging her, on the back seat, while I perched on one of the flip-down chairs. I said: 'I'm sorry, I didn't dare to interfere . . . in case . . .'

Even though they don't know their results, nearly everyone has decided to leave school this summer. Of the boys, that includes nasty people like Peter Davies, Darius, Robert Lester (though nobody sees him much these days anyway, he bunks off for months on end), as well as quiet people like Kampol, Gow, Stephen Harris; even Alexander's off, he's going somewhere else for his A levels. That leaves me with Gilbert and Dan Hair. Of the girls, Manmeet is leaving, and Sharon, and Yemisi, and Donna, and probably Claire and Ellen. Only clever girls like Melissa and Alison are staying on for A levels (or to retake their Os).

We had this party to celebrate the end of school. It lasted all through registration and the whole period after that. Ms Parsons – who's hardly any older than us, this is her first year as a teacher – brought along one of the school's record players, and everybody turned up with their favourite records, as well as drinks and snacks. Some of us brought in shandy as well as soft drinks, but we didn't think we could get away with actual beer. It was sad when the party ended, because, although I don't even like some of the people who're going, after next week I might never see them again – people I've known for *five* years.

Before we left, Ms Parsons gave each of us a reference to give out to employers. It's pretty stupid, her doing that, because she doesn't know anything about us. She isn't my teacher, she just takes the register, and half the time people don't bother turning up till the last minute – if at all. So she doesn't know the first thing about me. Anyway, I'd already told her I was staying on, whatever happened in the exams. She said I couldn't be sure what my results would be, but I let slip how I'd got all those As in the mocks. She asked if I'd been revising, and I said I didn't need to, but she reckoned I might be in for a nasty surprise if I took that attitude.

I had the final say, because I told her I would stay on for the sixth form *even to retake my O levels*, if I had to, so the reference was a waste of paper.

Anyway, towards the end of summer, I walked up through the park to fetch my exam results; I'd seen an article in the *Guardian* saying results were out today. Up by the sandwich bar in the park I met Samuel Thomas, who's become a complete dope-head: he even talks with a Californian accent even though he's never been there, *that*'s how bad he is.

When we got to the office, I was pretty gutted because I ended up with no As at all in the real exams, even though I'd got all As in the mocks. But at least I passed them all. Samuel failed some of his, but got five Es in the others. He was overjoyed, he said: 'Yeah, man, that's fuckin cool, check it out man, I got five O levels and I hardly ever did any work.'

He looked at my results and was really impressed, so I couldn't bring myself to tell him that E isn't really a pass, it's effectively a fail. I would have sounded like I was being a bighead. So I just said: 'Yeah fuckinell Sam, man, that's most excellent.' We had a coffee in the sandwich bar, then Samuel offered me a cigarette he'd rolled in green marijuana juice. While we were smoking it, this peacock followed us around the gardens.

Nearly everyone in my class failed most of their exams. Some people, like Gow, failed all of them. Gilbert failed quite a few, so he's staying on to retake, and so's most of the hippy gang. And Dan Hair.

Straight after the results came out, there was another of those open days for choosing the subjects you want to study. I couldn't believe it, teachers were imploring me to go in their class. It's true. Mr Brown is this Chemistry teacher who'd taken over my class from mad Mr Watson; Mr Brown's been around for ages – he even taught Anna when she was here, years ago. He practically *begged* me to do Chemistry.

But the only things I was sure I wanted to study were English and Maths. You know what? Nobody can study both of those because there's a timetable clash. So you have to decide if you're a science-type person or an arts-type. I asked the head of the sixth form which combinations were good for going to Oxford. He's a Science teacher, so I was looking out for bias in his answers.

'It depends what you want to study at Oxford.'

'Well – either English or Maths.'

'Why do you want to go to Oxford?'

'Because my parents went there.'

'Well, it's up to you to decide, which do you prefer, English or Maths?'

When I settled for English, he said a good combination would include a language (so that'll be French, then), and History. I hadn't done O-level History but he said that didn't matter, much.

Lower sixth

In the sixth form, you get privileges. During the morning break, you get coffee in a corner of the school hall; sometimes the teachers join you. It's just 5p a cup, and you can have tea if you'd rather. Also: cheese rolls.

In whole-school assembly, you sit on the top balcony – so if you want you can throw things at the younger people, you could even gob on them. And lessons are in Thorpe Lodge, classrooms with beautiful wood-panelled walls, and elaborate tiling, and windows that look on to the sixth-form gardens. You don't have lessons every period; in free periods they trust you to work under your own steam. In other words, you don't get in trouble if you go down the park instead of the library.

And in A levels, *everybody* in your class is civilized.

In English, I've got Mr Wilson again, but he's tons better now that the troublemakers have left. The other English teacher is Mrs Burns. She started us off with this book by a black woman from America called Alice Walker, *The Colour Purple*; that killed me, it was like in our old History classes, studying ethnic minorities all the time. The book is full of bad grammar, to reflect how the ignorant characters would speak, which is pretty corny, but what most annoys me is one of the main characters is a woman called Shug. What kind of a name's that? I mean, how do you pronounce it: does it rhyme with 'hug', or is it meant to be the first part of 'sugar'? How are you supposed to enjoy a book when you don't even know how to pronounce the name of the people in it?

I asked if we would do real *English* literature, which made Mrs Burns look fed up with me. She said the next book would be a Jane Austen, if I really wanted to know.

In History, the whole syllabus is about the twentieth century. One teacher, Mr MacDonald, does the British side, and the other, this new woman called Frida Chase, is doing Europe and the rest of the world – the Russian Revolution, the Depression, Hitler, both world wars, and all that. Not exactly kings and queens, but real history all the same.

For French we've got this woman who's got absolutely no common sense – she's thick, everyone knows. (Her name's Ms Avis.) The other one's Ms O'Reilly. I'm pretty excited about studying French literature actually, because we've never done any before, and I know a bit about it because my dad's mad about France, he studied it at Oxford. I've already read a book by Camus, and he's one of our set authors. The others are Sartre, Pagnol and Colette. I asked if we would be studying Molière, because my dad loves Molière and I once saw this play of his that's hilarious, but Ms O'Reilly said: 'I'm not rereading Molière just for *you*.' And she sort of sneered at me.

I couldn't believe it, we'd only just met, why did she have to take that attitude? Now I hate her, I can't help it.

Loads of posh people have joined for A levels, they come from famous private schools. For example, there are about seven girls from St Paul's, and some boys from Westminster, and a few others too.

I know where their old schools are. Mum used to work by Westminster School, it's right next to the Abbey, most of the buildings are probably medieval; there's a beautiful square for playing cricket. When I was small I walked past this group of boys at Westminster and one of them was the boy who acted as

Just William in the telly series with Bonnie Langford; I couldn't believe it. As for St Paul's, the girls who go there catch the buses at Hammersmith, I've been on the same bus as them loads of times. They wear a gingham uniform, like old tablecloths.

These people are just dropping out to be trendy, so they can say they've been to a hard school. But they don't understand what hard means, cause they missed out on the lower school; they probably think Holland Park's all about wood-panelled rooms and civilized classmates. A bit like their old place, most probably.

This pair of posh boys called Max and Robin are in my History class, and they're in one of the other A-level English classes too. They act like they own the place, even though they've only just arrived. Gilbert calls them 'your posh friends', but I've got more in common with him than with them, so why are they *my* posh friends? I never even *tried* to go to private school. My parents couldn't have afforded it, full stop.

The fact is, Gil's a bit intimidated by them: once when Max made a lame joke in the common room Gil laughed a lot, really politely, and he *never* does that usually. Another time, we all bunked off to play Stocks and Shares in an empty classroom, and Max stuck his head in to find out what we were up to. Gilbert said: 'We're playing Stocks and Shares, Max, man; do you want to join in?'

If that was anybody else, he'd have called them a nosy cunt and told them to fuck off. As it turned out, Max joined in and Gilbert wasted about half the lesson explaining the rules.

In Thorpe Lodge, this old kitchen has been converted into our common room. It's disgusting, the only reason to go there is to smoke. There're five old chairs, covered in burn marks where people must have rested a cigarette. The light bulb hangs down in the middle of the room, without a shade. If you want comfort, you have to fight for one of the broad window-sills. Not that there's anything to look at, much. The windows look over a couple of yards of paving towards a high brick wall, excluding everything but a strip of sky at the top.

People just sit around smoking and having a laugh, insulting each other. There's one guy, in the upper sixth, he does the nastiest insults you've ever heard. If anyone wanted, they could make fun of his face, which is terribly burnt; his ears are little stumps, like molten wax. But that would be too cruel. His name's Luke, but behind his back people call him Bernie.

One day, a teacher with terrible pock-marks, called Mr Wood-house, popped his head round the door and warned us that police were on the premises with a warrant to search for drugs: 'I don't want to know what you've got, but get rid of it.'

Everyone says Mr Woodhouse keeps a stash of cannabis plants in his room, shunting them into an annexe whenever he's got a class. Someone told me he saw Mr Woodhouse sitting outside a pub once, smoking a great fat joint. But I don't believe he'd do it that publicly. All the same, you've got to admit he's unusual among teachers. He refuses to be known as 'sir'. If you call him sir, he sits you down and gives you a long lecture about how he prefers to be known as Frank – or if you *really* insist on being formal, as Mr Woodhouse. Most cool people think he's sad as hell, trying to hang out with the kids as Frank, so I wouldn't be all that surprised if he does keep a pot or two of weed in his room. After all, look at him now, warning us about the pigs.

As soon as Mr Woodhouse left, about half the people in the common room unwrapped these packages of cling film and chewed up all their hash (they were off their heads all day).

Max from Westminster was sitting in the middle of the room watching. He said: 'Oh, man, this is most unreal,' with his phoney accent; a posh boy trying to sound American.

Tristan's in the upper sixth. He's stronger than anybody else, but he's not cruel, he only uses his strength in this game we play, Punching Circle, when we've drunk too much or smoked too much. All you do is, pass on the punch from the person on your left, until somebody squeals. The way you start the game is, somebody just shouts out, 'Punching circle.'

Everyone always keeps an eye out not to sit next to Tristan, in case somebody starts the game. Whenever we spot Ollie sitting next to Trist, we start a game before he moves. Ollie always loses, he gets hit hardest and complains most; he normally gets a lot of penalties too. If anyone breaks a rule, Tristan has to give them a haymaker. He puts his hands together as though for prayer, then meshes the fingers so the hands make a double fist, lifts them above his head, and brings them down hard on the offender's thigh. Even fat Jase couldn't take these blows. 'You cunt,' he said, as Tristan unclenched his hands – which technically meant Jase incurred another penalty.

After Tristan, Jase is next strongest, then Gilbert and Manuel, and even little Simon could give a vicious punch. I'm somewhere between Manuel and Simon.

I was sitting next to Tristan once and Jason called out punching circle, so I was gutted. But it got worse: Mark Rooney turned up. He left school last year, but he still thinks he rules the place; he likes to come and visit. So when he saw us playing this game, he came over to check it out.

So we told him the rules, and he sat on my other side. I got a punch from Trist, which nearly broke my fucking arm, and then I passed it on to Rooney. I had to do it quite hard, because I'd learnt my lesson that other time, with Geezer. But Rooney said: 'Ooh – cheeky cunt,' and slapped me before carrying on with the punching circle.

Strictly speaking, Rooney incurred a penalty by complaining about my punch, and another for slapping me. But none of us dared to say anything about him breaking the rules. None of us except Tristan, who shouted: 'Haymaker!'

Gilbert had to explain all over again to Rooney, who said:

'All right then, give me a haymaker.' We couldn't believe it. Tristan's got such cheek. Surely he wouldn't hit Rooney as hard as he hits the rest of us. But he did! He lifted his clenched hands and dropped them like some heavy medieval mace on to Rooney's thigh. It must've been the hardest shot Trist ever made. But Rooney, being so hard and everything, just sat there, he didn't even tense up his muscles for it. For a second, you could see he didn't know how to react. He was in shock, but he didn't want anyone to see that.

Then he grinned and said: 'Carry on.'

Bikes, books and shavers

One morning in registration Gilbert asked me if I'd come on my bike, and when I said yes he pushed me out of the room, down the corridor, out of the gates and into the park. He took me up a path, where the undergrowth was coming through the fence. Somebody had chained a racer to the fence without locking their quick-release wheels. They were expensive wheels, made of a lightweight alloy.

'Let's go,' said Gilbert, undoing the wheel at the front. I pulled up the lever on the back wheel and pushed against the gears and the chain, slipping the wheel out of the forks. We ran back towards the school, carrying the wheels, to Thorpe Lodge where I'd chained my bike.

Gilbert always carries some tools with him, so we got rid of my chunky steel wheels at once, before everybody began walking past to lessons. Working fast, we took off those crap wheels and replaced them with the lightweight ones we'd nicked.

I felt guilty about leaving the other bike with no wheels.

'We've got to leave him my wheels, like a swap.'

'All right.'

We ran back. As we got near the park I took hold of both wheels and Gilbert dashed ahead, on the look-out. The coast was clear, so I ran to catch up. We wedged my heavy wheels between the plundered frame and the fence – nobody would nick them – then headed back to class.

'Thanks a lot, Gil,' I said.

'No problem, mate.'

Now I've got a good bike: I saved up for a top-class frame, Ollie gave me a spare saddle he'd nicked, Gilbert gave me the Shimano gears, Ashley gave me some other bits (he carried industrial wire cutters in his school bag so he could nick bike parts whenever he saw them); and now I had a pair of excellent wheels. My bike's nearly as good as everyone else's.

But not quite. Ollie and Ashley came across this bike in Notting Hill Gate with a Reynolds 753 frame, which costs hundreds, and they nicked that. Ashley already had a 753, and now Ollie had one too, though it was far too big for him, he couldn't get his feet on the ground. Their bikes were loads better than anybody else's.

One evening after school we were in the Gaiety, off the Gate, having a few beers. We'd locked our bikes up together outside, all eight of them, so people had to step off the pavement to walk past, and this tall, thin bloke came over to us. He was being all friendly, he said: 'Are you lot the bike nuts?'

We all said yeah.

'Some of those bikes are fucking nice.'

'Cheers,' said Ashley.

'Whose are the 753s?'

Ollie and Ashley said they were theirs. The guy asked what they were like to ride, and stuff like that. He said Ollie looked a little short, no offence, to have such a giant frame. The rest of us stopped paying much attention cause Ollie and Ashley were showing off – but when he went, Gilbert suddenly had this idea.

'Fucking hell, Ollie, man, that's probably the geezer whose frame you nicked.'

We couldn't see him anywhere. Perhaps he'd gone for the police. We abandoned our drinks and rushed out, unlocked the bikes and cycled off to a quiet corner of Hyde Park, to smoke a spliff and calm down.

Ollie should've painted over his frame, but he was too proud of the 753 sticker.

Gilbert and Manuel have got excellent jackets for nicking things, baggy leather jackets with elastic at the bottom which stops stolen goods from falling out.

We go to W. H. Smith in Notting Hill Gate. It should be safe because I haven't spotted that old manager for years, the one with the tinted glasses, and anyway, we look like eager students, walking thoughtfully round the book section upstairs, instead of eyeing up sweets. We nick new hardbacks and sell them to the bloke round the corner at the second-hand bookshop. We do it nearly every day, it raises easily enough cash to score all the dope we need.

Because I'm doing A-level English, I'm the expert on which books to nick. I told Gilbert and Mans that I read the book reviews in the newspapers to find out which ones were best, and they couldn't believe it. But when they got over that, they spotted a business opportunity: they told me to point out the books with the best reviews because that way they'd get more dosh second-hand.

I tell them to nick *Money* by Martin Amis, and *Coasting* by Jonathan Raban, and *Waterland* by Graham Swift (because I've read those three, and they seemed pretty good); and also anything by the Best of Young British Novelists. I was given a free bookmark at Waterstones in High Street Ken, when I bought my copy of *Coasting,* and it had a list of the Best of Young British Novelists; so even though I've never read anything by Kazuo Ishiguro, if Mans picks up one of his books and says 'Is this any good?' I can easily say yes.

Mr Wilson goes on about Martin Amis all the time, especially *The Rachel Papers*; he persuaded me to buy it. But he said: 'The trouble with young Amis is that it's virtually impossible to find a single passage which would be appropriate for studying in class: it's all full of swearwords and sex.'

The bloke at the second-hand bookshop is a miserable bastard, he always rips us off. We give him perfect, new copies of books that cost, say, £10.95, and he gives us a quid. Still, we always get about a fiver altogether, which is enough for about an eighth.

We were outside Boots in High Street Ken, sitting on the edge of this flowerbed, wondering what to do next. We'd bunked off the whole afternoon cause Manuel and Jase wanted to nick some shaving gear. In a single raid, Mans scored two boxed shavers, the ones advertised on telly (they cost tons). Jase only managed one box of aftershave, which he doesn't even wear.

People like me and Gilbert and Simon wanted to go to Kensington Gardens to smoke up, but Ashley was jealous of Mans' shavers, so he wanted to stay and nick some more.

Then this policeman appeared in front of us on a giant white horse.

Simon said: 'Whoah, heavy trip, man.'

Anyhow, the copper jumped down and started talking to this woman with crinkly hair that we hadn't noticed before. She had a walkie-talkie in her hand, and a badge with the Boots logo on it. A plain-clothes detective!

So the copper started asking who we were, and if we shouldn't be at school. He didn't bother to remove his riding helmet, but he took off his gloves and dug in his pocket for a pad and a pencil. Then he started at one end with me and Gilbert. I asked him why he wanted my name, and whether I had to give him it.

'After all, I haven't done anything wrong, so I don't see why I should tell you.'

'Look, this is only so there's a record of who I've been speaking to, and when I spoke to them. It doesn't mean you're under arrest, necessarily.'

So I gave him Alexander Ford's name and address. Then he asked if I'd empty my pockets, so I did that and gave him one of those looks Gilbert does when he's innocent – wide eyes and shoulders up by your ears. He patted my pockets to check they were empty, then moved on.

Gilbert gave him a false name too, before emptying his pockets, but Simon gave his real name and address, which was a bit shocking. Then Ollie gave his real name too, but complained that this was police brutality: 'This is harrassment, man,' he shouted, 'we haven't done nothing.'

The copper stared at Ollie sternly, saying we'd been spotted inside the shop stealing shavers. But he didn't bother checking Ollie's pockets after Ollie had emptied them. That was lucky, because Ollie was carrying a £10 draw of weed inside his jacket.

By the time the copper got to Jason, we were bricking it. Jase was going to have to hand over the aftershave. But he gave his real name and address – as if he was innocent – and when he emptied his pockets there was nothing there. The Boots detective pointed at Mans, the last one in the line, and said: 'He's the one I saw with the shavers.'

But Mans did the same as Jase. He gave his full name and address without any complaints, he was even smiling. Then he emptied his pockets, putting a dirty hanky into the copper's glove. So the copper looked behind us in the flowerbeds but couldn't see anything.

'Well, then, lads,' he said, 'I'm sorry to have bothered you.' And he got back on his horse and trotted off, taking care not to slip on the marble paving. The detective gave us a snaky look, as if to say, I know you did it, then went back in the shop.

We headed straight for Kensington Gardens; everybody was dying for a smoke to get over it all. I asked Mans how he'd got rid of it. It was brilliant, such quick thinking. As soon as the pig on a horse appeared, Mans had dug a little hole in the flowerbed and buried the boxes, with Jason's aftershave. Then

229

he'd covered it up with mud and stuck his finger down his throat to make himself puke on the earth above the stolen merchandise. He puked so quietly that nobody even heard him do it.

But the next morning the Boots detective uncovered the buried treasure beneath his dried-up puke and Mans was arrested for shoplifting. He took the blame for the aftershave too.

In the common room, we devised a practical joke in honour of Mans and his puke. We bought a can of vegetable soup and each of us concealed a couple of spoonfuls in our mouths. Then we ran up to a group of girls and pretended to puke on their table. At first, because of the diced carrots, they thought it was real, and screamed.

Speed

Around Easter, for the sixth-form five-a-side contest, Gilbert decided our class needed special preparation: 'We all have to take speed, so that we have more energy.' Gil was team captain.

The evening of the contest, outside the Sports block, he handed out little yellow pills to each of us. 'Everyone has to take it now, cause I don't trust you,' he commanded. We put the pills in our mouths and took swigs from a can of Coke that Ben, our goalie, had brought.

The three separate Sports halls had been opened up into one large space, with the wooden walls folded back, and proper five-a-side goals in place. Several teams were already kitted up and passing the ball around. Up on the balcony, a big audience was watching. One or two boys who had never shown any interest in football – fat Raphael, for one, and Max and Robin too – stood leaning over the railings. But most of the audience was girls.

None of us spoke as we filed into the empty changing room. We chucked everyone's bags on the floor, to make room for our own.

'All right, lads?' said Mr MacDonald, my History teacher. He loves football, he supports Man U (but he's bald and bearded, so he looks like Notts Forest's Archie Gemmill). He was referee for the contest.

'Yes, sir.'

'Yes, sir.'

We didn't even *kick* a ball for nearly half an hour. Our first game was the last one in the knockout. I wondered if the drug would have any effect on me. Speed was hot stuff: Anna told me about some bloke she knew who'd taken speed in an O-level exam. He'd wasted the entire three hours scribbling his name and candidate number all over the paper. But the little yellow pill hadn't made *me* feel different yet.

Then Mr MacDonald blew a whistle and called us on. Gilbert had allocated our positions – he'd be in midfield, Ben in goal, and I was to look after defence. The others would float towards the front with him – but like in all five-a-side we had to be flexible.

Gilbert called heads and won the toss, so we kicked off. I placed a foot on top of the ball, before tapping it towards him. Then everything changed. We didn't stop running.

In the normal course of things, we might have displayed some appreciation of tactics, and fancy passing. But not this time. I had tunnel vision. I ran as fast as I could, all over the place. Did I look for space, shout out for a pass? No. I joined the others, all chasing furiously after the ball. We dashed straight for it, and when we got close, we kicked it along the straightest route for goal, and galloped after it again. As we whizzed past them, people in the crowd actually gasped.

I was gasping myself. My breathing made me swell up. *Bom, bom, bom*. My heart beat ten times as fast as normal, echoing inside my head. My face was purple, and so was everyone else's. Mr MacDonald, who tried to keep up with us, with the whistle in his mouth and his eyebrows permanently raised, looked worried that one of us might keel over.

After every goal – even the fifth – Gilbert scooped the ball up from the net and ran back to the centre spot so the opposition could kick off as fast as possible.

Ben was protected from the opposition by our sheer energy. But all the same, he was permanently hunched up like a professional goalie facing a penalty, with his hands splayed in front of him – even when the ball was miles away. Looking out for danger, his eyes bulged wildly.

The speed worked excellently. In the face of our determination, the other team simply gave up.

We had one match to rest while the first semi-final took place.

Then we were on again, with our reputation to keep up. The crowd was clearly on our side, and we ran as hard as we could to please them – not that we seemed to have any choice. Again, my vision locked on to the ball, excluding everything else. My legs felt too long and too fast, as if they weren't really mine. Again, we scored five goals without any trouble, and got through to the final.

But we didn't get any time to catch our breath: the final began immediately. I was empty, totally lacking energy. I asked Ben to swap places after a couple of minutes, and borrowed his gloves. He raced out, but the rest of the team was winding down, dangling a leg as opponents raced past them. A big bloke on the other team rushed towards me and smacked the ball straight in my face; then tapped in a goal on the rebound.

I lay there stunned. Ben trotted back, and returned the ball to the centre spot, but the rest of the team was folded in half, out of breath. Ben tapped the ball to Gilbert, who made to pass it back, but the other team intercepted, and rushed at me again. I dived early, to protect my face, and the ball went the other way.

In the end, they scored about eight.

In the common room Sean West said he was going up to All Saints Road to get a £5 draw, and did anybody want to chip in? Well, Mans and Ashley already had enough, so we said no thanks, but a couple of others went along – a girl called Geraldine and a couple of boys from the upper sixth called Mark and Red.

Then when they got back, three-quarters of an hour later, we spotted them skinning up just outside the gates. It was a bit obvious, so it came as no surprise to hear they were caught. Some teacher upstairs happened to look out of the window and spotted them.

All the same, we pretended to be sympathetic, the next day, when we heard about it. Sean came in the common room and told us.

They'd met Daniel Murphy outside the gates and he'd asked if they had any dope. So they stopped right there and offered him a share, for cash, and then Mark started rolling up, without thinking.

But Sean was worried, so he stood well clear, and when the teacher pounced on them, Sean and Dan somehow escaped. That's about the luckiest thing that ever happened to old Big Hair.

The other three were taken to Dr Rushworth. He stood and shouted at them, telling them how stupid they were, saying they stood no chance in their exams if they wasted time on drugs. Then he phoned their parents and announced that they were indefinitely suspended.

Sean felt terrible about it, he phoned them that night and asked if he should give himself up. But Geraldine said there was no point him getting in trouble too.

The thing is, the school doesn't want to get rid of them because it's too embarrassing. You won't believe it, but Geraldine's mum used to teach here, and Red's aunt is still a teacher, and Mark's dad's some famous writer.

So they'll all probably be allowed back.

Snogging

In the pub the other night, Ellen told me Becky fancied me, she said I should steam in. So I bought Becky a drink and told her I wouldn't mind taking it outside so we could talk.

Becky was drunk, so she kept trying to brush my hair. She had a brush in her bag, and whenever I looked away (to check if we were being spied on) she took it out and tried to groom me. I hate brushing my hair, if I wanted it brushed I'd do it myself.

One time, she grabbed me by the neck and pulled down my head towards her. I thought she was going to brush my hair again, so I said: 'Oh come on, Becky, please don't . . .'

But in fact she started snogging me. She was so drunk her tongue was out of control. Her lips were all floppy. The thing is, I do fancy Becky a bit, but I didn't want to take advantage, so I asked her if she knew what she was doing.

She kept saying yes, and falling into my arms, and trying to snog me. So in the end I snogged her with a clear conscience.

But the next morning, in registration, the girls gave me a load of grief. Ellen took the piss, doing an impression of me.

'Oh *darling*, are you sure, are you positively *certain* you don't mind if we snog?'

Alison joined in: 'Oh honey, I don't want to take advantage of you . . .'

Everyone was killing themselves.

I couldn't believe Becky told them that. What a traitor. I mean, at least I *asked*, I could have been like Desmond and just *forced* her to snog me.

I love *The Rachel Papers*, it's like a guidebook to being cool. I wish I was Charles Highway, getting into Oxford without much effort and putting a copy of Blake by my bed to make girls desire sex.

There's one bit I thought might come in handy. It's when Charles Highway's getting off with this girl Rachel for the first time: he does her ear. I read it over and over again, it goes like this:

> I 'did' her left ear with the index finger of my right hand. If 'done' skilfully this can cause the subject to become ga-ga with arousal. The thing is *hardly to touch* the ear, to touch it as lightly as possible consistent with touching it at all. The nearer you get to not touching it the better. (I knew because I had had it 'done' to me, in the St Giles bus shelter, by a wonderful waitress. I had almost fainted, but I was seventeen then.)

Amazing what you can learn from books. I wonder if Mr Wilson 'does' ears, and if he knew about doing ears before he read Martin Amis? Anyway, I learnt that quote off by heart so I could test it.

I tried it out at Ashley's party. Most of the people there weren't from Holland Park, so it didn't matter if I got it wrong; word wouldn't get back.

After a few cans of Heineken, I was sitting on this sofa when a couple of girls came and sat at the other end of it, to chat. The nearest one had her back turned to me, which I thought was a bit rude, but I had checked her out on the way over and she looked OK. So after a decent interval, I leant over (watching out not to spill my beer) and positioned the index finger of my right hand over her left ear. Then I started *hardly to touch* it. She looked round straight away and saw me sprawling across the sofa. I thought it was best to make out there was nothing odd about what I was doing, so I said, 'Hi, how's that?'

She picked up her bum and moved a little further away from me. After a second I tried again. I tried *hardly to touch* her ear, but I wasn't well balanced, so I probably touched it too firmly. She looked round again and said: 'Do you mind?'

I said: 'Not at all, if it gives you pleasure.'

She got up and walked off, leaving her friend behind. So I told her friend all about Martin Amis, and Charles Highway, and asked if *she*'d like her ear done. She smiled and said all right, so I moved up closer and gave it another go. Then she snogged me.

After a few minutes' snogging, we paused for breath, and I spotted Gilbert giving me encouraging faces, and *her* friend giving her *dis*couraging faces.

She said her name was Helen: 'Let's go in one of the bedrooms.'

I followed, holding her hand. Inside my pants, my dick was going crazy.

After we'd jammed a chair under the doorhandle, I sat on the chair to make double sure and invited her to sit on top. I'm so audacious. I asked her to take her top off, acting like it's the sort of thing I say all the time. I could hardly believe it, but she agreed. She had a white bra, with frilly bits – not like the ones I spotted when June and Kylie were getting changed, which were smooth and grey.

I told her to take her bra off too, but she said I was getting a bit ahead of myself and sat on my lap for some straight snogging. She told me she could feel my dick digging into her thigh. It was a bit embarrassing, so I just said: 'Yeah.'

While continuing to do her left ear with my right hand, I managed to slip down one of her bra straps, so I could check

237

out one of her breasts (I'd never seen one before). Now, I admit I'd drunk a few Heinekens, but I simply couldn't *believe* how many bumps there were on her nipple. I'd always thought it was a big dark circle with just one bump, like in cartoons, but actually that bump was more like *two* bumps with a fine line between them, and all around it were hundreds of tiny bumps. I stroked them to see what would happen, but suddenly the door behind my chair flew open and all my friends came in to see what I was up to.

Helen was on the floor with one breast sticking out and me on top of her. She was furious, she started swearing and pushed everyone out, while she pulled her bra on. She pushed me out too.

Camp

The freaks, or the hippies, or whatever you want to call us, we've all decided to go camping on an acid weekend.

It was Ashley's idea, based on some Freak Brothers comic. Ashley loves that stuff, he always wears T-shirts from Ken Market showing Fat Freddy's Cat with a spliff in his mouth.

There's one tent between nine of us, and it only fits three people, but Gil said that doesn't matter because we won't want any sleep anyway, we'll be tripping.

If you want to know the truth, I don't know how I'm going to get out of this one, without losing my friends. They take acid all the time, but the last thing I want is to jump off a cliff, or out of a tree, or walk down the tube tracks like Shelley. A few weeks ago, Ollie went to Glastonbury with Simon, Ashley and Andreas. They bought powerful tabs of acid from somebody, and Simon started to see things: he thought Ollie's ear was an oyster, and bit off the lobe. Ashley made him spit it out, and took Ollie to hospital. His ear's still red where the two parts were stitched together, but even Ollie still thinks acid's a brilliant idea.

Cause he's so small, Ollie's a bit of a natural victim. Even this kid in Crispin's class had a go at him, calling him a wanker outside Thorpe Lodge. They had a fight, and Ollie was embarrassed as hell because he only managed a draw.

We all met at Gilbert's house, with our bikes. Andreas (whose dad's rich) has got a moped, so he brought that, and carried the tent. The rest of us had little rucksacks for drinks and sandwiches.

Before we left, Gil showed me the tabs. They had Batman on them. He slipped two into a cup of coffee for his big sister, Sonia, then gave it to her. After he'd watched her finish it, we cycled off. Everyone was killing themselves about what a trip she'd have. She wouldn't even know she was tripping.

But inside my head I was thinking, We shouldn't have done that, it was dangerous – what if she runs under a car, or jumps out of the window?

Anyway, we cycled all the way to Putney before stopping for a revitalizing doobie. Then we carried on to somewhere in Surrey, way outside London, miles from anywhere.

Straight away, Simon, Ashley, Mans, Ollie, Andreas, Tristan and Jase dropped their tabs and walked off into the wood so it could get started. Me and Gil set up the tent, and made a bonfire. Then Gil took his own tabs, and handed me one. I washed it down with a swig of beer, then Gil rolled a doob to keep me calm.

I was desperate. I imagined all these psychedelic images appearing, but that wasn't the acid, it was my imagination. I said: 'Gil, don't let me do anything dangerous.'

'All right, mate.'

'And I'll keep an eye on you.'

We sat staring at the fire, passing the spliff, as the sun went down.

It was pretty dark when Ashley returned. He was already tripping, he said the pores on my skin looked like they were fish mouths, opening and shutting.

Then the others came back too. We all sat by the fire, amazed by its patterns. After a few minutes Gil went into the tent with a torch and we saw him making patterns on the side with the light, spinning circles round and round. He was mumbling: 'Yvonne, Yvonne . . .' It lasted for hours, then we noticed each other watching him, and laughed.

Although it was dark, you could see the trees swaying in the wind, lit up by the campfire. I thought they looked like tired old ladies, bending over, but I could still tell that they were trees really, so I didn't think I was tripping yet.

Ashley drained our last bottle of beer and said: 'We need some more byoooooze.'

So Simon dug into his pockets and told Andreas to fetch some from an off-licence, on his moped. Everyone thought that was a good idea, so we all emptied our pockets, we gave him every penny.

But Andreas didn't want the pigs to catch him riding his moped while he was off his head. Jason told him to drive without his headlamps; then no coppers could see him.

And that's what he did, he put on his helmet, revved up, and started riding through the trees without his light. We laughed like mad.

But then everyone got worried in case Andreas crashed, or was murdered by a mad woodman. We sat round the fire mourning him, staring at the pattern of the flames. I didn't dare look beyond the circle of the fire, because I could hear pirates approaching. Once I looked up and I saw Smee from *Peter Pan* running off to hide.

We sat there for hours, worrying. Simon said his acid had worn off, so he rolled a super-strength spliff, mostly weed, with a little tobacco added for flavour. We smoked it in honour of our dead friend Andreas. I stared at the flames of the bonfire as though it was Andreas' funeral pyre. I had tears in my eyes.

We had to collect some more sticks, but everybody was scared of the wood, so we went as a group, all eight of us sticking close together. By the time we got back there was still no sign of him.

Then we heard a police helicopter buzzing overhead. It was getting closer all the time. We couldn't see any lights.

But it wasn't a helicopter: Andreas burst out of the wood on his moped, still driving without his headlamps. You can't believe how happy we were to see him. Everyone gave him a hug, and patted him on the back fifty times.

Then Ashley said: 'So where's the byooooze, Andy, man?'

Andreas sat down and explained. After a long drive through the woods, he'd found a road, and followed it until he saw an off-licence. 'I spent every last penny on hundreds of those little bottles of beer,' he said, and we all cheered.

'There were so many bottles, I didn't think I'd be able to carry them. So I asked for a black bin bag and put it all in that. Then I drove with just one arm, carrying the bin bag in the other.'

'Excellent!' said Jason.

'Murdah!' said Gil, pretending to be black.

'But the thing is, guys,' said Andreas, 'I got really paranoid after a while, and decided to stash the beers before driving back here. It took me hours to spot the bonfire.'

'So where did you stash it?' asked everyone at once.

'Well, the truth is, I just don't remember. It's somewhere in the wood.'

That was all our money gone, but we didn't really mind. Jason jumped on Ollie and told him to take off his jumper and his jeans. Ollie didn't really want to, but he was so pleased to see Andreas again he did what he was told.

Then Jason threaded a stick through the clothes and dangled them over the bonfire, burning them in honour of Andreas. Ollie sat down on a rock, wearing nothing but underpants and socks, sulking.

Upper sixth

After retaking their O levels, practically *all* my friends left school. No more Gil, no more Manuel, not any of them.

Sometimes at the weekend I see the hippies at parties. But mostly I don't. There's nobody left to smoke dope with, so I've more or less given up. I never go in the common room now, I leave it to the lower sixth. It was hilarious, but I want to go to Oxford, and you have to do *some* work for that.

Julia and Kylie are in some of my classes, they've kind of adopted me, for sitting next to and writing silly messages. Then there's girls like Alison and Melissa – I stopped seeing much of Naimh last year after she snogged some boy in the upper sixth; I missed my chance. (Anyway, she's left too.) But let's face it, even though girls are sexy, they aren't the same as *friends*.

Most of the time, school's just incredibly boring.

At home, I've started reading tons of novels, but I've more or less abandoned hope in History and French because in History I get an E for *every single essay*, and they never tell me where I'm going wrong. As for French, Ms Avis is too stupid to help, and Ms O'Reilly doesn't want to. I wish I had Dr Bowes again, I really like him; when I talk to him in the corridor, I reckon he'd be brilliant for A level.

The only ones who get me fired up are Mrs Burns and Mr Wilson. They recommend all sorts of stuff to read, tell me the names of books I'd enjoy. Not just Martin Amis. At the moment I'm reading loads of Dickens. The characters make me laugh, especially the ones with catchphrases – like that friend of Mr Brownlow in *Oliver Twist* who says 'I'll eat my head.' They're eccentric as hell.

Mr Wilson lent me the school's videotape of *Macbeth*, directed by Roman Polanski. I watched it again and again, learning the speeches with exactly the same intonation as the actors: Peter Finch, Martin Shaw (from *The Professionals*), and this woman called Francesca Annis as Lady Macbeth, going nuts and walking about naked. It should help for my exams.

Mrs Burns tried to get me on to Jane Austen, which is one of our set authors, but I can't really see what's so good about it. Nobody does anything much, except sit around at home or go visiting their neighbours. Mrs Burns told me I'd grow to like it eventually. I was put off slightly by this other teacher, Mr Scunthorpe, who told me Jane Austen was boring. Now, Mr Scunthorpe's this sad bastard who wears string vests and fake tan to impress the girls. He's a total phoney, and he's cruel too: he keeps a little dog, a red setter, trapped inside his car all day, only letting it out for a run at breaktime. Once he jogged past a group of us, his hair streaming behind him and a medallion jiggling about on his chest – but he slipped on to his arse, virtually squashing the dog to death. Everyone in the whole school spotted that and laughed their heads off. So if it came to an argument between Mr Scunthorpe and Mrs Burns, about Jane Austen or anything else, I'd stick with Mrs Burns.

My dad gave me a credit card for Waterstones – it's purple like their bookmarks, with a big golden W – so I can buy whatever books I need. There's a limit on it, but I still spend a hell of a lot. I go on my own, I never nick any books. I'm building up a crime-free library.

The gay man in charge of the High Street Ken branch sometimes tries to chat me up, which is embarrassing, because somebody might be looking.

* * *

Some people who started A levels last year have given up because they're crap. Only people who have a reasonable chance of success still turn up. Now everyone in my classes is posh – except some of the teachers.

None of them say 'fucking' (except occasionally, for impact), and they all enunciate properly, no dropped Hs and Ts. Max drives to school in a Peugeot. Robin lives in one of the grandest streets off High Street Ken. They both wear designer clothes. Nowadays, if I was to turn up at school with expensive tracksuit tops, like Bug Eye's Fila, or a Pringle jumper like John McGuire's, or a Gabbicci roll-neck with frayed jeans like Gilbert, I'd be laughed at by the posh kids. They'd call me a casual. Just like Bug Eye and John laughed at me for wearing bogus Marks & Spencer imitations.

Nowadays you've got to get clothes in Ken Market: expensive jackets, shirts with paisley patterns, and patent-leather Doc Martens.

I have to change my whole character all over again.

When I turn up for interview at Oxford, it's no use being the same person who went out smoking dope with the freaks. I'll need to revert to what I'm *really* like, underneath it all. I'll be the slightly posh – well, not *posh*, but definitely middle-class – son of parents who were at Oxford before me.

The day after the Oxford entrance exam, I was walking down the north corridor staring into space, trying to remember what I'd written for one of the answers, when this gang of boys from two or three years below me approached. There wasn't anybody else around, so the biggest one – not much smaller than me – said: 'Oy, give me 10p.'

I couldn't believe it. In the old days, when Justice or Paul Grant picked on sixth-formers, they picked on plums. This boy's brother was in my year (until he left after O levels), his name was Lloyd.

I said: 'Don't give me that, man, I'm Lloyd's mate.'

He wasn't impressed. He said: 'You lying batty man,' and whacked me in the eye. He hit me so hard, I fell over.

They walked off, everyone in the gang having a chuckle. I got up and carried on walking to the English office, looking for Mrs Burns. She spotted blood coming out of my eye, so I went home and lay down.

After two whole years getting an E for every History essay, I was convinced I was going to fail. One of my History teachers, Mr MacDonald, told me he'd inflated my prospects on the university entrance because he liked me. He'd put me down for a C, which means, I suppose, that a D might be possible.

I went into that exam like a condemned man. I'd done just enough revision to have a few facts if I needed them. I started each essay with a gag – I thought I might as well amuse the examiner.

One essay was about the Wall Street Crash, I had to explain how dreadful that was. I started the essay: 'Two weeks after Dow Jones killed himself, the price of shares in New York was already 50 per cent higher than when he opened the window and jumped.'

Brilliant. Afterwards, I quoted it to Frida Chase, the woman who taught us foreign history, and she smiled. She was sitting close to me on the same desk, a bit *too* close considering there was nobody else in the room.

'Well done,' she said, 'let's just hope it's enough. After all, if you insist on going to an élitist university like Oxford you'll have to be pretty sharp.' Then she patted me on the thigh.

She hates Oxford, she's always going on about it like that; she probably got turned down for it in her youth.

I got turned down too. I got the letter after Christmas. I was gutted. Three of us had applied, but only one person got in:

Kylie. Next time I see Jason I must tell him. He'll never believe it, because Kylie is useless at Sport.

On the last day of the exams, there was a party at this bloke's house, but I didn't know anybody, so I drank loads of cider. I can't even tell you what time the party ended, because I've forgotten everything that happened after ten p.m.

I woke up this morning and couldn't think where I was. The first thing I saw was the sky, clear blue with a few small clouds whizzing across. I moved my hand from under my head and saw blood on the back of it. Then I noticed I was lying on the back seat of a car, with beads of broken glass under my head and all over the floor.

The window by my feet was broken. I sat up and looked out. The car – which I didn't recognize, was parked on Notting Hill Gate, on the main road. I must have broken into it after drinking all that cider, smashed the window and gone to sleep in a complete stranger's car.

Luckily I'd been woken by the early daylight: my watch told me it was only five-forty-five a.m., so nobody was around.

I got out as fast as I could, then spotted dried puke on the pavement near by, and matching traces on my shoe. At the nearest bus stop, I looked to see if the buses had started yet.

I felt in my pocket for my travelcard. It was gone, and with it the Waterstones credit card. After wiping the puke off my shoes, I started to walk.

PART III

The Rushworth Papers

I went to university, picked up two degrees in English, then joined my old classmates on the job market. Some of them, set free after O level, had already been employed for seven years; and as I sat in the jobcentre waiting for advice, I recognized that this gave them some advantage over me.

As a student I'd worked the previous summer at Inter Sport in High Street Ken. I'd grovelled at the knee of customers in search of chunky sports shoes, easing their stinking feet into trainers that I'd retrieved from the shop's basement. One day Samuel Thomas had walked in, wearing a suit, accompanied by a glamorous girl in a catsuit, as I sat cross-legged in front of a ten-year-old boy and his mother, lacing a pair of Adidas trainers. Samuel graciously acknowledged me, asking why I worked in a shoe shop, and telling me, unasked, about his worldly success, the flat he had in Ibiza, his plans to break into the emerging markets that had appeared when the Iron Curtain came down. Before leaving, Samuel asked his glamorous friend if I could fetch her anything to try on, in exactly the tone he'd have used if he were my employer.

Since then, I had heard that Samuel was going around using me as an argument against taking A levels and going on to higher education. 'Look at me,' he told people he met, 'I didn't do A levels and I'm doing fine, but a boy from school who went to university has ended up working in Freeman Hardy Willis.' The first time I heard that, I was stung, offended (he hadn't

251

even got the shop name right); but now I just wanted a job, any job. For weeks on end, I waited for my applications to turn into offers. I sat watching television with my brother, himself on holiday from university. He passed me a copy of a glossy magazine. 'Have you seen this?' he asked.

ES magazine, which comes free with London's *Evening Standard*, featured on its cover a picture of four Holland Park pupils. They were perching on a radiator in a grand corner of Thorpe Lodge. Two boys, two girls. Two clutching books to their chest, the others striking a pose. One black pupil, a couple of (I guessed) Asians, and a white boy whom I immediately recognized as the son of an actress, Una Stubbs. The coverline read 'Holland Park: the Ins and Outs of a Cool School'.

I flicked through to page 22, the opening spread. The headline read SCENES FROM THE CLASS STRUGGLE IN W8; beside it was a portrait of the current head, Maggie Pringle, who like Rushworth came to Kensington after a spell in charge of an East End comp. Opposite her was another photo of those four children from the magazine's cover. This time it was labelled: 'Joe Henson, Bindo Oye, Sepehr Sarkoob and Nora Kaissi'. Wild names, wild school, I thought, then turned the page and saw Dr Rushworth, peering out with his hands clasped and his tiny head craning forward, as though still waiting to hear why I hadn't finished my Latin homework. Beneath him was an old cartoon about Holland Park by Mark Boxer (*that*'s how fashionable the school had once been). And on page 26, *ES* reproduced a front page from the *Daily Mirror*. The headline: 1,000 CHILDREN IN RIOT AT A SCHOOL. Inevitably, the article was negative. I didn't like to see my own school run down so publicly. Unprompted, pride surged through me as I read Rushworth's bullish defence of the school. Especially when he said: 'There is a current wisdom – no, I won't say wisdom, I'll say stupidity – that bright children suffer in mixed-ability classes. It's heartbreaking to go through all the same arguments. It makes me despair about civilization.

However bad mixed-ability teaching is, it is better than streaming.'

Over the following week, I got to work on a letter. This would thank Dr Rushworth for all his efforts – including some I'd not heard of before, which were outlined in the magazine article – and it would also give me a chance to display to him my own verbal prowess.

I cast the letter in verse. It went like this:

To: Dr Rushworth

No other pupils took that class of yours:
Alone I had to study, clause by clause,
And battle on my own through *Gallic Wars*.
Great Caesar split his French work into three,
Your undivided Latin conquered me.
Your last and least good Latin student, I
Shall not forget you till the day I die.
Great praise perhaps, from one whose name
You'll maybe not recall (nor hear again),
But, Dr Rushworth, I can only pray
You also don't recall how, every day
You taught, alone I'd badly conjugate,
Decline, mis-call, and hopelessly translate.
Your spirits sunk (declined!) to weary state,
(This rhyme is easy with words Latinate!),
You must have cursed those hours that slowly passed
And wished that you'd *declined* to help when asked.
But now I've learned my *Path to Latin* books,
And anyone can see my notes, who looks.

It's five years since I left the school, since when
My friends have changed from nasty kids to men,
And I've grown up as well, and learnt the debt
That I, and countless others, can't pay yet –

Indeed, we'll never fully reimburse
Your kind hard work, so please accept this verse.
It shows at least that I'm not on the street,
And not on drugs, but firmly on my feet –
Iambic feet (I'm writing in my seat).
I'd like to say my life's no small success:
I'm happy, widely read, and liked no less,
And saying this should guarantee your pleasure –
Though I'm aware success has no true measure.
You said, and I agree, that when school's mixed,
The children's future lives are not so fixed,
For good or bad. There was a year or two
When I was sure I'd Sink, not Swim; but who
With more facility can quote from Pope?
And who of Byron more to know can hope?
Some few perhaps, and yet, is that to Swim?
It is for me, but not for him, or him.
To Swim, for Dan, from tutor-set 5.5
Was, 'Buy a van, and early learn to drive.'
These days, he takes cream cakes from store to store,
Returns to base, and fills his van with more.
He loves his work, and never thinks of rhyme:
He'd say, if asked, he doesn't have the time.
His day's work done, he props up public bars,
And talks of vans, and dreams of flashy cars.
He thinks this great success, which I think grim –
I gladly leave success like that to him.
I, like Descartes, can prove with little ink
I am (the school's success), *because I think*.

We all believe, and with much justice too,
That we are right to do the things we do,
Except unhappy sorts who can't decide
Which trip to take, and don't enjoy the ride.

Some few jump off: I know of three who died.
But all the blame for these by no means lies
With you, nor our old school, nor families
Which can't provide the homes we think they should:
Such circumstances also bring forth good.

You fought for what you thought was best for schools,
So though you helped the slow you brooked no fools:
Impatient at his son, my father's letter
You answered saying I could do much better:
And you were right, I'm not so foolish since.

Before the thugs I never saw you wince:
When school was hijacked one spring afternoon
By Paul and Des (and Rooney, their baboon)
And called to an impromptu soap-box session
On racists in the school, my painting lesson,
And every other lesson going on
Was stopped, to see you talking sense to Paul
Onstage (ironically, as I recall,
Fat Rooney was most racist of them all).
At last you won Paul Grant to give the mike
To you, and Des to make an exit, like
An actor who recalls his cue's long past;
Then fat Mark Rooney, last to leave, left last.
Assemblies never saw headteachers deft
As you, before you came, or since you left.

Some colleagues on your staff I'd like to thank include
My English teachers, Burns and Wilson, who'd
Be up there with the top headteachers now
If I could choose, and so would Mr Gow;
And Geoff MacDonald taught a lot of sense;
For six long years poor Dr Bowes taught French
With little thanks from me; my rhyme, again,

Sincerest praise distorts, for Tony Makin.
And you! Back home you had to bear your thankless
Work, when some thug gave you two broken ankles.

You'll maybe wonder why this note was penned
And worry that a boy from school could send
It to the right address. Perhaps you think
It's not so strange, it's just a waste of ink;
Perhaps you'll never read so far as here;
Perhaps my numbers grate upon your ear;
Or all or some or none of these are true:
But only know I wrote this stuff for you.
It's not a piece of homework set in class,
And I've been wasting days here on my arse
This page a blank before me. Never mind.
If you have read this far, you've been too kind.

Three years after I posted that poem, I determined to write this book. I spoke to Dr Rushworth several times, wrote to him and met him twice, to ask his advice and opinion. Initially, in the telephone call with which I first revived our acquaintance, he was welcoming. I sensed that he'd been grateful for my rhymes, despite their self-serving overtone.

I invited myself round to see him. When he opened the door to his house a week later he smiled warmly – though his pale blue eyes retained an icy quality that I remembered from school. 'You haven't changed at all,' I said, truthfully, as he nipped ahead of me up the stairs. He laughed that off, with a quote from Brecht – which I didn't recognize – suggesting that this compliment might be intended as backhanded.

At the top of the stairs, he ushered me into a book-lined study. A vast portion of the room was filled by a polished wooden table, which had been Dr Rushworth's desk at school – a gift on retirement.

'Would you like some tea?' he asked, then darted out to fetch it. Some moments later, we were discussing school when the door opened, and a hand reached in to place a cup of steaming tea, with matching saucer, on a level surface. Addressing the hand, Dr Rushworth said: 'Thank you, dear.' And then the hand withdrew.

Here I was, visiting Mr Chips; the end of the movie. For an hour and a half, we caught up with each other. Then, at my prompting, Dr Rushworth outlined some notable events in the history of Holland Park, and his own career. As he spoke, he came out with complete sentences from the magazine article which had reminded me of his existence three years previously. He even mentioned the 'current wisdom, no, stupidity' that mixed-ability teaching damages bright children. He must have read that article so often it had stuck in his brain.

He recalled the staff shortage: 'It was terrible at one stage, we were having to send sometimes two classes home each day. The worst was about 1973, I had a huge chart on my table to calculate the teachers. ILEA was recruiting abroad. People from the Antipodes would have been in a class within about ten minutes!'

And the unions: 'These were difficult days because of the union,' he said. 'The NUT is nothing like what it was in those days. There were lightning strikes at the drop of a hat. The NUT used to pass resolutions supporting any freedom movement anywhere. Once, around 1979, the union got everybody to hand in their resignation to the NUT representative, to give in if the ILEA did not agree to something or other.'

The door opened, and the woman's hand appeared again, bearing a plate with an apple strudel. This too was placed before me, though I still saw no more than the hand and forearm. 'Thank you so much,' I said, as the hand withdrew once more.

I asked Dr Rushworth about his own role, and how, towards the end of his headship, he had steered a merger with two other schools. 'Oh yes, that could have been ruinous,' he said. 'At

257

first the staff at the other schools were terrified. But we had an enormous number of discussions. I circulated every paper to every member of staff. That was very exciting, organizationally.'

And his assemblies? 'Assembly is very important, just for the school to see itself. Thinking of the assemblies was agony, every weekend. It was like a vicar preparing a sermon. I did one about the death of Jean-Paul Sartre and another about the death of Paul Robeson . . .'

'The assembly I remember you making most clearly', I interrupted, 'was about how black and white children should live together in harmony . . .'

'Really! Well that's fascinating that you mention that,' he said, rising from his chair and pulling a square piece of cardboard from a shelf. 'I was given this record just after I made that assembly, by my deputy head Dr Johnson. It's the song by that Beatle, McCartney, and Stevie Wonder. Do you know, it was in the charts when I gave that assembly, but I'd never even heard of it!'

Day in the life

In December 1995, the headmaster of a school in west London was killed when he intervened in a fight between teenagers outside his school. TV stories about Philip Lawrence consistently used a particular piece of old footage, showing him entering his school, and sitting behind his desk. One of many such occasions was the day a jury convicted the boy responsible for Mr Lawrence's death: those same clips were spooled into a report for the local BBC news. But that report lasted rather longer than the old Lawrence footage, so the BBC's reporter was obliged to splice into his package additional footage from an archive. Sitting at home watching this account of the trial, I saw shots of children milling about in front of a school library and sports block. But they weren't from Mr Lawrence's own school in Maida Vale, they were from Holland Park Comprehensive. Once again, the cameras had found Sir Leslie Norman's glassy walkways hard to resist. Implicitly, and presumably without doing it deliberately, the court report had linked Holland Park with the killing of a headteacher. Soon after that, a similar connection was made when the brother of Linford Christie was killed in a street fight. In a full-page feature on his troubled youth, the *Observer* pointed out that the sprinter's brother was educated at Holland Park.

A year or so before that, the *Independent* ran a photo on its front page which presented sneering Holland Parkers playing truant. In the caption, readers were informed that Holland Park had scored worse than virtually any school in the country in the national league table of bunking off. Not, certainly, the most helpful publicity – and the *Independent* is a relatively friendly paper: one of its three founders, Matthew Symonds, went to school at Holland Park; and Polly Toynbee, currently assistant editor, is the girl who transferred to Holland Park from Badminton with just four O levels, then scooped a scholarship to St Anne's College, Oxford.

Wherever you look, the comprehensive experiment undertaken by Holland Park finds discouragement. One of the biggest education stories of the 1990s concerned the choice of secondary school for Labour Party leader Tony Blair's children. Blair sent his oldest boy, Euan, all the way across London from Islington to the selective London Oratory, a near-neighbour of Holland Park, which had taken advantage of Conservative legislation by 'opting out' of local authority control, deriving its funds from central government as a 'grant-maintained' school. Labour policy at this time remained firmly against schools opting out – but Blair insisted he would not make a choice 'on the basis of what is the politically correct thing to do', and his friends pointed out that the Oratory suited the family's religious requirements; but all the same it's easy to contrast his choice with that exercised by an earlier middle-class Labour figurehead, Blair's near-namesake Tony Benn. Blair, like Benn, set a trend. Just as Tony Crosland and Roy Jenkins can be said to have followed Benn's lead, so, more recently, Harriet Harman followed Blair by dispatching her son to a grant-maintained school. Labour-voting supporters of the comprehensive system were devastated; some suggested the comprehensive system was finished.

Since I left Holland Park, education in England and Wales has changed considerably, with a sequence of Conservative ministers introducing numerous schemes designed to shake things up. This book could not be complete without paying a last visit to the school. I decided to interview the current head, Mary Marsh, observe some lessons, chat to pupils and teachers. Arrangements were made.

By chance, the date of my visit was historic. Just weeks before Britain was to throw out the Conservatives in favour of Blair's Labour Party – terminating the Tory rule which began only weeks before my first lessons at Holland Park, before all but the oldest of current students was born – I found myself in the thick of Holland Park's own election.

I stand outside the head's office, waiting for her to finish a meeting. Beside me is a boy from Year Seven, which I used to call the first year, waiting to be scolded for causing trouble in class (he tells me, without great pride, as if recounting an experiment which failed, that he made a girl cry). With his shaven head, he looks like some medieval penitent, but in no other respect does he suggest apology; on the contrary, he keeps clenching his fists. Beside my elbow stands an edition of *Chambers Encyclopaedia*, slightly older than the school itself. Flicking through one volume, I find a section concerned with education, containing the following sentence: 'In Britain, the general opinion seems to be that, where numbers permit, the advantage lies with separate classes for boys and girls.'

My reading is interrupted by the tannoy: one lesson ends and pupils begin to shuffle towards the next. Over the loud-speakers, a boy introducing himself as Marcel gives details of the Holland Park election. He says: 'There has been a fall in unemployment. Students must remember to bring library cards to vote in the sixth-form common room.'

Eventually the office door opens, and Mrs Marsh, an attractive woman scarcely old enough to be my mother, invites me in with a friendly smile. On the walls of her L-shaped room are countless drawings and paintings by students. In one corner is a table with ten seats round it, used, presumably, for committee meetings; but I'm offered one of four easy chairs by the window. I choose the very spot where, sitting in my first Latin lesson with Dr Rushworth nearly fifteen years earlier, I had watched through the curtains an episode of bullying masterminded by Shelley, the boy killed on Tube tracks, who's now been dead for longer than he was ever alive.

Mrs Marsh, who came to Holland Park from a grant-maintained school in Bushey, Hertfordshire, won the job against competition from thirty-nine other candidates. She's a thoroughly modern headteacher. On her desk squat pieces of technology which Dr Rushworth managed without: a TV, a computer, a printer. Most heads, these days, have this type of equipment at their command, but few can claim to have served on the Information Technology Working Group which formed a part of Sir Ron Dearing's curriculum review. Mrs Marsh, however, did precisely that. She's an IT nut. No longer, under her headship, are the school's stairways decorated with copies of old masters – Bruegel's *Fall of Icarus*, Manet's *Bar at the Folies-Bergères*. Instead, on the stairwells hang a series of blown-up photographs depicting pupils at work on computers. As well as the IT expertise, Mrs Marsh has a masters degree in Business Administration, and she's a member of the independent think-tank, Demos. Impressive credentials, and altogether appropriate for a woman who has been described by the *Times Educational Supplement* as possibly the country's highest-paid teacher (the post was originally advertised at £46,000–£62,000 plus car).

With around 150 staff, including special-needs teachers, and ten times as many pupils, Holland Park is now the only fully comprehensive school in the Royal Borough of Kensington and Chelsea. To show its commitment, the local authority has thrown money at it – around £4 million was recently spent on the buildings alone. Even the gardens, heavily trampled during my time, look well tended. Among headteachers, this must be a dream post. What could possibly top it? 'I don't know what you do after running Holland Park,' says Mrs Marsh, modestly; before popping out of her office and into the corridor for a word with some boys who are making too much noise as they move to their next lesson. Then she returns, shuts the door, and we talk.

Mrs Marsh proves masterly at 'selling' Holland Park. She hands me a videotape containing a six-minute feature on the school, largely upbeat, which was shown on *Channel 4 News* a few months earlier. The TV cameras, she explains, were back last week, when Holland Park played host to the Prime Minister, John Major, and a couple of his ministerial colleagues. That had turned out to be Major's last official function before he finally called the long-awaited general election. Having only received thirty-six hours' notice of the visit – officially in recognition of the school's sports programme – Mrs Marsh is satisfied that it proved a success. 'We were on *Channel 4* and *Sky News*,' she smiles. But it's clear that, at this school perhaps more than others, a visit by Conservative politicians, in the run-up to a general election which they look certain to lose, is not entirely good PR. 'We tried to do it very low-key,' adds Mrs Marsh; and indeed I later discover that angry teachers have insisted on discussing the merits of the visit at a forthcoming union meeting.

It seems unlikely that Mrs Marsh rose to her current eminence by sounding off angrily at union meetings. Before coming to see her, as well as swotting up on recent educational reform, I had found a few dissident teachers, and asked them to prime me with questions. One especially bitter figure urged me to ask Mrs Marsh whether she intended to impose a dress code on teachers; another told me speeches at leaving parties were banned after one of my own former teachers had used the occasion of his departure to speak 'bluntly' about his colleagues. But she sidesteps all my traps.

Does she bear a grudge against the prosperous local residents who continue to send their children to other schools? Nope: on the contrary, she insists that parents sometimes tell her they've been troubled by their conscience, and they 'want to give Holland Park a chance'.

I reel off a list of well-known figures who have sent their children to Holland Park since it opened: entertainers and artists such as Ivor Cutler, Jim Dale, Jimmy Jewel, Bob Monkhouse, Molly Parkin, the American film director John Huston; writers like Jeffrey Bernard, Gavin Ewart, Ian Hamilton, John and Penelope Mortimer, Philip Toynbee; musicians Alexis Corner and Michael Nyman; and other public figures such as Peter Parker, Tony Benn, Tony Crosland and Roy Jenkins. Mrs Marsh, nodding, observes that celebrities continue to send their offspring: one who does is the actress Francesca Annis. (How embarrassing for her children. Just suppose that old video of *Macbeth* were shown during a cover lesson. At the first sign of a naked madwoman, classmates could shout, with absolute truth: 'It's your mum!')

All right, Mrs Marsh, but many of the pupils at Holland Park are not so – *ahem* – elevated. What about troublemakers, at least ten of whom were sent to off-site units during the last year? Of course, she responds, hands still calmly folded on her lap, there'll always be difficult pupils: some of them come from rather disturbed backgrounds.

And all those children who can't even speak English? Don't they pose a problem? She turns this into an opportunity to boast: 'We have about three hundred pupils, out of 1500, whose parents have come here as refugees.'

OK, but out of 240 children who joined in Year Seven, a hundred had already left by Year Nine: isn't that a shockingly high turnover? There is indeed, she accepts, a high pupil turnover, but that is at least partly accounted for by the movement of refugees.

And you've introduced 'setting' in some subjects; does that mean you've abandoned the principle of mixed-ability teaching?
'No.

'Many people's idea of what goes on in schools', smiles Mary Marsh, 'is distorted. Parents are 80 per cent satisfied about their own children's school. Some do believe that there are terrible schools, but the inspectors have said schools are good and well-organized places. Senior businesspeople in eminent positions are quite clearly amazed when they come in and see how much we do with limited resources.' What sort of businesspeople? 'Chief executives of Fortune 100 companies and other senior directors, national business leaders, many of them people who might send their children to independent schools or else to a state school in a leafy suburb, or a shire county.'

Mrs Marsh guides me through the subject of league tables. In some such score-charts, such as the one recording absenteeism which had won Holland Park its picture on the front page of the *Independent*, the statistics are provided by schools themselves. Some choose to doctor the information, others don't. At least Holland Park is honest. Or again, consider the statistics which show the percentage of successful exam candidates. Schools like Holland Park allow even unpromising candidates to sit exams, while rivals, with their minds fixed firmly on league tables, put forward only those pupils with a strong chance of passing. The result: Holland Park, with plenty of failures, moulders at the bottom of government tables, while rivals who refused weak candidates the chance to take exams achieve as much as 100 per cent success.

'If people are not reaching the level expected for the average child – well, that can't be possible for everyone! Some children start with a big disadvantage, it takes them longer.' As for the tests, so much is expected of them that finding the right questions can prove difficult: 'We want to assess the child, inform the child, inform the parents, assess this year's group against last year's, also compare schools, assess the local authority and also measure national trends. That is a lot of measurements to get out of just one instrument.'

Let's move on, shall we, to the National Curriculum. In general, Mrs Marsh considers this greatly improved since the early days, when too much was crammed in. It still limits the scope for teachers to use their imagination, but before the National Curriculum things had gone 'too far', she avers, 'with each teacher doing their own thing'. Critics of the National Curriculum say that, for schools such as Holland Park, it places too much emphasis on academic subjects: Mrs Marsh concedes that 'people who are less confident with written language are disadvantaged; even in Maths there can be too much writing. Even the brightest second-language students have some difficulty.'

If Mrs Marsh were Education Secretary, she'd make Music and Drama compulsory. 'And I'd find a way to allow good practice and success to be calibrated and shared; make better opportunities for teachers to be recognized when they do well. That must be possible for the inspection scheme, and local authorities should be able to do that.' She draws again on what she learnt from her MBA: 'In business you need constant improvement, you must constantly reinforce positively. It's just a question of credit where it is due.'

A classroom on the third floor of the East Block. The curtains have been drawn together to darken the room, but all round the walls I discern piles of red plastic trays, containing safety goggles, Bunsen burners and clamps. Towards the back of the class is a piece of apparatus comprising two massive lenses, with a thin blue light flickering across them. The desk in front of me is entirely covered in blue biro scrawls, most of them dealing with matters unrelated to Physics, the subject which is taught here.

Beside me sits Endrit Kumbaro, the son of Albanian diplomats. With a whisper, and a scribble on my notebook, he explains that among his six classmates I will find an Armenian, a Romanian and a Bulgarian. Endrit is in his second year of A levels (Maths and Chemistry are his other subjects); and Mrs Marsh has trusted him to give me a good impression of the school.

The Physics teacher, Mr Sherrington, is only a few months older than me. Naturally, I've long been aware that people of my own age manage to hold down jobs as teachers, but actually sitting in class before one of them comes as a shock.

Mr Sherrington is thoroughly engaging, and still, after some years' teaching, an idealist who says he'd 'always' known Holland Park's reputation and wanted to teach here – 'like all teachers', he adds. Before starting this morning's lesson, he reads to the class from his copy of today's *Guardian*. This being National Science Week, the paper has run a feature about some American physicist. Mr Sherrington, master of the popular voice, refers several times to this eminent gentleman as a 'geezer'; and once, pointing a finger at the accompanying photograph, as a 'science geek'. Despite the demotic tone, however, the teacher's appearance marks him out. Mr Sherrington wears a grey suit with moderately trendy glasses. Apart from a solitary girl, he's the only clean-shaven figure in the class. (As for that girl: like the boys, she is not, by many schools' standards, entirely presentable. Throughout the lesson she chews all in one go what appears to be an entire pack of gum.)

For this lesson, the A-level class will split into two groups to conduct an experiment. A century ago, says Mr Sherrington – hovering beside the massive blue lenses and indicating the faint thread of blue light which had necessitated the drawing of the curtains – a man called Thompson showed that cathode rays are actually electrons. 'This experiment is to prove that electrons are particles.' Then the teacher defines a range of factors which might vary in the course of the experiment. Using calculators, the pupils work out a number of sums, writing the results into their exercise books. This experiment is part of their modular exams; by now they've completed four out of six modules.

As head of Year Seven, Mr Sherrington must also play host, throughout the lesson, to a number of smaller children he describes as 'miscreants'. While the sixth-formers work out their sums, he hands out work to two Year Seven boys sitting isolated in far corners of the room. Then he pops into his office to see another boy in 'internal exclusion', a state of limbo created to satisfy conflicting demands, as Mr Sherrington explains: 'We have pressure from inside to expel people and from outside to keep them in.' This, then, is the hierarchy of punishment: really troublesome children are sent off-site, the next level of naughtiness secures internal exclusion, and mild bother wins a few lessons sitting in Mr Sherrington's class with sixth-formers. From an adjacent classroom comes a reminder of the frustration children can cause: a teacher shouts loudly, and a door slams twice.

At this point, one of the Year Seven miscreants raises his hand and points to his work, asking, 'Sir, why is the Dead Sea so salty?' Mr Sherrington attempts to answer, then admits he's not entirely sure, and congratulates the boy for posing such a good question.

Returning to the sixth-formers, Mr Sherrington poses a number of questions of his own, to which he occasionally receives an answer. Only rarely do pupils ask their own questions, which strikes me as odd, because these are supposed to be good pupils (Mr Sherrington has predicted A grades for each of them). It seems the department has improved considerably over the last few years. 'When I came here,' says Mr Sherrington, 'there were three people doing Physics in the upper sixth – and they all failed. We used to have a Chemistry teacher teaching this.'

Towards the end of the lesson, he writes a number of equations on the board for pupils to copy down. Then he tells them what the next day's lesson will cover; and while he does that electronic pips signal the end of the lesson. The pips are followed by another announcement over the tannoy; this time a woman's voice gives rehearsal times for *The Fall of the House of Usher*. After a few last jokes from Endrit and his classmates, today's Physics lesson is over.

I'm sitting in the park, just where I sat with Desmond eighteen years ago, when I cracked my joke about the Englishman, the Scotsman and the Irishman (but failed to put him off his hot-dog), and this time I'm talking to pupils about some of their teachers. They offer the following mini-profiles:

Mr Preston is excellent. He can handle any type of person; he's from Trinidad. He works round the clock, leaving school at nine-thirty every day. He gives himself to the school, but he does shout at pupils. Some teachers, if they gave a detention, you wouldn't bother going – but you would for him!

Mr Osborne is very good, but he always wears the same suit (sometimes he changes his T-shirt).

Mr Miller is excellent. He organizes university applications, he sorts you out on the spot, he does everything. He has a Mickey Mouse watch, he's also very entertaining. He's got personality and he can teach.

Mr Golden is a tough teacher.

Mrs Marsh is a nice person. She's a good manager, but not inspiring. She gives assembly every two weeks, she stands there with a piece of paper and it's rather monotone. She reads from dramatic literature: the examples are out of date. She tries to be really serious, she leaves long pauses between sentences.

Mr Rattenbury has organized a scheme encouraging people to go to the opera.

Mr Sherrington is good: not just in Physics but in person. Three weeks ago he brought in a tape of 1980s music that he did in a band. (*Groans*.)

Mr Scunthorpe is a smart-arse, he has long hair, he always

269

talks about sex, and prostitutes. Every lesson, he has to bring in sex. (Mr Scunthorpe is the phoney who tried to put me off Jane Austen, the one who once jogged past me and my friends, medallion jingling from side to side, then slipped, fell on his backside and almost squashed his dog.)

Ms Johnson is devoted, she's this tiny Irish woman who'll sort you out at once. Everyone likes her, she is mad (in a nice way). But if you have your foot on a chair – she'll take it off! (*Laughs*.)

'Last week,' says Endrit, 'when John Major came here, my friend William was shown on TV pretending to talk to me about his Labour policies. Channel 4 told me to put up a poster for the camera. Then they filmed another party putting a poster on top of it. I told them that was a bad idea; they were trying to make this into a joke.'

At Holland Park, where one pupil in five is the child of refugees, they take democracy seriously, though only a few pupils are old enough to vote in the real general election. To put that another way, only a few pupils were born before the Conservatives came to power in 1979. Or: only a few pupils were born when I started at Holland Park.

One of the few pupils born eighteen years ago is Jan Sabo, Liberal Democrat candidate in the school election. Though old enough to vote in the real election, Jan won't do so as he's not British. He's Slovakian. Not that he's one of the school's refugees: like Endrit and other bright pupils I meet, Jan is the offspring of diplomats. He's been in England for many years. Before the collapse of Communist rule in Czechoslovakia, he was obliged to attend a Russian school; and he laughs at the recollection of a photograph showing him in full uniform, saluting Marx's grave in Highgate Cemetery. Similarly, Endrit chuckles as he performs a series of salutes taught to children under various eastern European regimes.

Jan is incredibly earnest, ardently political. 'If you have only one comprehensive in the borough, it can't work, it becomes a sink school,' he decares, explaining: 'If it is on its own in a particular area, it will have to take pupils who have been rejected by other schools.' Later, he says: 'This school does not get the funds it needs.'

Jan approaches the school election with broadly the same agenda as adult candidates in the national election. Unlike his rivals. 'Some party leaders,' he reveals, 'promised they were going to increase breaktime.'

Both boys are proud of Holland Park's international flavour. Having studied the school in Sociology lessons, they claim that it features in record books for having the greatest number of nationalities among its pupils. 'I can say "How are you?" in about twenty languages,' boasts Endrit. Which is, undoubtedly, admirable; but the boys' conversation does tend to suggest something that you aren't probably meant to notice: Holland Park has a relatively low proportion of white-skinned, English children, certainly by comparison with its catchment area. Consider Jan's description of the sixth-form common room: 'Sometimes eastern Europeans hold sway, then Asians take over, then maybe Moroccans. The Spanish and Portuguese mix together quite a lot. In the sixth form there are about forty people from eastern Europe,' he explains, then adds confidentially: 'But we don't tend to hang around with the Yugoslavians because they tend to come as refugees from the war, and we are from embassies.'

A word about racism, from Jan: 'If you even mention racism you can have it rebound on you, it's dangerous to mention it. The school's so anti-racist that you can't even mention it.' Racism, it turns out, is not the only problem. Others are homophobia and extortion: 'In the lower school you do get a lot of people who say you're a "faggot", or "Lend me 10p."'

*   *   *

For the election hustings, the final chance to sway voters, an impressive array of pupils has congregated in the sixth-form common room. This is no longer some grimy back-room in Thorpe Lodge, the domain of dope smokers. Nowadays it stretches above the head's office, in the main building, with a wall of glass overlooking the sixth-form gardens and glazed doors at both ends of the room, allowing teachers to peep through. A previous election meeting, in the school's main hall, was 'wild', according to Jan. 'It was not very constructive. But in the sixth form you can talk more sensibly.' His hopes of elevated discussion appear somewhat threatened: as a one-off, lower-school pupils have been allowed into the sixth-form common room to hear the debate.

At one end of the room, behind the panel of candidates, posters promoting a wide range of universities have been plastered over the wall. In front of the candidates are row upon row of fellow-pupils, with the greatest concentration, as ever, at the back. A handful of teachers is present too, including the man who organized the election, Mr Preston. Mrs Marsh has yet to make an appearance: as I walked up here with Endrit, I passed her in the corridor, speaking to a policeman.

Only now, amid the hurly-burly, do I truly feel I'm back at school. The sheer energy of the children is astonishing – unlike anything one tends to come across as a grown-up, at the office, which is probably not a bad thing. In one respect, however, they appear to have changed. They look *smaller* (some of them, I'm sure, would fit in my bag). But this, clearly, is just a matter of altered perspective: I'm six foot three, but not any taller than I was in the sixth form, or even the fifth year. As for their clothes – well, let's just say the current pupils don't strike me as possessing an appreciation of fashion that would satisfy Bug Eye, or Manmeet.

The candidates are introduced by Mr Grodzinski, a Social Science teacher. They represent the following, conventional, parties: Conservative, Labour (the candidate, oddly, is absent) and Liberal Democrat; as well as the 'Eurosceptic Party' and the 'Opportunist Party'. Each candidate makes a short speech.

Conservative (a short, dark-skinned boy called Sonny): 'We are Eurosceptic about joining the ERM, but we don't want to get away from Europe because there is a higher court for people from Britain who can't get justice. We don't want to lose that right.' Moving on to health, he corrects a comment made at the previous hustings by his predecessor as Tory candidate, who stepped down a couple of days ago: 'Last week you heard that we wanted to fire doctors but that is not true. We want to *hire* doctors.'

Liberal Democrat (Jan Sabo): 'I will give you an outline of our party and the others. The Conservatives are tired and must go. My party supports the single currency: the long-term advantages will outweigh losing the pound. Labour has brought in fresh faces but their changes don't really tackle the problems like unemployment or the NHS. Labour changes are superficial. The Eurosceptic Party only exists inside the school and would be damaging if they existed outside. It is very useful that people can get justice in Europe, and also Europe offers co-ordination over the environment: a cloud of radioactive waste does not care about national boundaries. The Opportunists are just factional. Liberal Democrats believe in long-term solutions. We believe in cutting unemployment and paying for education. We believe in putting a penny on income tax.' (*Boos.*)

Opportunist (a tall black boy, Mike Topley, accompanied throughout by a younger, white, non-speaking party official, Joe Norman): 'We would like sports like volleyball and basketball at playtime. Going to the adventure playground in Holland Park is boring. I have been speaking to people across all the years, they want more sports. Jan said that we are a factional party but that's not true. We created a football tournament last year; we gave people the opportunity to realize their talent. If you

273

get behind me I will make sure that things happen. As for the Eurosceptics, if you take away the question of Europe, that is their only policy.'

Eurosceptic (a fifth-year boy with a strong African accent, Charles, who begins by criticizing spelling mistakes in a Liberal Democrat flier): 'Europe is a collection of rich countries, the United States of Europe. They exclude the poor countries. And what is going to happen to the poor? They are going to get poorer and poorer. What does Britain get from Europe? We all lose our currency and our identity. We lose also the right to choose who governs us. Why give power to other people? Why do we send billions to Brussels when that is spent without asking us? As for the school, when I first came here there were fights everywhere. But not any more. Now people are suspended whenever there is any trouble. Fights don't happen any more.' (*Boos*.)

Questions from the floor, delivered in shrill tones, and accompanied by forceful displays of enthusiasm from the rest of the audience, prove challenging.

'Mike Topley, changing the canteen had nothing to do with you, how can you claim that?' The Opportunist candidate adopts a soothing tone: 'My party is for giving people opportunities, I want to become an independent party giving people their needs.'

One question relates to the disappearance of the previous Conservative candidate: 'What happened to Akbar?' The present candidate appears edgy: 'Akbar was suspended for reasons that I can't go into.'

Another question for the Opportunist: 'You say that you organized things, but they were only for senior years . . .' Mike Topley replies: 'I didn't say that I had done everything, just that I had broken the mould by bringing Year Eleven into the soccer tournament.'

At this point the Eurosceptic intervenes: 'What about something else? Life is not just about games, life is serious, not about games . . .' This put-down inspires voluble cheering and booing across the room. When that dies down, the Opportunist responds: 'Well, what has the Eurosceptic Party got to offer apart from pulling out of Europe?'

Unasked, Jan Sabo offers a solution: 'We should think about the real issues and choose from the real-life parties. My party is the only one offering a real solution . . .'

But the Eurosceptic has a question for Jan: 'How would you raise the money for all your policies?'

Jan's reply: 'We do want to increase taxes. With both parties offering to cut taxes it's unbearable. The reason for privatization is to raise money for everything. One day the government might sell off the Post Office.'

Inexplicably, Jan's gloomy prediction fails to horrify the audience. One small boy at the back raises his hand and asks: 'If that boy at the end wants to raise taxes, why doesn't he pay for it himself?'

Finally Mr Grodzinski asks for a straw poll of candidates. Only two or three people raise their hands for any of the candidates. (A week later, I meet Endrit by chance in Hammersmith. He tells me the Opportunist won the election. Jan came second.)

As the common room empties, I wonder whether London Oratory, down the road, might have conducted its own election too. Would Tony Blair's son, Euan, stand as Labour candidate?

And if this is the Eton of comprehensives, what happens at the other Eton, the one in Berkshire? Do they too conduct a school election? Is Prince William allowed to represent a party, make speeches and put up posters? Or does he sit waiting, like his grandmother, for the winning candidate to present himself, all by way of practice for the real thing in twenty or thirty years?

Prince William should have gone to Holland Park. What an eye-opener it could have been. He'd have seen a world in which even those who call themselves Conservatives cling to the idea of Europe because it offers a higher court to ensure justice for people who can't find it in Britain. A world in which Eurosceptics denounce Europe *because it excludes poor countries.*

If nothing else, attending Holland Park would have enabled Prince William to see more of his mother: for Kensington Palace, Holland Park is the local school. To get there, the prince would simply have cut through the embassies, nipped up Church Street, then dashed along Bedford Gardens. He could have been at registration just five minutes after finishing his royal boiled egg.

It's possible that the prince might, like me, have buckled under peer pressure and failed to set a good example. Just imagine: Prince William nicking sweets and books from W. H. Smith. The future head of state masterminding a 'fighting league table'. Willy Windsor smoking dope in the park, taking speed in a five-a-side footy competition, dropping acid round a bonfire. Certainly, that's possible. But would it have done him any harm? And anyway, he could do any of this at Eton.

Holland Park might have done him some good. Picture the headlines: PRINCE WILLIAM LEARNS TO SEW! PRINCE WILLIAM (*pictured*) WITH THE MACARONI CHEESE HE MADE HIMSELF! PRINCE WILLIAM SNOGS A GIRL CALLED YEMISI!

There's more than one boy's future at stake. State education as a whole, so long ignored by the upper and middle classes, would have benefited enormously from royal approval. If Prince Charles is so worried about education – as he occasionally pleads – he could have done a lot to help by sending his own children to a comp.

Leaving the school grounds, I turn left on to Campden Hill Road. Ahead of me is one of my former teachers, returning to work for a parents' evening. I tell him what I've seen, adding that the school seems much improved.

Wildly staring, he contradicts me. 'A couple of weeks ago, a group of kids was had up against the wall by McDonald's in Notting Hill Gate and one of them had an axe on him. We've got a lot of trouble here now.' Then he stalks off, shouting back: 'Your Donna was par for the course.'

Has he gone mad? Is he making it up? Is that why I saw Mrs Marsh speaking to a policeman when she should have been watching the hustings? At the bottom of the hill, I head for McDonald's. Two police constables stand outside. Still somewhat nervous about speaking to coppers, I ask why they are there.

The taller one replies: 'A group of children were stopped here last week. One had an axe, and one had a bag of knives. That's why we're here now: there were twenty of them sitting over there, just a while ago. We have to let them know they can't carry knives. But they're not just from the school, they're people who have left the school and come back to meet their friends.'

I ask: 'What will happen to them?'

'They were arrested and they will be charged.'

I thank him and turn to leave.

'Thank *you*, sir.'

The Register

ALKAN, GILBERT, took his A levels at West London College, then went to work. For a short while, he contributed elaborate, unreadable reviews of the London dance scene to the *Big Issue*. Together with Andrew Smith – who recently finished a spell in prison after being caught in possession of Class A drugs – Gilbert runs a shop on Portobello Road. Outraged by the prices charged by shop fitters, Gilbert used some of the sewing skills he'd picked up at school to make his own curtains.

He sells imported American casual clothes, chunky watches and skateboarding gear, trying not to worry too much about credit-card fraud. Shoplifting is not something that worries him. After so many years as a poacher, Gilbert the gamekeeper has developed a theory about it: 'If you have a small shop, you'll be all right.' (Selfridges be warned.) Not that he's changed altogether: 'When your book comes out,' he promises, 'I'll nick a copy.'

ARROWSEED, DAVID, studied music at the Royal Northern College of Music. I once heard him play classical guitar in a state room at the NatWest Tower.

BEATON, ELLEN, who criticized Daniel's haircut but neglected to shave her own armpits, who carried love messages between Big Donna and Bug Eye, and collaborated with Lisa in drawing up a fuck list, became a firefighter.

BRADFORD, OLLIE, who'd helped to hold me down when Gilbert first blew cannabis smoke up my nose, whose earlobe was bitten off at Glastonbury, whose clothes were burnt in jubilation when Andreas returned to our campsite – even *without* any beer – designs graphics for tabloid newspapers.

CABLE, DONNA, works in the health service, in east London.

COLLINS, NAIMH, occasionally visits her mum in the Fulham Palace Road flat that I walked past so often.

CUNNINGHAM, JASON, grew out his Mohican and immediately landed a job working backstage on *La Cage aux Folles*.

DAVIES, PETER, works in the Co-op in Hammersmith, selling mobile phones. Three years ago, he met an old classmate talking to a woman in her eighties. At the top of his voice, Peter asked his old pal: 'Is that your pussy?'

DOMINGO REY, DIEGO, went to work for a bank, and was occasionally spotted around Earls Court, handcuffed to a briefcase. Towards the end of the 1980s, Tomato invited Alexander to his flat to watch a video. This showcased the funeral of Russian premier Yuri Andropov. Diego has since returned to Spain, standing successfully as a Communist candidate in local elections.

DOUGALL, ROSALIND, left Holland Park after three years to live in Paris. She briefly went out with a prince, but now lives in Kilburn. She works in research at the Royal Free Hospital.

FATODU, YEMISI, works as a fashion designer near King's Cross.

FORD, ALEXANDER, having endured years of abuse, suffered a mental breakdown after the fifth year and left school. He tried private schools, first Westminster as a day boy, then Mill Hill as a boarder, but got thrown out both times for calling the head a wanker. After that, his parents lost patience with him and threw him out of their home. He writes violent fantasy novels. His stick-like frame has filled out. His head eventually fought off the dandruff, but lost much of its hair in the process. Subsequently reconciled with his parents, he recently came into nearly £300,000.

GARDINER, JUSTICE, met Gilbert in a nightclub. Justice wore a pinstriped suit, with a gold watch-chain. Around him was a group of henchmen, all of them black, several of them wearing trilby hats. Justice asked Gilbert how he was; Gilbert said: 'All right, man.' They stood looking at the dancers for a while, nodding together. Then Justice said: 'D'you want a spliff?' Gilbert said yes. So Justice beckoned one of the men in a trilby, and told him to roll a 'damn big spliff for my good fren Gil'. The man went off and did it, bringing back the longest joint Gil had ever seen. They stood smoking it together, still nodding every so often to show appreciation. Justice explained that he wasn't allowed to carry any gear himself, but didn't say why. Gil said thanks and rejoined his own friends.

And that's not the only time Justice was spotted with his men in hats. Another time, Samuel Thomas was walking in Notting Hill Gate when he noticed an expensive-looking car. The rear electric window came down as Samuel approached, and a dark-skinned hand beckoned him over. He peered inside, and saw Justice in the middle of the back seat, with men in trilbies on either side of him, and two more in the front. 'You all right, Samuel?' said Justice. 'Um, yeah, thanks, Justice man,' said Samuel. 'See you later.' As the window went back up, Samuel noticed the men in hats nod their approval.

Since then, Justice got heavily involved in crack, not just using it himself but dealing too. Together with his older brother, he runs a jewellery shop in central London. The Child Support Agency is looking for him.

GRANT, PAUL, has disappeared.

HARRIS, STEPHEN, works with his father in a carpet-cleaning enterprise.

JOHNSON, MELISSA, by repute the lesbian lover of Rosalind, the girl who dropped me in it when I stuck another lesbian lie on a teacher's back, went to art school. She grew her hair long, put a ring through her nose and took to wearing dungarees. Living with a drummer in Hackney, she has a six-month-old son called Ezra.

LESTER, ROBERT, has disappeared.

LOUP, MAX, the Westminster boy who joined our sixth form, was called up for National Service in France. Desperate to leave, he held a gun to the forehead of an officer.

MAI NGRAM, KAMPOL, works in his parents' Thai restaurant. I met him on the tube, and he offered me a free meal.

MCGUIRE, JOHN, has disappeared.

MEARS, DESMOND, the black boy who'd gone for lunch with me on the first day, the boy who wore sellotaped trainers, and who pressured Naimh to snog him at the end of the fifth year, was one of a gang arrested for attempted murder around the time the rest of us sat down to our O-level exams. The gang had steamed a man walking through the park. They all got off. Later, Desmond was arrested for attempted rape, but again, not convicted. He subsequently enrolled on a teacher-training course, and now teaches Sport in schools. God help his pupils.

MILLER, CLAIRE, worked for three years with foster-children, but it made her depressed so she joined a direct-marketing outfit.

MOHAMMED, MANMEET, got married, despite the apparent disadvantage of her big nose.

MURPHY, DANIEL, who revealed the sinister art of wanking; failed to look trendy, be clever or hard; and never cut his hair to everybody's satisfaction, works as delivery man for his father's bakery. He's also become a dope-head, incapable of normal speech. Whenever he meets old classmates, he asks them for money.

MYERSON, JULIA, who got top marks in Drama CSE, went on to study Drama at university, then became manager of a trendy cinema near school.

NATTY, IAN, found a job stacking shelves and operating the till at an Indian-owned supermarket in Shepherd's Bush. He fell in love with his boss's daughter, but she was earmarked for arranged marriage to somebody else. When the parents found out, they sent the girl back to India, away from Ian. He was briefly employed by Gow, but Gow soon had to sack him for slacking; they're no longer in touch. Ian now works for the police in a clerical role; the Indian woman, back in England, lives with him.

NERUDA, MANUEL, who puked over his stolen haul in a plucky attempt to evade arrest, runs a shop selling clubwear, above a porn shop in Soho. He still plays footy with Gilbert.

NYLAND, DARIUS, was last seen approaching Alexander in a dole queue to apologize for being so horrible to him at school. He had a giant crucifix in his hand; and somehow looked a lot smaller.

PYE, MARK, never really broke into the first team at West Ham. Shame.

RAPHAEL, FAT, whose girth Justice prized for goalkeeping, became a printer.

RAWSON, GOW, left school as soon as he could – he didn't even take his O levels. For a while, he sold Smurfs from a stall in

Shepherd's Bush Market (when Donna bumped into him, he gave her a few for nothing). After that, Gow got work installing burglar alarms; then set up his own window-cleaning business. He married a girl who first met him on the Smurf stall; they were reunited when Gow was installing somebody's alarm. Their daughter, Ruby, is one year old.

RED, the boy without a surname who was caught smoking dope but not suspended, now works at a production company making commercials. Like his pregnant girlfriend, he is unable to shake off an enthusiasm for Class A drugs.

ROONEY, MARK, the expert on James Bond actors, the campaigner against racialism, works on a fruit-and-veg stall in Shepherd's Bush Market. He has also been employed as a bouncer. One old classmate met him outside a nightclub, and said hello. With uncharacteristic sleight of hand, Rooney picked a bogey out of his own nostril and wiped it in his old friend's mouth, saying: 'Gotcha, you cunt!'

SIMONS, JEREMY, met Gow a couple of years after school, cleaning windows. He said: 'I'd like to say thanks.' Gow asked him what he meant. 'For not spitting on my jacket that time.' Within six months, Jeremy's mother told Gow that Jeremy had killed himself.

ST JOHN, LISA, went on the game. She too is dead: a victim of cancer at twenty-six.

STERLING, KYLIE, left Oxford with a History degree and became a TV researcher.

THOMAS, SAMUEL, the bad influence who encouraged me to steal from W. H. Smith, the drug fiend who scored Es in his O levels (pun intended), teaches English as a foreign language in Thailand.

VAUX, ALISON, the Fox girl with the off-putting chocolate-drop mole on her hand, the girl whose breasts developed fastest, and into whose bed Gilbert inserted a crab's claw, studied Biology before landing work as a nature ranger. After living with an electrician for some years, she got pregnant, then married. They plan to lead a self-sufficient life in the Hebrides. Looking back, she surprises me by saying it was tough being seen as a posh girl: Donna's gang, it turns out, would frequently spit at her, and tear her clothes.

WHITTAKER, DAVID, the New Romantic with the silly fringe, white suit and synthetic tan, never got over his taste for fancy dress: he now works in the police force, at the station off High Street Kensington.

ZARAGOZA, JORGE, disappeared before school ended, rumoured to be a heroin addict. Gilbert told me Bug Eye died of an overdose, but eleven years later I saw him again. He was naked but for a lot of soapy lather, preparing to rinse himself under the shower at my local gym. When he caught my eye, he stuck his hand out and exclaimed: 'It's my old mate John!'

We went for a drink, and he told me what really happened to him. He'd been smoking dope with John McGuire when a teacher spotted them. They dropped the roach out of a window, ran into a girls' loo, then climbed on to a sink and out of the window. The teacher rushed in as the sink fell away from the wall. Both boys were sent to a special-needs school. Bug Eye behaved immaculately, desperate to come back. But a visiting teacher decided the special-needs school was doing him good, so he remained there until he was sixteen.

Several years later, he got a job with a video company, where he started a lucrative line in pirate films. After some months, the police swooped, but he refused to comment and, as Bug Eye had bribed the other staff to keep quiet, they didn't comment either.

Nowadays, having dropped the name Jorge in favour of George, he's building himself up to become a personal trainer in a gym.

We left the pub together, me in my jeans and linen jacket, Bug Eye in a shell suit, with chunky gold jewellery. As we came to say goodbye, beside one of the cafés that spill on to the pavement in leafy Belsize Park, a Ford Transit jerked towards us, driven by two boys. The older boy – who can't have been more than fourteen – lowered a window, and asked: 'Do yous guys want a video? We've got some in the back.' I said I didn't. Bug Eye hunched his shoulders, glanced left and right, then admitted under his breath: 'As it goes, John, I could do with a video.' He hopped in, and they sped away. I haven't seen him since.

LADBROKE GROVE

E

LATIMER ROAD

E

A

SHEPHERD'S BUSH

HOLLAND ROAD

D

OLYMPIA

A	POSH PEOPLE'S STREETS
B	INTERNATIONAL EMBASSIES
C	KENSINGTON PALACE
D	CARDINAL VAUGHAN SECONDARY
E	TOUGH ESTATES (FORMERLY SLUMS)
F	CENTRE OF 1958 RACE RIOTS
G	HIPPIES FORCE ME TO SMOKE DOPE
H	CARDINAL VAUGHAN BOYS ATTACK GIL
I	BECKY SNOGS ME IN THE PUB
J	GIL WITNESSES SHOOTING IN POOL HALL
K	MANUEL PUKES TO ESCAPE ARREST

N

HAMMERSMITH ROAD